e your

INSIGHT ● GUIDES

TUSCANY

Walking Eye App

YOUR FREE DESTINATION CONTENT AND EBOOK AVAILABLE THROUGH THE WALKING EYE APP

Your guide now includes a free eBook and destination content for your chosen destination, all for the same great price as before. Simply download the Walking Eye App from the App Store or Google Play to access your free eBook and destination content.

HOW THE WALKING EYE APP WORKS

Through the Walking Eye App, you can purchase a range of eBooks and destination content. However, when you buy this book, you can download the corresponding eBook and destination content for free. Just see below in the grey panels where to find your free content and then scan the QR code at the bottom of this page.

Destinations: Download your corresponding essential destination content from here, featuring recommended sights and attractions, restaurants, hotels and an A–Z of practical information, all for free. Other destinations are available for purchase.

Ships: Interested in ship reviews? Find independent reviews of river and ocean ships in this section, all available for purchase.

eBooks: You can download your free accompanying digital version of this guide here. You will also find a whole range of other eBooks, all available for purchase.

Free access to travel-related blog articles about different destinations, updated on a daily basis.

HOW THE DESTINATION CONTENT WORKS

Each destination includes a short introduction, an A–Z of practical information and recommended points of interest, split into 4 different categories:

- Highlights
- Accommodation
- Eating out
- What to do

You can view the location of every point of interest and save it by adding it to your Favourites. In the 'Around Me' section you can view all the points of interest within 5km.

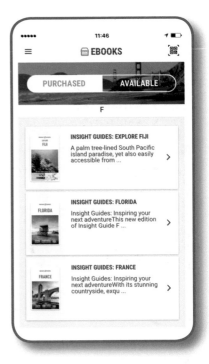

HOW THE EBOOKS WORK

The eBooks are provided in EPUB file format. Please note that you will need an eBook reader installed on your device to open the file. Many devices come with this as standard, but you may still need to install one manually from Google Play.

The eBook content is identical to the content in the printed guide.

HOW TO DOWNLOAD THE WALKING EYE APP

1. Download the Walking Eye App from the App Store or Google Play.
2. Open the app and select the scanning function from the main menu.
3. Scan the QR code on this page – you will then be asked a security question to verify ownership of the book.
4. Once this has been verified, you will see your eBook and destination content in the purchased ebook and destination sections, where you will be able to download them.

Other destination apps and eBooks are available for purchase separately or are free with the purchase of the Insight Guide book.

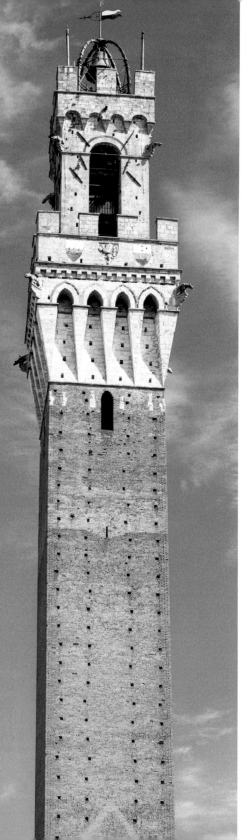

CONTENTS

Travel tips

TRANSPORT

A – Z

LANGUAGE

FURTHER READING

Maps

LEGEND

𝒪 Insight on
◎ Photo story

THE BEST OF TUSCANY: TOP ATTRACTIONS

△ **Val d'Orcia landscape**. With its farmhouses, abbeys and conical hills, this pastoral landscape was redrawn in the 14th and 15th centuries to reflect good governance and create an aesthetically pleasing picture that has inspired many artists. See page 222.

△ **San Gimignano, a medieval Manhattan**. As Italy's best-preserved medieval town, Tuscany's time capsule survives, with its bold towers signifying San Gimignano's prestige and prosperity. A beguiling spirit transcends the town's over-popularity. See page 193.

◁ **The Leaning Tower of Pisa**. Finally fully restored, this iconic symbol of Tuscan architectural genius stands alongside the gleaming Duomo and Baptistery on Pisa's aptly named Campo dei Miracoli – the Field of Miracles. See page 161.

△ **Hill towns of Montepulciano and Montalcino**. Montepulciano and Montalcino draw you in with their palaces, seductive lifestyle and cellars of famed wines. Sip Vino Nobile in Cantine Contucci or sample Brunello di Montalcino in the Fortezza. See page 219.

▽ **Florentine churches**. From Brunelleschi's dazzling Duomo to Romanesque San Miniato, Gothic Santa Croce and Michelangelo's Medici tombs in San Lorenzo, Florentine churches are mesmerising repositories of art and history. See page 101.

△ **Etruscan Tuscany**. Whether in Volterra's intriguing Etruscan museum or Chiusi's painted tombs, the colour and life of Etruscan art contrasts with the cold perfectionism of the Greeks and Romans. See page 31.

▽ **Wine-tasting in the Chianti**. Ignore the "Chiantishire" tag and visit a chequered landscape of vineyards, villages and fortified-wine estates that include the Castello di Brolio, birthplace of the modern Chianti industry. See page 193.

▷ **Tuscan spas**. Despite dating back to Etruscan times, Tuscany's new breed of thermal spas combine sophisticated pampering with authentic water cures in incomparable natural settings – as in Fonteverde Terme or Terme di Saturnia. See page 140.

▽ **The Uffizi Gallery in Florence**. The world's greatest collection of Renaissance art includes masterpieces such as Botticelli's *Birth of Venus*, and works by Leonardo da Vinci, Michelangelo, Raphael, Titian and other masters of the High Renaissance. See page 112.

▷ **Siena, the quintessential medieval city**. Siena, the feminine foil to Florentine masculinity, is the city that most lives enfolded in its own private world, from the compelling medieval mood to the pageantry of the Palio horse race. See page 205.

THE BEST OF TUSCANY: EDITOR'S CHOICE

CHURCHES AND MONUMENTS

Brunelleschi's dome. An incredible feat of engineering by the father of Renaissance architecture. See page 101.

Monte Oliveto Maggiore. A secluded 14th-century monastery set among groves of cypress trees. See page 216.

Sant'Antimo. An abbey church built of creamy travertine framed by tree-clad hills. See page 230.

Siena cathedral. A magnificent Gothic structure of banded black and white stone. See page 209.

San Michele in Foro in Lucca. A fine example of the exuberant Tuscan Romanesque style. See page 135.

Santa Maria della Grazia. The domed church just outside the Etruscan walls of Cortona is a hidden gem. See page 250.

San Pellegrino in Alpe. An ancient monastery deep in the Garfagnana mountains, with sweeping, glorious views. See page 151.

Abbazia di Sant'Antimo, southern Siena.

THE BEST TUSCAN HILL TOWNS

Pienza. The ideal Renaissance city is famous for its scenery and its production of tasty pecorino cheese. See page 217.

Monteriggioni. The Sienese hilltown encircled by walls and 14 towers is a truly spectacular sight. See page 193.

Massa Marittima. This town is perched on top of a high hill on the edge of the Colline Metallifere and is the loveliest springboard for exploring the Maremma. See page 188.

Cortona. An enchanting hill town in eastern Tuscany with attractions out of all proportion with its tiny size. See page 252.

Vinci. The genius of Leonardo is proudly celebrated in his birthplace, a tiny hill town situated between the cities of Florence and Pisa. See page 129.

Pitigliano. Once one of the most important settlements in southern Tuscany, this dramatic tufa haunt is found in a forgotten corner of Tuscany. See page 240.

San Miniato. An ancient town straddling three hills in the province of Florence. On a clear day, you can see Volterra and the Apuan Alps from this vantage point. See page 128.

The Pitigliano skyline.

TUSCANY FOR FAMILIES

Florence or Lucca by bike. Or, in the case of Florence, also by rickshaw, Segway or summer boat along the Arno. See page 259.

Giardino di Boboli. The gardens behind the Pitti Palace are fun for children to clamber around. There is an amphitheatre, strange statues and grottoes, and a handy café. See page 116.

Trips to the Tuscan islands. Explore the Tuscan archipelago with the ferries and hydrofoils that sail from Porto Santo Stefano to Giglio, and from Piombino to Elba. See page 179.

Giardino dei Tarocchi. A bizarre garden full of colourful fantasy figures. See page 238.

Parco di Pinocchio. Pinocchio's park at Collodi, near Pisa, has a certain old-fashioned charm. See page 139.

Associazione Mus.e in Palazzo Vecchio. Dressing up, model-making and other fun activities for kids in the Palazzo Vecchio bring the Renaissance to life. See page 98.

Ice cream. When all else fails, an ice cream on a town square, most of which are traffic-free, rarely fails to win them over.

TOP ETRUSCAN SITES

Volterra. Volterra has some of the best Etruscan funerary art to be found outside Rome. See page 183.

Chiusi. Etruscan tombs and tunnels are the highlight of a visit to Chiusi. See page 223.

Tufa towns. Superb Etruscan sites and trails are found around Sovana, Sorano and Pitigliano. See page 239.

Museo Archeologico. The Museo Archeologico in Florence has a fine collection of Etruscan art. See page 108.

Fiesole. An Etruscan temple and a Roman theatre a 30-minute bus ride from Florence. See page 123.

The Teatro Romano in Fiesole.

Talamone on the Maremma coast.

SEASIDE AND SPAS

Elba. A beautiful island with dramatic scenery and a series of small beaches and coves. Perfect for families. See page 175.

The Maremma. Backed by a nature reserve, it is one of the most unspoilt stretches of beach on the coast. See page 234.

Forte dei Marmi. With its villas and chic cafés, this cycle-friendly summer resort is a magnet for the beautiful people. See page 150.

Monte Argentario. A craggy peninsula with several chic fishing ports make it tempting to explore by yacht or by car. See page 236.

Spas. From the simple but charming (Bagni San Filippo) and the sophisticated and stylish (Grotta Giusti, in a villa) to a cool castle spa (Castello del Nero), Tuscany is Italy's most pampering spa destination. See page 140.

Sunbathing on one of the Tuscan coast's many pleasant beaches.

A TASTE OF TUSCANY

Wine tasting. As well as in the Chianti (see page 196), Montepulciano (see page 219) and Montalcino (see page 229), visit Bolgheri for the Super-Tuscans and Maremma for Morellino di Scansano (see page 234).

Food festivals. Tuscans are proud of their local produce, which they celebrate with festivals (sagre) – white truffles, chestnuts, Valdichiana beef, wild boar and pecorino cheese all have festivals dedicated to them.

Cookery courses. The best include: Cucina Giuseppina in medieval Certaldo (www. cucinagiuseppina.com); the Florence Chefs (www. theflorencechefs.it); and Badia a Coltibuono (www. coltibuono.com), where you can eat, sleep and cook.

Mushrooms. In autumn, mushroom-loving Tuscans forage for *funghi*. Wild mushrooms, especially the prized *porcini* and *tartufi* (truffles), are also on the menu. See page 81.

Sweet treats. These include candied fruit cake, *panforte*, sweet almond biscuits, *ricciarelli*, crunchy *cantucci* biscuits, and irresistible *gelati*. See page 213.

RENAISSANCE ART

Masaccio's Florentine frescoes. Found inside the Brancaccio chapel and Santa Maria Novella in Florence, Masaccio's sublime frescoes reflect a range of true Renaissance values: the importance of the human form, human emotion and the use of perspective. See page 106.

The Bargello. A major collection of Renaissance and Mannerist sculpture is housed in this building – a former prison. See page 120.

The Baptistery. Ghiberti's bronze doors are so dazzling, Michelangelo called them the "Gates of Paradise". See page 102.

Lorenzetti's frescoes.

Located in Siena's Palazzo Pubblico – a striking allegory of good and bad government, one of the earliest secular paintings. See page 208.

The two Davids. Michelangelo's *David* is Florence's icon, but Donatello's *David* was the first free-standing nude since antiquity. See pages 119 and 121.

Giotto's frescoes, Florence. Santa Croce church displays a significant departure from the flat Byzantine style. See page 108.

Piero della Francesca's frescoes, Arezzo. These are marvels of pastel shades awash with cool light. See page 245.

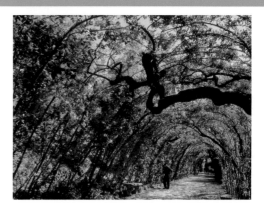

Walking in the Boboli Gardens, Florence.

VILLAS AND GARDENS

Giardino di Boboli. The regal gardens of the Pitti Palace, now a vast museum. See page 116.

Villa Medicea Poggio a Caiano. The perfect frescoed Medici villa, with beautiful gardens. See page 126.

Villa Demidoff and Parco di Pratolino. The gardens contain extraordinary Mannerist sculpture and grottoes. See page 126.

Lucchesi villas. The area around Lucca is rich in villas, all surrounded by beautiful parks. See page 137.

Villa Medici (Fiesole). A delightful villa and garden with superb views of Florence. See page 126.

Villa Medicea della Petraia. An elegant villa decorated with wonderful frescoes. See page 126.

Villa Medicea di Castello. This villa has beautiful Renaissance gardens. See page 126.

A detail of the magnificent bronze doors of the Baptistery, Florence.

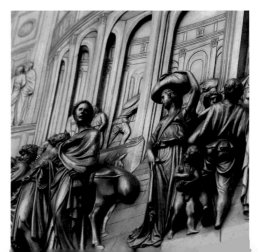

TUSCAN LANDSCAPE

The Crete Senesi. The dramatic landscape of rounded hills, stately cypresses and isolated farms; this is the Tuscany of postcards and posters. See page 216.

Parco Regionale della Maremma. Beautiful, unspoilt beaches backed by steep cliffs, parasol pines and wild Mediterranean scrubland. See page 235.

Chianti Country. Gentle hills cloaked in vineyards and dotted with medieval castle estates where wine-tasting is on offer. See page 193.

Parco dell'Orecchiella. A wild mountainous area, rich in wildlife, the region's most spectacular park. See page 76.

Apuan Alps. Behind the well-groomed beaches of the Versilia is a rugged hinterland of marble quarries, mountain ridges and narrow gorges. See page 152.

The Casentino. Ancient forests of the upper Arno valley. See page 247.

Monte Amiata. The site of an extinct volcano with a profusion of thermal springs and quaint hamlets. See page 240.

A typical landscape in southern Siena.

FESTIVALS AND EVENTS

Il Palio. Siena's traditional horse race is a heart-racing and passionate affair, involving all of the town's *contrade*. See page 214.

Lucca Summer Festival. This takes place in July and attracts some big celebrity names. See page 265.

Puccini Festival. This celebration of Puccini's musical genius is held at the composer's villa on Lake Massaciuccoli. See page 265.

Luminaria di San Ranieri. A lovely Pisan festival when thousands of candles light up the River Arno and celebrations are brought to a close with a boat race. See page 265.

Carnevale. Viareggio's riotous carnival is a memorable experience and one of the best carnivals in all of Italy. See page 265.

Estate Fiesolana. This enjoyable music and arts festival held in Fiesole in the province of Florence is well worth catching. See page 264.

Carnival fun in Viareggio.

The beautiful Val d'Orcia landscape.

Pisa's iconic Leaning Tower.

The azure waters of La Sorgente beach in Elba.

A parade during the Palio in Siena.

THE TUSCAN MIRACLE

Birthplace of the Renaissance, a strong tradition of village life, picturesque countryside: these factors and more contribute to the enigma that is Tuscany.

Bean crostini.

From the top of a village tower, the Tuscan landscape lies below: the most civilised rural scene on Earth. Yet driving through southern Tuscany at night, there is little sense of civilisation, still less of domesticity – even farm animals are kept indoors. In the distance, a succession of small lights trails across the black countryside: tenuous links with separate inward-looking communities. The spaces in between are remote, uncivilised. The blackness and emptiness of the countryside go back to medieval times and beyond; the "Tuscan Miracle" only illuminates the cities, leaving the gaps unfilled.

In giving birth to the Renaissance, Tuscany designed the modern world. In his paintings, Giotto projected Tuscany into space. Brunelleschi crowned space with his Florentine dome, the greatest feat of Renaissance engineering. In the Carmine frescoes, Masaccio peopled space with recognisably human figures. His *Expulsion from Paradise* reveals Adam and Eve in all their naked beauty. Gone is the medieval coyness; present is the palpable suffering of a couple who have lost everything.

Etruscan sarcophagus, Chiusi.

The Tuscan miracle, however, is not a frozen Renaissance portrait but a living procession of Tuscans completely at ease with their artistic setting and identity. Tuscans do possess an innate aesthetic sense but the Tuscan tapestry is a rich weave that has been created by many different threads. Literary Tuscany is a strand that can be clearly traced through Boccaccio, Petrarch and Dante. Republican Tuscany is best glimpsed through its fortified town halls, while humanist Tuscany is enshrined in poetry, sculpture and art, the fruits of patronage and craftsmanship. Aristocratic Tuscany still lingers in Medici palaces, villas and sculptured gardens, as well as the ancestral homes of the Rucellai, Corsini and Frescobaldi. Bourgeois Tuscany parades along Florence's Via Tornabuoni, patronises the arts and restores family farms. Peasant Tuscany traditionally takes a little of everything from the land: game, beans, chestnut flour, unsalted bread, olive oil and, of course, the grapes needed to make Chianti and Brunello. Tuscan cuisine combines proportion and variety to produce delicious, hearty fare. Like the Tuscans themselves, it is of good peasant stock.

TUSCANY TODAY

Despite the region's resounding popularity, Tuscany is not succumbing to "Disneyfication" – and a new environmental awareness means that the lifestyle is more seductive than ever.

It's a travesty to equate Tuscany to "Chiantishire", a parody of an English country-house party transposed to Italy. It is also misleading to reduce the region to Renaissance art, Florentine architecture and Chianti vineyards. The Tuscan landscape is as beautiful as the art. The soothing scenery, dotted with hill towns, inspired the Renaissance masters and nurtured a lifestyle with timeless appeal. This rose-tinted Tuscan lifestyle is arguably now the greatest lure, with villa-living or farm-stays the ideal way of living the dream. The Tuscans seem to have found a perfect balance between country and city living. And, as bedazzled fans, we come in search of the secret, as if it lay in the princely countryside, the pasta feasts and the pampering hot springs.

Pienza is perfect Tuscany. This tower-capped outpost overlooking sun-baked valleys is all an Italophile could wish for – so much so that this town of 2,200 has around 100,000 visitors a year. In the rush to enjoy the rural idyll, we risk turning high-season Pienza into an elbow-to-elbow mêlée. And this is Tuscany's dilemma. Her beauty is in danger of becoming her beast. While Rome does government and Milan does commerce, La Toscana does cypress-lined rolling hills and the Renaissance. The region's wealth is her landscape and heritage, and the question for the future is how to preserve this while finding room for some 10 million visitors a year.

THE PRICE OF PARADISE

As Italy's most popular region, Tuscany's long-standing relationship with tourism is finely balanced. Pisa is grappling with the quick-fire habits of the tourist in search of little more than a snapshot of himself, arms askew, mimicking the Leaning Tower behind him. Florence is reeling.

Dining alfresco in the Piazza Cisterna, in the popular medieval hilltop town of San Gimignano.

The city that caused Stendhal Syndrome – the dizzying disorientation some visitors experience when they overdose on Florentine Renaissance masterpieces – is in danger of sending tourists' heads spinning in front of the Uffizi Gallery.

While ostensibly true, this snapshot is still misleading and restricted to tourism "hotspots" such as the Leaning Tower, the great Florentine galleries and San Gimignano. Beyond these beautiful bottlenecks, Tuscany is as spacious yet enveloping as ever it was. Many evocative hamlets on Monte Amiata see far too few visitors, as do Maremma's Etruscan sites, wild Garfagnana and cities of the stature of Massa Marittima. But even just beyond San Gimignano's walls, you can still lose yourself on walks through epic countryside that has been cultivated since time immemorial.

ENVIRONMENTAL FACTORS AND "SLOW TRAVEL"

Tuscany has also woken up to environmental issues, with classic hill towns, such as Montepulciano, closed to traffic, or partly pedestrianised, as is Siena. Florence is dabbling with trams to the suburbs and electric buses in the historic centre, with a futuristic Norman Foster-designed rail hub due to hopefully open in 2021. And Tuscans, not

of completeness. Tuscan towns go against the grain, shunning spurious modernity if it simply means homogeneity. Instead, without being fossilised, Florence is becoming more Florentine and Siena more Sienese. For a Tuscan, city life feels narrow but it is also invitingly deep. The watchwords are tradition, civility, good taste and a sense of ease with the past.

THE HERITAGE SCENE

Temperamentally left-wing, Tuscans can be deeply conservative when it comes to heritage

Cycling through southern Siena – a fantastic way to see the stunning countryside.

just tourists, have taken to cycling, especially in Pisa, Lucca, the Chianti and the Versilia coast. Pisa currently boasts more pedestrians than cars, and more bicycles than motorcycles and mopeds. Despite traffic restrictions, cities such as Siena, Lucca and Massa Marittima are more liveable than ever, big enough to take tourism in their stride, but small enough for civic pride to define who they are. Equally harmonious are Volterra, the Val d'Orcia villages, Montepulciano, Pietrasanta, and the "tufa towns" (a type of local stone) around Pitigliano.

Such places embody the essence of "Slow Travel" – confident enough to be revitalised by tourism, careful not to be denatured by it. The secret of Tuscan identity lies in each town's sense

– and with good reason. Apart from being the cradle of the Renaissance, Tuscany boasts no less than seven Unesco World Heritage Sites: from Florence, Siena, San Gimignano, Pisa and Pienza to the landscape and lifestyle of the Val d'Orcia via the Medici villas and gardens. The Pisan Unesco site was expanded to embrace the cluster of sacred buildings on the Campo dei Miracoli beyond the legendary Leaning Tower.

Safe in its historical time capsule, Florence has often struggled to break free from its self-serving reputation as a museum-city, marooned in its glorious past. In recent times, its sleepy attitude to culture post-Michelangelo has been shaken up by the success of the Palazzo Strozzi, which has put the city on the contemporary art map.

The duality of the Tuscan temperament when it comes to heritage – conservatism with a dash of radicalism – is reflected in the Renaissance Palazzo Strozzi, and its contemporary-arts space, La Strozzina. The Establishment space can stage art blockbusters, leaving its cutting-edge sister to play with new trends and talents.

RECONCILING THE CULTURAL PAST AND PRESENT

Florence's former mayor, the charismatic Matteo Renzi (who went on to be Italy's prime minister until 2016), triggered a cultural revival in his native city, still very much in place today. The Palazzo Vecchio stays open until midnight in the summer season, and there is pressure on the more staid State-owned museums to follow suit. The greatest, the Uffizi Gallery, has opened new rooms and the city also has a new opera house and auditorium. In addition, former convents, a fortress, a station and even a prison have been converted into cultural centres, concert halls, libraries, galleries and venues for fashion shows, exhibitions and eclectic events. This new dynamism is not

Florentine belle.

Reading a daily newspaper in Florence.

⊘ THE NEW MEDICI OF WINE

A relatively large number of Tuscan wine estates are still the preserve of aristocrats who trace their lineage back to Medici Florence or beyond. The noble names include the Antinori (the largest family-run wine business in Italy), Frescobaldi and Ricasoli. But now the rock stars are moving in as the new Medici of wine.

In Tenuta degli Dei, flamboyant Florentine designer Roberto Cavalli creates Tuscan Merlots at his wine estate and stud farm in the heart of Chianti country (www.deglidei.it). Tuscan opera legend Andrea Bocelli also dabbles in wine-making (www.bocellifamilywines.com), his greatest passion after music and

horses. Sienese rock star Gianna Nannini crafts Sangiovese-style reds in a former monastery near Siena (www.certosadibelriguardo.com). In gentleman-farmer mode, superstar Sting sells his wine, organic oil and honey on his Tenuta il Palagio retreat in Chiantishire.

Tuscan actors and artists are equally keen to till the soil. Actress Stefania Sandrelli produces genuine Chianti on her estate, and artist Sandro Chia makes award-winning Brunello. Castello Romitorio, Chia's 12th-century estate, is dotted with arresting artworks that would have caught the Medici eye. (www.castelloromitorio.com).

restricted to Florence. Prato's Pecci museum of contemporary art is thriving, and an elite group of Tuscan arts festivals are gaining international recognition, from Florence's Maggio Fiorentino to Cortona's Mix Festival and Lucca's celebrity-studded summer music festival.

But there's no escaping the constraints of the 16th-century straitjacket. If the glory of Florence is that it contains the world's greatest concentration of Renaissance art and architecture, the price is responsibility to future generations, and perpetual restoration. Critic Mary McCarthy put the dilemma forcefully: "Historic Florence is an incubus on its present population. It is like a vast piece of family property whose upkeep is too much for the heirs, who nevertheless find themselves criticised by strangers for letting the old place go to rack and ruin."

RENOVATION AND PROTECTION

Yet there is much to celebrate in the capital and in Tuscany as a whole. In Siena, the glorious pilgrims' hospital of Santa Maria della Scala has become a magnificent medieval museum. In Pisa, the (slightly straighter) Leaning Tower was finally unveiled in 2011. In the Maremma, Sovana's monumental Etruscan trails have recently been restored. A welcome trend in conservation is the return of artworks to the churches for which they were created. In Florence, Michelangelo's wooden Crucifix returned to Santo Spirito, as did Masaccio's fresco of the Trinity to Santa Maria Novella. More recently, a once-neglected Crucifix has been restored, declared a genuine Giotto, and returned in glory to its home in the Ognissanti church.

Even so, restoration is never-ending in Tuscany, with each project accompanied by public scrutiny from some of the most artistically aware citizens in Europe. In Piero della Francesca's superb fresco cycle in Arezzo, for instance, the restorers were accused of repainting rather than simply restoring. As for major sculpture, the threat of pollution means that "cloning" carries the day, with restored statues replaced by copies. In a sense, the pattern was set by the removal of Michelangelo's *David* to the Accademia. The cloning issue divides critics, with realists opting for copies and romantics preferring the works to grow old gracefully, or disgracefully, in the place for which they were created. But given Florence's new environmental initiatives, more sculptures may well remain *in situ*.

TUSCANS AND THEIR LANDSCAPE

The counterpoint to the compact urban artistic heritage is the endless countryside. Etruscans cultivated it, Tuscans civilised it, and foreigners romanticised it. Tuscans still prefer living in large villages or small towns, echoing the Etruscan ideal, which was confirmed by the rural perils of medieval Europe. These deeply urban people cultivate a close relationship with the land, but it is a wary bond that doesn't imply mastery. Even so, rural traditions have deep roots. Lucca's olive trees date back to Roman times, while the

Young boys wearing the colours of their contrada, drinking from a fountain during the Palio, Siena.

region's ancient vineyards are terraced on slopes that have been cultivated for centuries.

World War II shattered rural life in Tuscany – ending the feudal *mezzadria* system of land being governed by the wealthy nobility. With the ancient paternalistic social structure gone, thousands of farmers and villagers abandoned their homes and headed for the cities in search of jobs. Villages that had been the hub of rural life for thousands of years became ghost towns. Although the medieval *mezzadria* system of sharecropping (in which a landowner allows a tenant use of the land in return for a share of the crop produced) was banned in 1978, old traditions die hard. Apart from large wheat and cattle farms in the

Val d'Arno and Val di Chiana, farming is mostly labour-intensive, under-mechanised and organic. Partly through poverty and tradition, Tuscany has gained a reputation as a leading region for small-scale sustainable farming.

THE COUNTRYSIDE REVIVAL

Even so, beyond the sought-after wine and oil estates, the countryside has been suffering from depopulation. The influx of the olive-nibbling classes has helped to reverse the trend, with tumbledown farmhouses being snapped up by the Chiantishire set. Villas, castles and fortified estates have been turned into sleek spa resorts. Semi-abandoned villages are being reborn as boutique retreats, as in the case of Il Borro, a resort restored by the Ferragamo family. Castelfalfi is the most ambitious rural resort, with a hotel, villas, farmhouses and a golf course developed by TUI, the huge German tour operator. Critics mutter about "the German conquest", but the lovely village, with views towards Volterra, was previously abandoned. Other slumbering villages are being saved by novel local schemes. Pari, a depopulated

Enjoying the sun in Castiglione della Pescaia on the Maremma coast.

⊘ TUSCANY IN THE CINEMA

Tuscany is cinematic by nature, with its rolling hills and quaint villages perfect for expat dramas, from *Room with a View* (1985) to *Under the Tuscan Sun* (2003). Bernardo Bertolucci's *Stealing Beauty* (1996) plumped for Chiantishire, while Jane Campion's stylish *Portrait of a Lady* (1996) preferred the Lucca countryside. Franco Zeffirelli's semi-autobiographical *Tea with Mussolini* (1999) is set in wartime Florence, a period also perfectly evoked by Anthony Minghella's *The English Patient* (1996). In the last film, Piero della Francesca's frescoes in Arezzo's Basilica di San Francesco are revealed by flares to the enchanted Hanna (Juliette Binoche).

Tuscan film sets transcend period drama. Ridley Scott made his epic, *Gladiator* (2000), in lush Val d'Orcia, while *Hannibal* (2001) saw the charismatic psychopath lap up Florence, from the Ponte Vecchio to the Porcellino. And Carrara's marble quarries saw action in *Quantum of Solace* (2008), with the film thundering to a climax during Siena's Palio horse race.

Artier films include Zeffirelli's Oscar-winning *Romeo and Juliet* (1968) and Tarkovsky's *Nostalgia* (1983), set in the mysterious spa pool at Bagno Vignone. And just when many feared that Tuscany had fallen out of favour with directors, along came a vampire story, *Twilight: New Moon* (2009) and a romantic drama, *Letters to Juliet* (2010).

village between Monte Amiata and Petriolo, has been running a "reopen the shutters" project to win back young families, offering to pay their rent for three years. Proof, indeed, that tourism is not the only answer.

In fact, beyond the Florence–Siena axis, the effects of tourism fade away. Here another Tuscany emerges, in the Apuan Alps and Garfagnana, with their rugged mountains, plunging valleys and marble mines. And to the west, the Maremma is still imbued with a sense of mystery, its wild pine groves a reminder that Tuscany is blessed with

Dantesque grandiloquence and Renaissance finery, Tuscany's heart is rural. Its largest city is home to less than 400,000 people, and the nickname for Tuscans is *"Mangiafagioli"* (bean eaters). So it is perhaps not surprising that the province's best-loved son comes from the Arezzo countryside. Italy's tragicomic clown-prince – Oscar-winning actor Roberto Benigni – speaks lovingly of his homeland as "a region of hunters and hares, of large peasant women and wild and poetic beauty". And who would argue with Tuscany's *"grande Roberto"*?

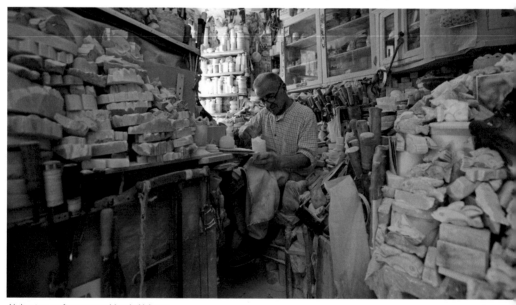

Alabaster craftsman working in Volterra.

more forest than any other region in Italy. These remote swathes are the riposte to those who decry Tuscan "Disneyfication". The same is true of the beaches, such as Marina di Pisa, Castiglione della Pescaia and the silver coast of Monte Argentario, which win Tuscany awards as one of the cleanest coastlines in Italy.

In Tuscany, quality of life is cultivated like an olive grove: few would jeopardise this heritage by turning to heavy industry. The industries Tuscans speak of with pride, such as Siena's *panforte*, Carrara's marble, Volterra's alabaster and Arezzo gold, date back to medieval times. In keeping with tradition, true Tuscans are provincial, conservative and independent; civic culture and rural pride are their touchstones. For all its

⊘ CHIANTISHIRE COMMUTERS

Peasant farmers could not believe their luck when crumbling, empty farmhouses began to be seen, in the 1960s, as an opportunity to create a rural idyll. A British presence in this revival gave birth to the nickname Chiantishire. Tuscans often protest that the Chiantishire commuters have priced locals out of their native villages, but foreigners argue that they saved places such as Sovicille near Siena, or Bugnano near Lucca from total abandonment. *Agriturismo* (farm-stays) helps to generate funds for further restoration. What's more, many foreign residents are now well integrated, as evidenced in the marble-carving town of Pietrasanta.

DECISIVE DATES

ETRUSCANS AND ROMANS

800–500 BC
Etruscan civilisation flourishes in the region. Etruria Propria, a confederation of 12 states, includes Arezzo, Chiusi, Fiesole and Volterra.

480–290 BC
Romans annexe Etruria and found colonies at Ansedonia, Roselle, Volterra, Luni and Lucca.

80 BC
Faesulae (Fiesole) becomes a Roman military colony.

59 BC
Colony of Roman veterans founds Florentia (Florence) on the banks of the Arno.

AD 200–600
Region invaded by Lombards, Goths and Franks.

AD 306
Constantinople becomes the capital of the Roman Empire; the Byzantine period follows.

AD 476
The Fall of Rome.

MEDIEVAL TUSCANY

1000–1300
Germans conquer Italy; warring between Guelfs (supporters of papacy) and Ghibellines (supporters of Holy Roman Empire).

1062
Pisa triumphs over the Saracens in battle off Palermo.

1115
Florence becomes an independent city governed by a mercantile-class council.

1118
Pisa Cathedral consecrated.

1125
Florence begins expansion with takeover of Fiesole.

1173
Bonnano Pisano begins Pisa's Leaning Tower.

1246–50
Work on Florence's Santa Maria Novella begins and Bargello built.

1260
Sienese defeat the Florentines in battle of Montaperti.

1294
Arnolfo di Cambio begins Florence's Santa Croce.

1296
Di Cambio begins Florence's Duomo.

1310
Siena's Palazzo Pubblico is completed.

1314
Dante Alighieri begins *The Divine Comedy*.

1334
Giotto begins Florence's Campanile.

c.1345
Florence's Ponte Vecchio is erected by Taddeo Gaddi.

Lorenzo de' Medici.

1348
Black Death hits Florence.

1390
John Hawkwood becomes Captain General of Florence; inter-city wars.

THE RENAISSANCE

1406
Pisa is defeated, becoming part of Florentine state.

1420
Papacy returns to Rome.

1434–64
Cosimo de' Medici rules Florence.

1436
Brunelleschi completes dome for Florence's Duomo.

1452
Alberti's *Ten Books on Architecture* is published.

1469–92
Lorenzo de' Medici rules Florence.

1478
Sandro Botticelli paints *La Primavera*.

1498
Savonarola hanged for heresy in Florence's Piazza della Signoria.

1504
Michelangelo completes *David*.

1513
Niccolò Machiavelli writes *The Prince*.

1527
The Sack of Rome.

1530
Republic of Florence ends as armies of Pope Clement VII and Emperor Charles V besiege the city.

1550
Giorgio Vasari's *Lives of the Artists* first published.

1554
Siena is defeated, becoming part of Florentine state.

1564–1642
Galileo Galilei discovers the principles of dynamics.

GRAND DUCHY TUSCANY

1716
Grand Duke establishes Chianti wine laws.

1737
Gian Gastone, the last male Medici, dies.

1796
Napoleon's first Italian campaign.

1815
Grand Duchy absorbed into the Austrian Empire.

MODERN TUSCANY

1848
The War of Independence.

1861
Kingdom of Italy proclaimed.

1865–71
Florence capital of Italy.

1915
Italy enters World War I on the Allies' side.

1922
Benito Mussolini elected.

1940
Italy enters World War II against Allies.

1945
Mussolini executed.

1946
Italy becomes a republic.

1957
The Treaty of Rome; Italy a founder member of EEC (now EU).

1966
Massive flooding in Florence – artworks damaged.

1993
Mafia bomb kills five and damages Uffizi, Florence.

1994
Right-wing government ushers in Second Republic. Silvio Berlusconi elected premier (re-elected in 2001 and 2008).

The aftermath of the 1966 flood.

2004
Val d'Orcia declared Unesco World Heritage Site.

2005
Pope John Paul II dies, succeeded by Benedict XVI.

2011
Restoration on Pisa's Leaning Tower ends after 20 years of work. Oldest-ever Etruscan necropolis found near Livorno.

2013
Medici villas and gardens designated Unesco World Heritage Site.

2014
Former mayor of Florence and Democratic Party leader Matteo Renzi becomes Italy's prime minister. Dario Nardella, from the same party, replaces him as Florence's mayor.

2016
Matteo Renzi resigns as prime minister and is succeeded by Paolo Gentiloni.

2018
General election held in March results in a hung parliament. In June Giuseppe Conte, a lawyer with little political experience, becomes prime minister of a coalition government between the far-right League and Five-Star Movement.

THE ETRUSCANS

Long before the Romans left their mark on the landscape, the Etruscan people established their own sense of regional identity, humanistic values and peaceful society in Tuscany.

The story of Tuscany begins with the Etruscans, its earliest known inhabitants, whose origins are shrouded in myth and mystery. The Romantics and latter-day writers believed that the Etruscans sailed from Asia Minor. However, Dionysius, writing as the Etruscan civilisation neared its end, held that the Etruscans were natives with an indigenous culture too deeply ingrained to be oriental. Most modern scholars believe that the Etruscans migrated from Eastern Europe over the Alps and represent the flowering of the early Italic tribes. What is clear is that between the 8th and 4th centuries BC "Etruria Propria" flourished as a confederation of 12 city-states in central Italy.

Part of the fortification wall at Chiusi, one of Tuscany's major Etruscan sites.

> Northern Etruria, roughly equivalent to modern Tuscany, included Arezzo, Chiusi, Cortona, Populonia, Vetulonia and Volterra.

Etruscan seafarers and merchants first settled on the coast and began smelting iron ore from Elba and importing oriental ceramics, glass and silverware. Greek naval supremacy meant an opening to Hellenistic culture: ships sailed to Corinth with honey, gold and bronze figurines, and returned to Vetulonia and Populonia with perfume and painted wine jars. The inland cities such as Chiusi and Volterra thrived on hunting, farming and trade. Over the next two centuries, the Etruscans allied themselves to the developing Roman power, and by the 1st century BC, all Etruscan territory was annexed. Although Etruscan and Latin co-existed, Etruscan culture was crushed; its role degenerated

into the provision of soothsayers, musicians, dancers and fighters for Rome.

ETRUSCAN SOCIETY

The original confederation had a complex urban and social structure: each city was originally run by a king, later by local aristocrats, and finally by a priestly oligarchy. The lords owned large landholdings or navies and were served by serfs and slaves. Whereas the serfs were rewarded with agricultural plots, the slaves danced and sang for their supper. With urbanisation, an independent class of artisans and merchants began to emerge. The granting of the same Roman citizenship to the middle classes as to the aristocratic priests and magistrates was a severe blow to the Etruscan princely tradition.

The Etruscans were expert builders. Their cities followed the contours of the land and sited the necropolis below the city walls and the living city above. If cities of the dead predominate today, it is by accident and not by design. Public buildings, constructed of wood and clay, did not survive. From what remains of the cities, there was enough to impress Roman and Renaissance architects. Volterra's Porta all'Arco, a deep gateway inspired by Mesopotamian architecture; the huge drystone walls at Saturnia, rebuilt to defend the city against Roman incursions; the neat town plans of Pitigliano and Sovana – all these scattered remains are evidence of the vitality and ingenuity of Etruscan builders.

New discoveries of Etruscan artefacts continue to be made around the region. Recently, east of Livorno, archaeologists unearthed a 3,000-year-old necropolis, dating from the end of the Bronze Age, and the oldest Etruscan site ever found. To trump that, a Palaeolithic man, Tuscany's oldest *Homo sapiens*, was found in Monteriggioni in

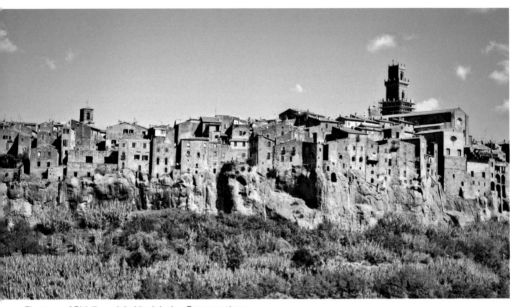

The town of Pitigliano, inhabited during Etruscan times.

⊘ BEST ETRUSCAN SITES

Scrape the surface of the most enigmatic Tuscan towns and an Etruscan spirit lies beneath, with temple walls recycled into Roman buildings, or ancient epigraphs encrusted within Renaissance palaces.

In Volterra, the Porta all'Arco Etrusco reveals a Roman arched vault, incorporating three Etruscan basalt heads, on massive Etruscan bases. The superb Etruscan Museum displays *The Shadow of the Evening* sculpture. Although over 2,000 years old, this bronze figure seems modern in both message and design. Florence's Archaeological Museum boasts the reconstructed Inghirammi Tomb, a semicircular Etruscan tomb from Volterra. Finer still is the museum's bronze *Chimera* from Arezzo.

Chiusi has one of the best museums, stuffed with *bucchero* ware and Canopic urns, cinerary urns with an idealised effigy of the deceased on the lid. The only painted tombs in Tuscany are here, along with underground galleries and a mysterious labyrinth that reputedly conceals the sarcophagus of Lars Porsenna, mythical king of the Etruscans.

In the Maremma area, Sovana is riddled with deep, ravine-like Etruscan roads and "pigeonhole" tombs, niches cut into the rock. In Vetulonia, the remote, rural setting contrasts with tangible proof that this was once one of the richest cities in Etruria.

2011. In Sesto Fiorentino, outside Florence, the Etruscan Tomb of La Montagnola is now opened to the public, with its impressive secret vaulted corridor and noble burial chamber. At Poggio Colla, two Etruscan depictions of a woman in childbirth were discovered in 2011 while a 227kg (500lbs) stele bearing the name of fertility goddess Uni was unearthed in 2016.

ETRUSCAN ART

Fascinating tombs, in every shape and form, can be seen in the Etruscan necropolises: "temple"

Friezes of serene married couples, tender lovers, absorbed wrestlers, erotic dancers or grieving warriors reflect the fullness and variety of Etruscan life.

Noblewomen enjoyed freedom, influence and social status. They are frequently depicted attending banquets without their husbands, riding covered wagons to their land-holdings and playing flutes or lyres at funerals. The men are rarely still: they charge through games, boar-hunts, processions, journeys, dances, banquets and diving competitions. The "ordinary" Etrus-

Sarcophagus dating from the 2nd century BC, Tarquinia.

tombs at Saturnia; melon-shaped tombs at Cortona; oriental "trench" tombs at Vetulonia. It is the tombs that remain as a cultural testimony to the power, wealth and beliefs of their owners. Death reflected life: the poor were often buried in shallow graves or their ashes put in small urns; the rich were buried in chamber tombs and stone sarcophagi decorated with pottery.

Since there is no extant Etruscan literature, our knowledge of the living Etruscans is oddly dependent on a reading of this funerary art for clues. We know them as they would like to be known, these idealised aristocrats elevated by Greek myths. The women were depicted as pale, while the men were uniformly reddish-brown, either suntanned or ritually painted.

can is only glimpsed in passing: a prized blonde courtesan flits past dancing slaves; a serf mourns his dead master.

THE ROMAN LEGACY

Rome annexed Etruria in 351 BC, and, from the 3rd until the 2nd century BC, as part of the massive road-building programme that was to transform the entire country, four great Roman roads were built across the territory: the Via Aurelia, which ran up the western seaboard to Pisae and the naval base at Genua in Liguria; the Via Clodia, which stopped at Saturnia; the Via Cassia, built in 154 BC to connect Rome with Florentia; and the Via Flaminia, built in 220 BC to connect Rome to Umbria and the Adriatic Sea.

Etruscan roads were all designed to connect the interior with the coast, whereas Roman roads all led to Rome, thus the axis was turned 90°, from east–west to north–south. The more impressive new Roman roads purposely avoided the great Etruscan cities, which slowly fell into decline, whereas the new Roman cities such as Pistoriae (Pistoia), now better connected, grew in importance.

New colonies were founded at Ansedonia, Fiesole, Roselle, Populonia, Volterra, Luni and Lucca. The cultural identity of the Etruscans was gradually absorbed into that of the Romans, a process that was accelerated in 91 BC when Roman citizenship was extended to the Etruscans.

The Romans learnt many things from the Etruscans – principally, the Tuscan arch, which they developed as a key element in their extraordinary aqueducts, bridges and buildings, relegating the classical columns of Greece to a more decorative role in their architecture.

Certainly, the Etruscan influence on the Romans was considerable. Apart from intro-

The remains of the Roman theatre in Volterra.

⊘ MYSTERY LANGUAGE

The Etruscan language may be as mysterious as the people's origins, but its unintelligibility is still part of a glamorous myth. Although the alphabet is borrowed from Greek, the language, read from left to right, belongs to no known linguistic group. True, there are no external keys such as dictionaries or bilingual texts, but the core grammatical and phonetic structure is known, and most of the 10,000 shorter texts can be read accurately. These texts are mostly funerary inscriptions and religious dedications. The one known book, a priest's manual discovered wrapped around an Egyptian mummy, has only been partially deciphered.

ducing to Rome the purple toga, an abundance of gods and competent soothsayers, the Etruscans also added a set of religious, humanistic and regional values that far outlived the Roman Empire itself. But by creating the roads and major cities of Tuscany, the Romans also left a permanent imprint on this part of the Italian landscape.

A millennium later, the ruins of their great bridges, amphitheatres and city walls were the inspiration for the next great blossoming of Italian culture: Tuscany's coming of age, the Renaissance. The art critic John Ruskin even saw an unbroken line of tradition from the tomb paintings of the Etruscans to Giotto and Fra Angelico.

ROMAN TUSCANY

Apart from the roads, the Romans' greatest legacy is their template for the classic town plan, with the forum – evolving into the piazza – the focal point.

It's hard to imagine the impact that Roman roads, giant engineering projects, must have had on the colonised Etruscans, as regimented teams spanned rivers with elegant stone bridges, built drains to prevent their new roads from flooding, and at times even cut through the hills themselves.

ROMAN TRACES

Detective work is necessary to unearth Roman Florence, Florentia; the Roman gridiron street plan is clearly visible in maps, with the Piazza della Repubblica following the outline of the old *castrum*. Nearby, Fiesole, which possibly dates from the 8th century BC, was an Etruscan settlement but, as Faesulae, became a Roman military colony from 80 BC and later became the capital of Roman Etruria. The Piazza Mino da Fiesole occupies the site of the Roman forum. The archaeological site, set on a hillside near the Duomo, features a remarkably well-preserved Roman theatre, still used for performances. Beyond are Roman baths, and on the far side, the ruins of a Roman temple, both 1st century BC, as well as a 3rd century BC Etruscan temple, set against the Etruscan city walls.

In Lucca, the original street plan is also still evident. Lucca began as a military colony in 178 BC and featured a 10,000-seat amphitheatre, outside the walls. In time, it was largely dismantled, and most of its remains are below street level. During the Middle Ages, however, houses were built using the remaining walls of the amphitheatre, thus fossilising its outline and four main entrances. Fragments of it are still visible from the surrounding lanes, incorporated in the outer walls of the houses. Volterra, which became an important Roman municipality in the 4th century BC, also recycled its history, as well as retaining the ruins of the 1st century BC Roman theatre beyond the city walls.

Luni, called Luna by the Romans, was founded in 177 BC and was the springboard for the conquest of the Ligurian tribes. The Roman city, its forum, a number of houses and its amphitheatre have been excavated.

Another extensively excavated site is at Roselle, the Roman Rusellae, one of the most important Etruscan cities of northern Etruria. Originally an island, the Etruscan city was taken by Rome early in

View from the Teatro Romano, Fiesole.

the 3rd century BC. The ruins are satisfyingly complete, with Romano-Etruscan walls, a Roman forum, paved streets, basilicas, villas, amphitheatre, workshops and baths.

Ansedonia, the Roman Cosa, was founded as a Roman colony in 273 BC. The ancient hilltop city has been excavated, and the site contains the ruins of a main street, forum, walled acropolis and the *capitolium* – a tripartite sanctuary for the triad of Jupiter, Juno and Minerva. The city's 1.5km (1-mile) wall is virtually intact, as are many of its 18 guard towers and forum. The site is slightly overgrown, and many of the ruins are covered in brambles, creating a beguilingly elegiac mood, but it has fabulous views out to sea and is worth a visit.

Procession of the Magus Balthasar (fresco from the Magi Chapel of the Palazzo Medici Riccardi) by Benozzo Gozzoli (c. 1420–97).

THE RENAISSANCE AND THE MEDICI

From feuding factionalism to the rise of the Medici, the aspirations of small city-states to remain independent were often dashed – but wealth, power and patronage still fostered an artistic flowering.

Between the ending of the Roman Empire in the 5th century AD and the beginning of the foreign invasions in the 16th century, the story of Italy is a catalogue of conflict between its cities, each of which was a sovereign state. In Tuscany, a three-way battle was conducted between Florence, Pisa and Siena.

THE *CONDOTTIERI*

In the early stages, the battles between the city-states were conducted by the citizens them-selves, but when Florence crushed Arezzo in 1289 at Campaldino, the bloodshed was so great that thereafter the cities began to fight out their differences with mercenaries, the *condottieri*.

Throughout the 14th century, the *condottieri* held the balance of power. Commanding com-panies numbering thousands of men, they sold their services to the highest bidder. The city that could afford them – and control them – domi-nated its neighbours. Few could control them, however, and that is why the *condottieri* system failed. The *condottieri* had a vested interest in conflict: from being paid to fight on behalf of a city, it was a short step to blackmailing that same city into paying you not to attack them.

Some *condottieri* were bought off – Sir John Hawkwood, the piratical leader of the much-feared White Company, was given a palatial villa and a substantial estate as his reward for retir-ing gracefully from the fray. Hawkwood craved immortality and wanted an equestrian statue to be erected in Florence – instead, the miserly Florentines opted for the less expensive solution of an illusionistic fresco, painted by Paolo Uccello to look like a statue, in Florence Cathedral.

The burden of paying the *condottieri* fell to the merchant class. They were caught on the

Detail from Ambrogio Lorenzetti's Effects of Good and Bad Government (1338).

horns of a dilemma, desiring domination over their trade rivals, and yet aware of the high cost of war, in terms of both taxes and eco-nomic instability. When they waged war on neighbouring cities, they often did so in the name of "Guelf" or "Ghibelline" partisanship. The Guelfs were broadly made up of the ris-ing merchant class, bankers and members of the trades guilds, who nominally supported the papacy in its long battle against the Holy Roman Emperor, and who wanted a greater role in city government. Conversely, the Ghibellines, the old feudal aristocracy, supported the emperor, because he seemed the best guarantor of their virtual autocracy. Since the emperor was often

German or Spanish and an absentee ruler, paying nominal allegiance to such a distant figurehead was far preferable to the threat of the pope exercising real and temporal power much closer to home.

Outside Tuscany, many city-states fell under the dominion of a single ruler – some of them former *condottieri* who ended up rulers of the cities they once protected, founding dynasties. The Tuscan city-states and republics maintained their independence far longer, but eventually even they fell to a dynastic power, as the Medici transformed themselves from private citizens to grand dukes.

THE RISE OF THE MEDICI

Ruefully reflecting on the mistakes that had led him to be imprisoned and tortured before being cast from office, Niccolò Machiavelli, former Chancellor of Florence, wrote his masterpiece *The Prince*, in which he admiringly recounted the ruthless methods used by the Medici to claw their way to absolute power in Tuscany. Even more remarkable is the way that the dynasty threw up gifted

The map known as the Carta della Catena showing Florence around 1470.

⊘ DANTE'S FLORENCE

In the medieval heart of Florence, an unassuming tower-house is reputedly the birthplace of Dante Alighieri (1265–1321), Italy's most revered poet. His epic poem, *The Divine Comedy*, set the Tuscan dialect as the model for Italian literature. The Casa di Dante is an evocation of Dante's Florence rather than an insight into the poet's genius.

As a citizen of Florence, Dante's horizons embraced the Bargello, the Baptistery and the Badia Fiorentina. The museum presents the Guelf-Ghibelline political struggles, including family crests and battle maps. Unjustly cast into exile after disputes within the Guelf faction, Dante declared himself "a Florentine by birth but not by character". The poet died in exile in Ravenna, but his native city belatedly redeemed itself with a Dante memorial in Santa Croce.

On display in the poet's home is a copy of Henry Holliday's Pre-Raphaelite painting, *The Meeting of Dante and Beatrice*, alluding to the doomed infatuation that inspired much of the poet's work. The earliest-known portrait of Dante was recently discovered in the medieval meeting hall of the Magistrates Guild. Now both a museum and restaurant, the vaulted walls of Fishing Lab Alle Murate reveal portraits of other Florentine legends, including Petrarch and Boccaccio. (Fishing Lab Alle Murate: 16R Via del Proconsolo, Florence; www.fishinglab.it. Casa di Dante: Via Santa Margherita, Florence; www.museocasadidante.it).

individuals, generation after generation. The Medici were masters of realpolitik and military strategy but also patronised the arts, helping to make Florence and Tuscany the engine of cultural regeneration that we know as the Renaissance.

The man who laid the foundations for the family's meteoric rise was Giovanni de' Medici (1360–1429), founder of the Medici bank. This was just one of 100 or so financial institutions in 15th-century Florence, but Giovanni's master-stroke was to develop a special relationship with the Church, eventually securing a monopoly over the collection of the papal revenues.

Giovanni's son, Cosimo, developed this relationship still further: one of his great coups was to attract the prestigious General Council of the Greek Orthodox and the Roman Catholic churches to Florence. These two great Christian churches had been at loggerheads for six centuries. Their assemblies in Florence were intended to find ways of burying their differences and creating a unified Christian church. This they failed to do, but the meetings had a lasting impact on Florence. Not only did they create a stimulating climate of theological and intellectual debate, out of which the Renaissance was to grow, but also they fuelled artistic debate. The pomp and pageantry of the papal entourage, and the flamboyance of its Greek counterparts, provided artists with an array of exotica.

Cosimo himself eschewed such riches. He took pride in simplicity, ordering Brunelleschi, the temperamental genius behind the dome of Florence Cathedral, to modify his designs for the Medici palace, as they were too ostentatious. More to his taste was Michelozzo, who designed the marvellously airy library in San Marco, Florence, as a repository for the Medici book collection, the world's first-ever public library. Such generosity was typical of Cosimo, who spent a fortune endowing Florence with public buildings. Among his friends he counted humanists who shared his thirst for classical knowledge, for this was an era in which the lost classics of Greece and Rome, including works by Plato and Cicero, were being rediscovered.

Though a devout Christian who regularly retreated to his private cell at San Marco, Cosimo believed strongly that God's grace was best leavened by human reason. This made him an effective and humane ruler – even if, following his father's advice to "keep out of the public eye", Cosimo never sought public office. Instead, he wielded immense influence behind the scenes.

> "Whoever desires to found a state and give it laws must start with assuming that all men are bad and ever ready to display their vicious nature whenever they may find occasion for it."
> (Niccolò Machiavelli)

A portrait of Lorenzo de' Medici.

⊙ GOOD AND BAD GOVERNMENT

In Siena's Palazzo Pubblico, Lorenzetti's great frescoes, *The Effects of Good and Bad Government*, served as a lesson to the city's medieval rulers. *Bad Government* depicts a countryside ravaged by bandits, with fields left uncultivated, churches in ruin, and women raped in broad daylight. By contrast, *Good Government* depicts a city-state populated by peaceable citizens, attentive students and prosperous merchants. The adjoining room is dominated by a portrait of Guidoriccio da Fogliano in ceremonial battledress. As the city's *condottiero*, he was responsible for delivering the peace that underpinned the Sienese social order.

Lorenzo de' Medici inherited his father's love of the classical philosophers, and his gift for diplomacy. An outstanding poet in his own right, he promoted the study of Dante in Tuscan universities, elevating the Tuscan dialect to equal status with Latin. His greatest gift was peace. By using his diplomatic gifts to hold the great rival powers of the papacy and the Holy Roman Empire apart, Tuscany enjoyed a period of relative prosperity, in which merchants thrived and great fortunes were made. With the countryside no longer ravaged by war or held to ransom by lawless mercenaries, wealthy individuals began to build the villas that are still such a characteristic feature of the Tuscan countryside. Lorenzo himself led the way, staying regularly to his rural retreats at Fiesole and Poggio a Caiano.

THE MEDICI LOSE SUPPORT

Prophetically, Pope Innocent VIII declared that "the peace of Italy is at an end" on learning of Lorenzo's death in 1492. A period of turmoil ensued when Lorenzo's successors, who lacked the political acumen of their forebears, were

Painting depicting Cosimo I planning the conquest of Siena in 1555.

⊘ BONFIRE OF THE VANITIES

From 1494, Girolamo Savonarola, a Dominican preacher, filled the Florentines with anti-Medici zeal. He argued that their fondness for pagan philosophers and the artistic depiction of heathen gods would bring God's wrath on the city. In 1497, erotic sculptures, fine clothes, secular poetry, mirrors and paintings were burnt in what Savonarola termed "the bonfire of the vanities". Even Botticelli supported the movement, renouncing his past attachment to humanist ideals, and turned to painting Christian allegories, such as *Nativity*. But the Florentines tired of their firebrand friar, and burnt him at the stake in Piazza della Signoria.

expelled from the city and Savonarola, a firebrand preacher, took centre stage.

But the Medici swiftly returned in 1512. Michelangelo had carved his *David*, the boy hero standing up to the bullying giant Goliath, as a symbol of the city's desire to rid itself of the Medici. He also fashioned new defences for the city, but when the combined forces of the Medici and the Holy Roman Emperor held the city to siege in 1530, he took himself off to hide – irony of ironies – in the Medici mortuary chapel, attached to San Lorenzo. Vasari attributes his cowardice to the artistic temperament, and while he was in hiding he worked the masterly reclining figures of *Dawn, Evening, Day* and *Night*, which now adorn the Medici tombs.

Alessandro de' Medici, who led the victorious siege, rubbed salt into the wounds of his fellow citizens by having himself crowned Duke of Florence, claiming absolute power where his predecessors had been content with influence. When he was murdered in 1537 by his own cousin, with whom he had been having a homosexual affair, the city sought a successor. Cosimo, descended from Giovanni de' Medici via the female line, emerged victorious, partly by convincing his fellow citizens of his probity.

the region, he also set up an effective civil service to administer the dukedom, based in the Uffizi (literally, the "Offices") in Florence. This proved effective right up to the point when Tuscany joined the United Kingdom of Italy in 1861. So effective was this civil service that Tuscany continued to be ruled effectively even when Cosimo's successors proved to be corrupt, incompetent, self-indulgent or mad. Few made a major mark on the city, though Cosimo II did the world a great favour by patronising Galileo, making him court mathematician to the Medici

Detail from a painting by Vasari portraying Florence's victories over Pisa and Siena.

Once in power, Cosimo revealed his true colours, as he systematically set about destroying all opposition. Not only was he unrelenting in his pursuit of the republican leaders who had opposed his election, tracking them down in their exile and bringing them back to be tried and executed in Florence, he also set about conquering old enemies – Pisa, Siena, Massa Marittima, Montepulciano – with a ruthlessness and brutality that is still remembered and resented to this day. The whole story is told on the ceiling of the Palazzo Vecchio council chamber in a series of bloody frescoes painted by Vasari to honour Cosimo I in 1563–5.

To his credit, Cosimo not only forced Tuscany into political unity and established security in

and providing him with a home after his trial and excommunication by the Inquisition.

THE MEDICI ART COLLECTION

The dynasty also amassed an astonishing art collection, which Princess Anna Maria Lodovica, the last of the Medici line, bequeathed to the city of Florence upon her death in 1743, along with all the Medici palaces and gardens, ensuring that many of the greatest works of the Renaissance were not sold off or dispersed, but would remain in the city that gave them birth. Today, these priceless works of art form the backbone of Florence's three main galleries: the Uffizi, the Pitti and the Bargello.

For more about Renaissance art and architecture, see page 55.

VIA
S. AGATA

MODERN TUSCANY

After the Renaissance, Tuscany became an economic backwater. Italian Unification, international conflict and political corruption have all had an impact on modern Tuscany, and the "Tuscan model" is now often seen as a wise balance between prosperity and a peaceful pace of life.

Since the glories of Rome and the Renaissance, Italy has written little history. The head of Italy's Bureau of Statistics likens modern Italian history to a muddle, "a happy antheap where everyone is running about and no one is in control". The alternative is the "strong man" view of recent history, as expressed in the Florentine saying, "Whose bread and cheese I eat, to his tune I dance". But, while Rome danced to martial music, Tuscany sometimes starved or burned.

Tuscany has been buffeted rather than enriched by its recent past. Well-kept war memorials in shabby towns attest to the loss of two generations, one abroad and one at home. Look at Asciano, a village dwarfed by its *carabinieri* stronghold, built by Benito Mussolini and still used to this day to maintain law and order. Visit Montisi where, for the price of a drink, locals will describe the German bombing of the village tower, a story complete with sound effects, gestures and genuine sorrow. Ask proud Florentines why the medieval houses on the south side of the Arno are lost for ever.

THE EFFECT OF ITALIAN UNIFICATION

In 1865, Florence briefly became the capital of the newly united Italy. Although its exalted role would only last five years before Rome was then made the permanent capital, Florence underwent profound and rapid change during this time. An ambitious plan of expansion and modernisation sadly led to the demolition of, among other things, the old city walls, and their replacement with a wide ring of avenues punctuated with large piazzas in keeping with the French urban taste of the times. Quarters for the middle classes and the Piazzale Michelangelo were built. Later, old areas of the centre,

Illustration of 1860 depicting the event of Tuscany becoming part of a newly unified Italy.

including the Ghetto, were declared to be in dangerous condition and unwholesome, and were razed; the soulless Piazza della Repubblica was created partly in their place. The square remains a bold flourish of nationhood, but when the capital was transferred to Rome, Tuscan allegiance unquestionably remained in Tuscany. Unification, under the leadership of Count Camillo Benso Cavour, a French-speaking Piedmontese, was seen as a foreign threat to the *de facto* sovereignty of Florence and the smaller city-states. Defenders of the Risorgimento, the movement for Italian unification, appealed to nascent patriotism. Critics of unification cited Dante's pleas to Tuscan liberty, before both sides settled down to start subverting the power of the new rulers. The merging of Tuscans into Italians started promisingly enough, but the end result is still only to be seen abroad or at international football matches.

WORLD WAR I

Unification represented a missed chance for Italy. By failing to help shape a national identity, Tuscans also fell victim to the clearer vision of a "strong man". Even before World War I, Mussolini was making inflammatory speeches while a weak parliament practised the art of "timely resignation", a ploy used ever since to stage-manage a new coalition.

Although the pre-war Tuscan economy thrived under weak government, it was no match for growing social pressures and a deepening gulf between society and state. With few real policies, one of the last liberal governments blundered into World War I. Italy's unpopular late entry into the conflict cost Tuscan lives and support. The pyrrhic victory was exacerbated by a power vacuum, economic

Bagni di Montecatini - Piazza Umberto I

Montecatini in the early 1900s.

⊘ THE GROWTH OF THE GRAND TOUR

The most anglophone city in Italy, Florence has been a magnet for foreign visitors since the 17th century, when daring adventurers explored this strange land. By the 1700s, rich aristocrats were attracted to the region's alien psyche, perfect climate, low cost of living and undervalued art.

Florence became an essential stop on any European tour and, in the 18th century, the middle classes joined the aristocratic *dilettanti* and *literati* on the road to Tuscany. Art was on the agenda, with foreign visitors flocking to see the Uffizi sculptures and Botticelli's *Birth of Venus*. By the 1850s, visitors from Victorian England had made Florence *"une ville anglaise"*. "They toil not, neither do they spin" was the cool judgement on his contemporaries by Irish novelist Charles Lever. Lever's biographer, William Fitzpatrick, damns the expatriate circle as "the society of diplomats and demireps, swells and snobs, princes and pretenders, wits and worthies, snarlers and social men".

By the 20th century, the Anglo-Florentine community was well established, though World War I chased many away. The Grand Tour resumed in the 1920s, mainly for society figures and intellectuals. The tradition continues today, with sons and daughters of the Establishment coming to learn Italian and attend art courses on the Renaissance – occasionally enjoying the designer labels rather than the artistic treasures.

problems and a revolutionary working class. Benito Mussolini, from neighbouring Emilia, wasted no opportunity in claiming, "Governing Italy is not only impossible, it is useless", before proceeding to govern it impossibly but fairly usefully for 20 years.

By 1922, the corporate state was literally under construction. The economic benefits lasted until 1929, but the aesthetic effects linger on in functionally "improved" cities all over Tuscany. Florence railway station was the first Functionalist station in Italy.

captured by the Allies, individual Fascists held out, firing from the rooftops. Surprising loyalties emerged: while the director of the British Institute was a known Fascist sympathiser, the German consul risked his life to protect Florentines who had been denounced. After the liberation he was granted the freedom of the city.

Florence was liberated in August 1943, but Mussolini and the German forces survived the winter behind the so-called "Gothic Line" in the Apennines. Apart from Florence, the partisans were very active in the Monte Amiata area,

Santa Maria Novella railway station in Florence, one of the key architectural works of Italian Modernism.

WORLD WAR II

At the outbreak of World War II, most Tuscans were cautiously neutral. Mussolini, despite having signed the Pact of Steel with Germany, only entered the war in 1940, after the fall of France. By 1943, the north was under German control, but the Allies were progressing northwards from Sicily. Allied bombing, German entrenchment and an emerging Tuscan Resistance transformed Tuscany into a battleground.

Anti-Fascist cells had been secretly set up by the Communists and Catholics in key towns under German and neo-Fascist control. Florence was split: while it was the intellectual centre of the Resistance, it also harboured strong Fascist sympathisers. Even after the city was

as well as in the Val d'Orcia, where the writer Iris Origo, an Englishwoman married to an Italian *marchese*, sheltered many refugees and prisoners of war in her villa, La Foce.

Writing about it at the time, she observed: "In the last few days I have seen Radicofani and Cortignano destroyed, the countryside and farms studded with shell holes, girls raped, and human beings and cattle killed. Otherwise the events of the last week have had little effect upon either side; it is the civilians who have suffered."

Nor were the Allies completely blameless. The modernity of Grosseto, Livorno and Pisa today owes much to Allied bombing in 1943. The British War Office reports naturally exonerated the Allies: "No damage of any significance is

FOREIGN WRITERS IN TUSCANY

Generations of enraptured writers have penned paeans to Tuscany, which often say more about themselves, and their romantic projections, than they do about Tuscany.

Shelley pronounced Tuscany a "paradise of exiles" tempted by art, adventure and escape from persecution. But the exiles' motives were as varied as their prose styles. The Scottish writer Tobias Smollett (1721–71) failed to appreciate the entrepreneurial nature of the Tuscan aristocracy, finding it undignified

Virginia Woolf saw "loneliness" in the landscape.

for "a noble to sell a pound of figs or to take money for a glass of sour wine". The Romantics were more enthusiastic. Lord Byron was "dazzled, drunk with Beauty" in Santa Croce. Shelley adored Pisan landscapes and Livornese seascapes, tragically drowning near La Spezia. Tuscany soon became a place of pilgrimage for the later Romantic poets, such as Tennyson and Wordsworth.

STENDHAL SYNDROME

Although officially a diplomat in Florence, the French novelist Stendhal spent most of his time absorbing Renaissance frescoes and planning his novel, *Le Rouge et le Noir* (1830). As with Byron, the Santa Croce Effect sent Stendhal reeling: "I walked in

constant fear of falling to the ground." This aesthetic sickness is now known as Stendhal Syndrome.

Henry James was one of the few foreign writers able to see through Tuscany's literary and artistic veil, taking a more pragmatic approach. His *Portrait of Places* gives an opinionated but sensitive picture of the region in the 1870s.

THE BROWNINGS

The most romantic Victorian couple was undoubtedly the poets Elizabeth Barrett Browning and Robert Browning. Robert brought his wife to Florence because of her poor health. There he used Chianti to wean Elizabeth off her addiction to laudanum. Their 15th-century *palazzo*, redecorated in Victorian style, is now a museum.

A ROOM WITH A VIEW

The 20th century brought E.M. Forster, with his ironic analysis of the resident English community at play. Forster's *A Room with a View* portrays the heroine's encounter with an alien culture and alien passions. Virginia Woolf saw her own image reflected in the landscape, "infinite emptiness, loneliness, silence", while D.H. Lawrence, living in his "grave old Tuscan villa", imagined that he was communing with the original Etruscans.

World War II prevented further literary flowering, but in *War in Val d'Orcia*, Iris Origo, an Anglo-Florentine, painted a dramatic picture of the Tuscan battlefield. Soon after the war, the Welsh poet Dylan Thomas came to Tuscany and was entranced: "The pine hills are endless, the cypresses at the hilltop tell one all about the length of death, the woods are deep as love and full of goats." He apparently enjoyed a hedonistic lifestyle, vegetating in the sun and devouring strawberries and wine.

AN ENDURING LOVE

Tuscany still draws literary pilgrims. Frances Mayes' bestseller, *Under the Tuscan Sun* (1996), brought a fresh wave of American tourists in search of the Tuscan dream. This book and her ensuing memoirs, *Bella Tuscany* (1999) followed by *Every Day in Tuscany* (2010), are only the latest in a long line of tributes penned by besotted foreigners.

attributable to Allied action [in Florence]." The Allies issued their troops with booklets listing various buildings to be protected, including the tricky prospect of safeguarding the "living museum" of Florence: "The whole city of Florence must rank as a work of art of the first importance." According to one report, "the great monuments, nearly all of which lie north of the river, escaped practically undamaged because, though the enemy held the northern bank against an advance, our troops deliberately refrained from firing upon them".

locally. Until 1994, this meant Christian Democracy at national level and Communism at regional level. On the surface, this appeared a rather curious recipe for success.

Given the level of national opposition to Communists, the Communist Party evolved an aggressively pro-regionalist stance. The reward was the "red belt" across central Italy, run by left-wing coalitions since the first regional elections in 1970. Red Tuscany formed the central strand between Emilia Romagna's model economy and rural Umbria. Despite the transformations in the

Hitler and Mussolini salute at Florence's Tomb of the Fascist Martyrs.

Despite Allied concern and care, Florence nevertheless lost innumerable bridges, streets, libraries, churches, *palazzi*, paintings and Tuscan lives. But, in contrast to the "mutilated victory" of 1919, Italy lost the war but won the peace.

Massimo Salvatore, a supporter of the partisans in Florence, saw the war as a character-building exercise: "Without it [we] would surely have sunk into a morass of low politics and intrigues." That was still to come.

"RED BELT" TUSCANY

Tuscans may be conservative by nature, but they are also fiercely independent. Since World War II, they have tended to vote for right-wing governments nationally, but for left-wing councils

> *Commendable feats of Allied bravery included the penetration of enemy lines via the Vasari Corridor, a secret route used by the Medici in similar crises.*

"new Italy", left-leaning Tuscany survives as one of the most efficient of regional governments.

The Tuscan left believes in a broad but increasingly secular Church. Civic culture, regional pride and fierce individualism form the real faith. The power of the left is as much a reflection of regional hostility to Roman centralisation as an espousal of social democratic principles. Even in "red belt" Tuscany, the region's most popular newspaper is the right-wing but regional *La Nazione*, not the left-wing but national *La Repubblica*. How could a Roman product possibly compete with a Florentine/Sienese masterpiece?

At a national level, however, by the early 1990s, more than 50 post-war "swing door" governments had come and gone. To many observers, the source of this crisis lay in Italy's administration and dubious morality. Senior party leaders tended to die in office, governments suffered from opportunism, not lack of

opportunity. *Partitocrazia* (party influence) supplanted democracy, extending from government to public corporations, infiltrating banking, the judiciary and media, and the public tacitly condoned this "old boys' network".

CORRUPTION AND TERROR

The early 1990s saw a series of political scandals involving bribes, and the result was the *Mani Pulite* ("Clean Hands") campaign under the fiery leadership of Antonio di Pietro, a former magistrate who became Italy's most popular

Paintings from the Uffizi laid out for restoration after the 1966 flood.

⊘ ECCENTRIC EXPATRIATE COLLECTORS

Anna Maria Gastone, the last of the Medici, left centuries of art treasures and palaces to Florence in perpetuity. In her wake came a succession of patrons who left treasures that can still be seen *in situ* today. Among connoisseurs, the 19th-century race for progress produced an artistic backlash, a desire for escapism coupled with nostalgia for an idealised past. In response, the Florentine foreign collectors pursued a private Arcadia. Often the reaction took the form of a romanticisation of the Gothic era, a period perceived as a heady amalgam of medieval chivalry and costumed romp. Other collectors were inspired by the Florentine heyday, conjuring up a Renaissance stage set.

The art historian Herbert Percy Horne (1864–1916) left his idealised Florentine Renaissance *palazzo* to posterity. Frederick Stibbert (1838–1906) was the classic case of a collector who succumbed to *fin de siècle* aestheticism, leaving behind his museum of armour in a villa steeped in decadent Gothic gloom. Charles Loeser, heir to Macy's store, bequeathed his collection of Old Masters to the Palazzo Vecchio in 1928. The art historian Bernard Berenson (1865–1959) pioneered Renaissance studies and his villa, I Tatti, is now Harvard's Centre for Renaissance Studies. The Anglo-Florentine aesthete Sir Harold Acton (1904–94) left Villa La Pietra, his home and art collection, to New York University.

moral crusader. A vast network was uncovered, in which public contracts were awarded by politicians to businesses in return for bribes. Italian public life was convulsed by the scandal, dubbed *Tangentopoli* – literally, "Bribesville". Dozens of MPs and businessmen were arrested, with others committing suicide. The Christian Democrat Party, which had dominated Italian politics since the war, collapsed under the weight of its own corruption. Two former prime ministers – the socialist Bettino Craxi and the Christian Democrat veteran and seven-time former prime minister Giulio Andreotti – were investigated.

Craxi died in self-imposed exile in Tunisia in 2000, while Andreotti, charged with Mafia ties, was eventually acquitted. The appeal judges found Andreotti to have enjoyed "friendly" and direct relations with the Mafia "up until 1980", but not later – so "Beelzebub" escaped prosecution thanks to the statute of limitations.

In the midst of the political upheaval, in May 1993, Florence suffered a devastating blow when a bomb planted by the Mafia behind the Uffizi gallery rocked the city. Five people were killed, priceless paintings and sculptures damaged and a handful destroyed. The Uffizi's buildings were damaged, and several medieval buildings around the corner were virtually destroyed.

The Mafia's aim was to use the attack, and others in Milan and Rome, to force the Italian state into submission, and to agree to a deal of mutual convenience with the Mob, as had been enjoyed with the Christian Democrats. The jailed Sicilian Godfather, Salvatore "Toto" Riina, was sentenced to life for the Uffizi bombing in 1998. Meanwhile, while no area of Italy appeared to have been left untouched by corruption, including Florence, in the end few, if any, *Tangentopoli* politicians served much real time in jail.

In a frank interview in July 2005, the film director Bernardo Bertolucci told the *Corriere della Sera*: "Italy lost a great opportunity after *Tangentopoli*. It should have had a real examination of conscience, in order to understand how on earth it could be that there were so many corrupt figures populating our landscape, accomplices of a system which goes from small tips in return for small favours, to large *tangenti* (bribes) for big contracts. And instead we have wound up with an illegal prime minister, who was elected amid conditions of

almost complete control of the media." He was referring to Silvio Berlusconi, the media tycoon-turned-prime minister.

SILVIO BERLUSCONI

Berlusconi, the populist, perma-tanned tycoon, was first elected premier in 1994, on an anti-corruption ticket, and has led two further administrations. Ironically, Berlusconi's career has been dogged by charges of everything from conflict of interests to embezzlement and false accounting. His classic response is that such

Bettino Craxi, former Prime Minister of Italy.

⊘ THE FLOODING OF FLORENCE

When the Arno broke its banks in 1966, the havoc caused to the city's heritage was immediate: Santa Croce was soon under water; the Duomo lost sections of its marble facade; panels from the Baptistery doors were swept away; over a million historic books and illuminated manuscripts were destroyed; and countless artworks were damaged. Although most works have been restored to their original state, Cimabue's *Crucifix* in Santa Croce was controversially left semi-restored. Instead of recreating the missing sections of the work, restorers simply painted in the spaces with patches of neutral colour, intended to symbolise the city's "wound".

allegations have been politically motivated by rivals and a biased judiciary.

Clowning, corruption and "bunga bunga" sex scandals aside, Berlusconi has dominated Italian life, as much by his oversize personality as by his vast wealth. Some see Berlusconi as a product of Italian culture, tapping into the traditions of patronage and family. The billionaire's business empire spans the media, entertainment, insurance, construction and sport (the tycoon owns AC Milan football club). Berlusconi's fans felt that only a successful businessman could transform a recalcitrant country into a model business. His critics cite conflict of interests, including the media mogul's ownership of three television channels, and undue influence over the public-broadcasting networks. They believe that Berlusconi entered politics to protect his empire and evade legal charges. The right may wear the trousers in Rome but, almost as a matter of regional pride, far fewer Tuscans voted for Berlusconi than in other regions.

Berlusconi's second term, from 2001–6, made him the only post-war prime minister to govern for a full five-year term. Despite bringing a semblance of stability, the empire-builder narrowly lost out to Romano Prodi in 2006, ceding to a fragile left-wing coalition whose eventual collapse prompted fresh elections. Disillusionment with a lack of leadership from the left led to the right regaining power in 2008, masterminded by Berlusconi's People of Freedom party. The flamboyant billionaire businessman was elected on a platform of reducing public spending, lowering taxes, reforming the judiciary, and modernising the infrastructure.

The consensus is that Berlusconi, bogged down by personal scandals and pursuing his own interests, failed to deliver on all fronts. By mid-2011, the country was in a perilous position amid fears that it would fall victim to the eurozone debt crisis. Despite being its third-largest economy, Italy has not embarked on reforms or tackled public debt. After faring badly in local elections in 2011, Berlusconi's chances of surviving until the general elections in 2013 looked slim. He was

Aftermath of the Uffizi bombing.

⊘ A TUSCAN HALL OF FAME

There's a saying that Tuscany is "equally blessed by the genius of man and nature". And history has proved the proverb, with the greatest Tuscans achieving worldwide fame. Unsurprisingly, many are from the world of art: Giotto, Leonardo da Vinci, Michelangelo, Donatello, Masaccio and Cellini were all born in or around Florence, as was the architect Brunelleschi. The painter and art historian Giorgio Vasari is famed for his *Lives of the Artists*.

Literary celebrities include the triumvirate of Dante, Petrarch and Boccaccio (born in Paris, but raised in Florence). In the music field, the composer Puccini hailed from Lucca, and opera itself was born in Florence in the late 1500s. Tuscany was also home to the astronomer Galileo, mathematician Leonardo Fibonacci, political theorist Machiavelli, and merchant-turned-explorer Amerigo Vespucci. Alas, in the banking field, the great Florentines are anonymous, including the creators of the florin (*fiorino*) in 1189, and the inventors of double-entry book-keeping.

Many famous modern-day Tuscans are linked to the fashion world: Emilio Pucci, Guccio Gucci and Salvatore Ferragamo (a transplanted Neapolitan), plus Roberto Cavalli. Showbiz representatives include the singer Andrea Bocelli, film-maker Franco Zeffirelli, and comedian Roberto Benigni.

also involved in four trials, with charges ranging from illegal sex with an underage prostitute to corruption and perverting the course of justice.

After dominating the political scene for 17 years, Berlusconi, the country's longest-serving post-war prime minister stepped down in 2011. Overwhelmed by the scale of Italy's debt crisis, the consummate survivor finally made way for respected economist Mario Monti, who formed a government of technocrats to steer the country through uncharted waters. Monti's time in power was short-lived: his centrist coalition Civic Choice lost the 2013 general elections and he was replaced by Democratic Party's Enrico Letta, whose time in the limelight was even shorter as he resigned in early 2014. A new government was formed by Matteo Renzi, also from the Democratic Party. Renzi was the first ever Italian politician to become prime minister while holding the post of city mayor (2009–14). In late 2016, Renzi was forced to resign as PM after conceding defeat in the referendum on his proposed constitutional reforms; he was succeeded by the Democratic Party's Paolo Gentiloni. The Italian Parliament was dissolved in December 2017, yet the general election in March 2018 resulted in a hung parliament.

FLORENTINE REVIVAL

When he was elected Florence's mayor in 2009, Matteo Renzi was the youngest mayor in Italy. He rejuvenated the Tuscan political stage, declaring that Berlusconi's sleazy generation of politicians should stand aside. Apart from introducing merit as the main criterion for council jobs in Florence, Renzi appointed women to half of the posts. Meritocracy was a bold new concept in such a closed, clubby and recalcitrant political culture. Elected on a platform of making the city cleaner, more liveable and more accountable, the mayor's first public act was to pedestrianise Piazza del Duomo, since extended to other areas, notably Piazza Santa Maria Novella and chic Via de Tornabuoni. Visitors can now savour the Duomo without the din of traffic, apart from the clatter of hooves from the horse-drawn carriages. You can even take in the stripy Gothic facade of Santa Maria Novella without fear of being hit by careering cabs shooting out of the station.

The changes went beyond pollution-cutting measures and spruced-up squares. Culturally,

the revitalisation was extended to revamped galleries and museums, more cosmopolitan nightlife, and a fresh perception of Florence as a creative, contemporary city, not mired in the past. Bicycles were made more readily available, inspired by schemes in Paris and London, while Segway tours and rickshaw rides were also encouraged. Museums became more user-friendly, with longer opening hours and better ticketing. Major galleries started taking invisible masterpieces out of the store-rooms and put them into the public domain. A "Fire-

Matteo Renzi, mayor of Florence from 2009 to 2014.

nze Card" was finally introduced; currently it gives access to all the top museums while the Firenze Card Plus combines museums and public transport).

When Renzi was elected prime minister in 2014, he was replaced as Florence's mayor by Dario Nardella, another young and dynamic Democratic Party politician. Nardella actively supports sustainable and innovative policies, such as the various new car-sharing schemes. In 2015, he approved the Smart Florence Plan, promising to improve the Florentines' quality of life by 2050. A professional violinist himself, Nardella is also a fervent promoter of the arts. The next mayoral and council elections are scheduled to take place in 2019.

The Massacre of the Innocents (c.1305) by Giotto.

RENAISSANCE ART

Art historians divide the Renaissance into three waves: the trecento (1300s) was the era of the workshop and fresco; the quattrocento (1400s) welcomed a new realism featuring perspective and emotion; the cinquecento (1500s), or High Renaissance, was the apogee followed by a sharp decline, as political and economic decay eventually took its toll.

One of the great myths of history provides a kind of Hollywood scenario for the "birth of the Renaissance", linking it to the fall of Constantinople in 1453, when scholars were supposed to have escaped, clutching their precious Greek manuscripts, to Italy. There, these manuscripts became a kind of magical seed, taking root, growing and bearing fruit almost immediately as "the Renaissance".

Of course, this is nonsense; like any other human phenomenon, the Renaissance had roots deep in history. It was the political fragmentation of Italy that created the Renaissance, each little city-state contributing something unique to the whole. But the process certainly started in Florence, and the city dominated the cultural scene until the early 16th century. Again and again over the centuries, attempts have been made to analyse the causes of the Florentine flowering, with reasons ranging from the poverty of the soil to the quality of the light. But it is no more possible to "explain" this than it is any other mystery of the human spirit.

Detail from the Dying Slave (c.1513), one of four "unfinished" Slaves by Michelangelo (Accademia), intended for the tomb of Pope Julius II.

DEFINING THE RENAISSANCE

The very word "renaissance" is a Florentine invention. In his book *Lives of the Most Excellent Architects, Painters and Sculptors*, first published in 1550, Vasari, first of the art historians, remarks that the reader "will now be able to recognise more easily the progress of [art's] rebirth *(il progresso della sua rinascita)*".

But what, exactly, did Vasari mean by *rinascita*? What was being "reborn"? Vasari was referring to a rebirth of the art and architecture of classical times, that is, before Emperor Constantine transferred the seat of empire to Constantinople at the beginning of the 4th century AD, causing it to become the centre of art and culture. A distinctive architecture, based on Roman models, using bricks and featuring domes and cupolas, was developed. Byzantine art was hierarchical in style, using flattened forms and no perspective.

Architects drew and measured the ruins of the Roman cities, rediscovering their building techniques and their rules of proportion, the "classical orders". Vitruvius's *Ten Books on Architecture*, the only surviving manual from classical times, was studied anew and became the basis, in the 15th century, for Alberti's treatise of the same name.

Painting, which of all the arts is pre-eminently *the* art of the Renaissance, owed little to antiquity, partly because no Roman examples survived to be used as models. Renaissance artists broke new ground, discovering perspective and observing the natural world that surrounded them. The 14th-century Florentine artist Cennino Cennini gave good advice to his fellow artists. "If you wish to draw mountains well, so that they appear natural," he wrote, "procure some large stones, rocky, not polished, and draw from these." The idea of a handful of

Detail from the Coronation of the Virgin (c.1330) altarpiece by Giotto (Santa Croce, Florence).

stones standing in for the Alps or the Apennines might seem ludicrous, but it was a pointer to the new road the artist was taking, the road to reality in nature.

The classical world provided the inspiration for the artist to rise above the narrow medieval world, with its emphasis on theological studies. But, once he had started, he went his own way. What was reborn was an artistic sensibility but not a recycled past.

THE TRECENTO

Until the quattrocento (15th century), the term "artist" had no particular significance, being virtually interchangeable with "artisan" or "craftsman". All were members of guilds, or *arti*: there was an *arte* for the shoemaker, no more and no less valid than the *arte* for the goldsmith, itself a subdivision of the immensely powerful Silk Guild. Everything was linked to the power of the guilds and the emergence of artistic workshops.

The growing popularity of the process known as *buon fresco* also demanded a cooperative approach. The medium of fresco painting had been introduced about a century earlier, and time had shown that it was the most permanent of all forms of mural art to date, since the colouring became an intrinsic part of the plaster itself.

In addition to large commissions, the workshop (or *bottega*) would produce a variety of smaller articles for sale, ranging from painted scabbards to holy pictures and statues. There was widespread demand for religious art, which provided the bread and butter for hundreds of small *botteghe*. A peasant might have scraped together enough for a tiny picture; a parish priest might have a large sum at his disposal to commission a mural or even an altarpiece; or a wealthy merchant might be anxious to propitiate fate and show an appropriate level of piety.

The potential client had little interest in the identity of the craftsmen producing his order. But, if expensive colours were used (gold, silver, or blue made from the semi-precious lapis lazuli), then the fact was clearly stated in the contract, along with the date of delivery of the finished piece. Commissioned work was almost invariably recorded in a contract that, in addition, usually specified how many figures were to appear in the finished

⊘ BYZANTINE ART

Byzantine artists covered interiors with mosaics, a Roman decorative device that became a sumptuous art form, with myriad glazed-stone fragments catching the light in a way no fresco ever could. Inspired by cupolas in Constantinople, the best Byzantine art in Italy is in Ravenna, dating from the 5th century. But the style prevailed in 11th-century Venice, and even influenced 13th-century Florence. But to its Florentine critics, notably Vasari, Byzantine art was static and stiffly formalised. It was this aspect that Vasari decried as "a certain residue of the Greeks" – and that was completely overthrown by the Renaissance artists.

painting, as well as their activities and attributes. Sacred art touched on the delicate area of religious orthodoxy, and the wise craftsman ensured that his client stated exactly what he wanted.

The identity of most of the workers in the *botteghe* is unknown. They were conscientious and skilled, rather than brilliant, but they formed the subsoil from which the genius of the quattrocento could flourish. The actual working pattern of the *bottega*, whereby a group of lesser craftsmen would paint the main body of a picture, leaving it to the identified master to put the finishing touches to it, would continue into the High Renaissance, the cinquecento. This made it difficult, at times impossible, for the most skilled art critic to say that such a painting was, beyond a doubt, the work of a particular famous artist.

EARLY RENAISSANCE ART

Comparing trecento (or Gothic) paintings in any Tuscan art gallery with the work of quattrocento (or early Renaissance) artists reveals a compelling difference: whereas Gothic paintings are iconographic, revelling in the use of celestial gold and presenting a spiritual Madonna and Child for worship and contemplation, the same subject in the hands of Renaissance painters becomes a study in living flesh, the figures of mother and child endowed with attitudes, character, emotions and psychological motivation. Scholars argue endlessly about why this great change occurred, but there is near-universal agreement on who started it: Giotto di Bondone (1267–1337), who, according to Vasari, "restored art to the better path followed in modern times".

But Giotto was not entirely alone in injecting life, and naturalism, into art. Nicola (1223–84) and Giovanni (1245–1314) Pisano the father-and-son team, were achieving similar advances in sculpture at the same time as Giotto was breaking new ground in art.

When the Pisani were living and working in Pisa, it was the fashion for Pisan merchants to ship home Roman sarcophagi from the Holy Land or North Africa for eventual reuse as their own tombs. Scores of them still line the cloister surrounding Pisa's Campo Santo cemetery. Inspired by the realistic battle scenes carved on these antique marble tombs, the Pisani created their own versions: great pulpits sculpted with dramatic scenes from the life of Christ,

which can be seen in Pisa's cathedral, and in Sant'Andrea church in Pistoia.

In architecture, the classical inspiration that helped to define the Renaissance had never disappeared to quite the same degree as it had in art. The very term Romanesque – meaning derived from or in the Roman style – indicates the essential continuity between the architecture of Rome and that of Tuscany in the 1300s. Churches were still built to the same basilican plan as those of the late Roman period, and, though the facades of many Tuscan churches

Scene from the Life of St Nicholas (c.1327–30) by Lorenzetti (Uffizi).

look quite unclassical, they are still based on the geometry of the Roman hemispherical arch, as distinct from the four-centred arches of Venice or the pointed arches of French Gothic. What distinguishes Tuscan Romanesque from Lombardic or Piedmontese is the exuberant use of polychrome marble to create complex geometrical patterns. Pisa was the seminal influence here – trade links with Spain and North Africa led to the adoption of Arabic numerals in place of Roman, and to the fondness for surface patterning in architecture, copying Moorish tilework and textiles. From Pisa the oriental influence spread to Lucca, Prato, Pistoia, and even to Florence, where it was to pave the way for the great polychrome Campanile designed by Giotto.

THE QUATTROCENTO

A great breakthrough took place in Florence at the beginning of the 15th century, a moment so important that it can be dated to within a few years, and a new philosophy of life flowed through the city. Until the 1470s, Florence was a dynamo, providing light and energy for the entire peninsula. The city retained its dominance in art for barely a lifespan, however,

Adoration of the Magi (1423) by Gentile da Fabriano (Uffizi).

Ø THE GUILDS

The guilds extended their control over the decorative as well as the practical arts. Sculptors and architects were enrolled with the masons, and painters formed a subdivision of the apothecaries, as they needed a grasp of chemistry to prepare their colours. Far from resenting the obligation to join associations, painters and sculptors formed their own groups, or *compagnie*, within larger guilds. This meant members could help one another, sharing profits and losses. Increased teamwork also meant that several men might be engaged at successive stages in the shaping of a pillar, from rough hewing to final carving, conveyor-belt style.

because it exported so much of its native talent – which ensured the spread of Renaissance values but, with them, ensured Florence's own relative eclipse.

The breakthrough began when the Florentine *Signoria*, or government, decided to refurbish the ceremonial centre of Florence: the group of buildings consisting of the cathedral, the Campanile – begun by Giotto in 1334 and finished after his death but to his design in 1359 – and the octagonal Baptistery. This little black-and-white building had a special place in Florentine affections, and when, in 1401, it was decided to offer a thanksgiving for the city's escape from plague, the Baptistery was chosen to benefit. The wealthy Wool Guild announced that it would finance the design and casting of a second set of bronze doors that would be even grander than those of Pisano. The design for them was thrown open to competition.

Out of the many entrants, seven were chosen, each to execute a panel on the same subject: the sacrifice of Isaac. Two of the entrants, the 21-year-old Brunelleschi, later credited as the creator of the "Renaissance style" in architecture, and the 20-year-old Lorenzo Ghiberti, produced work that caused considerable difficulty to the judges. Both the panels exist today, one preserved in the Museo dell'Opera del Duomo, the other in the Bargello museum. Comparing the two, posterity finds it impossible to say which is "better". The *Syndics*, at a loss to choose, came up with a compromise, suggesting that the artists should share the work. Brunelleschi declined and set out for Rome, while Ghiberti began work on the doors, completing them 22 years later.

He was offered the commission to produce a second pair: these took him 27 years. During the almost half-century that he worked on the project, it is possible to see in his contracts the changing status of the artist. In the first contract he is treated essentially as an artisan, expected to put in a full day's work "like any journeyman".

In later contracts for his employment, he is treated far more as a free agent, permitted to undertake commissions for other work. Ghiberti, too, made explicit this change by boldly including his own self-portrait among the reliefs on the door.

LEARNING FROM THE ANCIENTS

Meanwhile, in Rome with his friend Donatello, Brunelleschi was discovering how the ancients had built their enormous structures. In an entirely new approach to the past, he examined originals rather than copies of copies. One of his findings – or, possibly, inventions – was the *ulivella*. Intrigued and puzzled by the existence of regular-shaped holes in the huge stone blocks of the ancient buildings, he assumed that they had been made to allow the block to be gripped by some device, and designed a kind of grappling iron to fit. Whether or not the Romans had actually used such a device, it was very useful – and a demonstration of the benefits to be gained by studying the past.

Brunelleschi returned to Florence at about the time that the *Syndics* of the Wool Guild, who also had the responsibility for the cathedral, were puzzling over the problem of completing it. Arnolfo di Cambio had begun it in 1296, and it had been completed, all except for the dome, by 1369. Nobody knew how to bridge this immense gap, which, for half a century, had been covered by a temporary roof.

In 1417, a special meeting was called to debate the problem and consider suggestions, and Brunelleschi put forward his solution. He

The Battle of San Romano (1432) by Paolo Uccello (Uffizi).

⊙ GIOTTO DI BONDONE

Tradition has it that Giotto (1267–1337) was working as a shepherd boy until Cimabue, himself a pioneer of greater naturalism in art, discovered that Giotto could draw a perfect circle freehand, and offered to train him as an artist. Pupil soon surpassed master, and Giotto went on to create the great *St Francis* fresco cycle in the Upper Basilica in Assisi and the *Life of Christ* fresco series in the Scrovegni Chapel in Padua. In Florence, his main masterpiece adorns the Franciscan church of Santa Croce, where his work covers the walls of the two chapels to the right of the choir. To measure the breadth of the Giotto revolution, it is enough to compare his frescoes with the static 13th-century altarpiece nearby.

Despite Giotto's supposedly rural background, in his work nature is formalised and subservient to humanity. It is the figures who occupy the foreground, vibrantly *alive*. Giotto was ahead of his time in introducing character and individuality to his art. Straddling two ages, Giotto has been claimed both as a Gothic artist and as the pioneer of the Renaissance. Perhaps if war and the Black Death had not ravaged Europe from the 1340s, the Renaissance might well have blossomed sooner than it did. As it was, another 60 years were to pass before the naturalism pioneered by Giotto was to re-emerge, this time as a mass artistic movement.

was mocked for it because it dispensed with the wooden centring over which architects traditionally built their arches and vaults, supporting their weight until the keystone was in place. But, in desperation, the *Syndics* offered him the job. Brunelleschi solved the problem by building a dome that was pointed in sections, supported by ribs with the lightest possible in-filling between them. He built two shells, an outer skin and an inner one: one way in which the crushing weight of the dome, the problem that had prevented its construction, was considerably reduced.

Trinity (c.1425) by Masaccio, the pioneer of perspective (both in Santa Maria Novella, Florence)

The work took 16 years, and was completed on 31 August 1436. This was the first Renaissance dome in Italy, the largest unsupported dome in Europe, bigger than the Pantheon in Rome, which Brunelleschi had studied, bigger even than the great dome that Michelangelo raised a century later over St Peter's in Rome.

It was Brunelleschi's successor, the scholar Alberti, who first applied the classical orders to domestic architecture and created what we now think of as the Renaissance palazzo. Whereas Brunelleschi introduced the columns, pediments and cornices he copied from Roman ruins into his churches, there were no surviving examples of Roman domestic architecture for the 15th-century

Florentines to copy. When Rucellai, a wealthy Florentine merchant, asked Alberti to design a palace for him, Alberti took as a model the Colosseum in Rome and applied its tiers of arches to the facade of a three-storey palazzo. Although it was the only palazzo he built, and though Brunelleschi's design for the Medici Palace never got beyond the model stage, these two architects developed a new type of building, a system of proportion and an elegance of line that is still in use today.

Brunelleschi's other major breakthrough was his use of perspective. Alberti described its effect to a generation for whom it appeared almost a magical technique: "I describe a rectangle of whatever size I wish, which I imagine to be an open window through which I view whatever is to be depicted there." Donatello (1386–1466) eagerly used the technique in his bas-relief of *Salome Offering John's Head to Herod*. The observer is looking at a banquet where the diners are recoiling in horror from the offering. Beyond the banqueting rooms can be seen a succession of two more rooms, giving a remarkable and, for contemporaries, almost eerie sense of depth.

A NEW PERSPECTIVE

Like the difference between Giotto's mobile, dramatic figures and their static, formal predecessors, perspective gave a new vista to civilisation. Its most dramatic form was that employed by the young Masaccio. His great painting of the *Trinity*, in the church of Santa Maria Novella, is an intellectual exercise in the use of perspective that is also infused with religious awe. Beneath a trompe l'oeil classical arch stands the immense figure of God the Father, half-supporting a cross on which there is an equally immense figure of Christ; below them are various saints and donors and a *memento mori* of a skeleton in a sarcophagus revealing an ancient warning: "I am what you are, and what I am, you shall be."

The huge figures stand out from the background and appear to loom over the observer. As a young man, Michelangelo used to stand before these, copying them again and again to fix the style in his mind. Eventually, therefore, some essence of this experimental period of the Renaissance found its way into the Sistine Chapel, that shrine of the High Renaissance dominated by Michelangelo's work.

The classical arch in Masaccio's painting is a pointer to a curious development that took place during the quattrocento – the clothing of biblical figures in a totally anachronistic way, either in classical Roman attire or in contemporary Florentine dress. The frescoes that Ghirlandaio (1449–94) painted in the Sasseti Chapel within the church of Santa Trinità supposedly concern the prophecies of Christ's birth, and the location should be Augustan Rome. But it is a Rome that bears a remarkably close resemblance to 15th-century Florence, and the people waiting for the awesome news are all citizens of Florence in normal dress. Lorenzo de' Medici is there, as is his mother, his children, friends and various colleagues.

Early Renaissance painters were preoccupied with technique. Their subject matter remained largely unchanged: religion was still the most important concern. But in the second half of the quattrocento a new, exciting and somewhat disturbing element began to appear: the mythological and the allegorical. The supreme practitioner in this field was Sandro Botticelli, who worked with Leonardo da

Birth of John the Baptist (1485) by Ghirlandaio.

⊘ BOTTICELLI'S SPRING

La Primavera (1478) is Sandro Botticelli's most famous painting – and certainly the most mysterious of the Early Renaissance. Hung in the Uffizi, it depicts nine supernatural creatures placed in an exquisite natural setting. On the left, a young man is pointing at something. Next to him a group of grave-faced women are performing a solemn ritual dance. On the right is the only figure who seems to be aware of the observer: Botticelli's stunningly beautiful "mystery" woman with a provocative half-smile. Beside her what appears to be an act of violence adds a discordant note: a bluish figure is leaning out of the trees and clutching at a startled girl.

In the background, but dominating the whole, is the most enigmatic figure: a pale woman whose expression has been variously described as frowning, smiling and melancholy; whose stance has also been described in conflicting ways, as dancing, as that of a consumptive, as pregnant and as offering a blessing. The figure is claimed to be both Venus and the Virgin Mary. Botticelli was trying to restate classical mythology in Christian terms while remaining true to the original – and to his own quirky self. However, he was later influenced by the gloomy, savage friar Savonarola and, almost overnight, ceased his joyous mythological paintings, concentrating instead on orthodox religious subjects.

Vinci in Verrocchio's workshop but developed in a totally different direction.

THE HIGH RENAISSANCE

Even to the untutored eye, there is a profound difference between the work produced before and after the 1520s in Tuscany and elsewhere, most noticeably in Florence. Partly this was the result of an immense political crisis. Italy had become a battleground, invaded again and again by warring foreigners. In 1527 a savage army, composed partly of mercenaries, sacked Rome and held the pope to ransom. Italy was never to recover from that experience, which was the curtain-raiser for a period of foreign domination that would not come to an end until the 1800s.

The apogee of the Renaissance – in Florence, at least – was ushered in with Leonardo da Vinci and Michelangelo. But the decline swiftly followed, particularly when Michelangelo and Raphael left for Rome, to work for Pope Julius II. Other artists followed suit: the major Florentine families – other than the Medici – could no longer afford to make commissions, so the art scene moved on.

La Primavera (1478) by Botticelli (Uffizi).

⊙ MICHELANGELO IN FLORENCE

A Vasari anecdote describes how a 13-year-old Michelangelo Buonarroti (1475–1564) made a drawing of the tools in the workshop. His master, Ghirlandaio, was so impressed that he told Lorenzo de' Medici, who invited Michelangelo to enter his princely household and study with his own children.

Michelangelo also worked for the next 40 years on a thankless task: the great tomb for his patron, Pope Julius II. The unfinished statues for this tomb, the famous *Slaves*, are now in Florence's Accademia gallery. Five centuries later, the sculptor's technique is still clearly visible; shallow depressions surrounding the figure, made by the rounded head of a chisel, seem to be "freeing" the figures.

Florence boasts many statues by Michelangelo; although often unfinished, they always reveal the chisel strokes of a master. They include the iconic *David*, and the statues of *Dawn*, *Evening*, *Day* and *Night* in the Medici Chapel. Florence's Casa Buonarroti (Via Ghibellina), once owned by Michelangelo, showcases the sculptor's working drawings and a few early works. The quintessential Renaissance man is not fully represented here, either in spirit or in sculpture. Still, thanks to his descendants, the palace conveys the atmosphere of a family home and remains a touching tribute to the great sculptor, painter, architect and poet.

Shortly after the sack of Rome, the Medici Pope Clement VII clamped down on his native city of Florence, ending republicanism and preparing the way for the first dukedom. Meanwhile, in the world of art, the glory was departing from Florence, as the impetus of the Renaissance shifted to Rome and Venice. From the middle of the 16th century, Florentine artists tended to be court artists, dancing attendance on the Medici dukes. Among them was the artist-turned-art historian Giorgio Vasari (1511–74).

Until recently, Vasari's work as an artist was dismissed almost as contemptuously as his work as an art historian was received enthusiastically. However, posterity owes him a debt of gratitude, both as an architect and as a painter. In 2011, worldwide celebrations to mark the fifth centenary of his birth provoked a re-evaluation of his artistry. Not only did he build the Uffizi for Duke Cosimo I, and the Vasari Corridor, but he frescoed the interior of Brunelleschi's dome. Vasari also remodelled the Palazzo Vecchio and decorated its parliamentary chamber, the great Salone dei Cinquecento, with outstanding contemporary representations of the city and its surrounding countryside.

LEONARDO DA VINCI

Although the glory was departing from Florence, the sunset was stupendous. It could scarcely be otherwise with two such giants as Michelangelo and Leonardo still on the scene. Leonardo, born in 1452, trained in Verrocchio's *bottega*, thus carrying the medieval systems on into the new era. One of Vasari's anecdotes claims that Verrocchio, on seeing his young apprentice's work, laid down his brush and never painted again. Unlikely though the incident is, the anecdote shows that Leonardo was recognised as being almost a freakish genius in his own lifetime.

Leonardo left Florence for Milan at the age of 30. He returned in 1502 when commissioned by the *Signoria* to create the great mural, the *Battle of Anghiari* in the Council Chamber, and eventually crossed the Alps to become court painter to François I of France. His contribution to the history of ideas is incalculable, but his legacy in Tuscany is restricted to several Madonnas and the unfinished paintings of the *Battle of Anghiari* and the *Adoration of the Kings*, all in the Uffizi. The two best-known masterpieces, the *Mona Lisa*, set against an exquisite Tuscan background, and the *Virgin of the Rocks*, are in Paris (London's National Gallery has a later version of the latter). However, there is at least a museum of his fantastical creations in Florence, which displays working models of his flying machines, armoured tanks and swing bridges, all before his time (see page 101).

Michelangelo is another story, however. His greatest work, the Sistine Chapel, is also situated outside Florence, but he did leave an enduring imprint upon his home city, in the

A sketch in charcoal by Leonardo (Uffizi).

form of the walls that gird it and the sculptures that grace it.

MICHELANGELO

Michelangelo was nearly a generation younger than Leonardo, born in 1475 when the Renaissance was approaching its apogee. His father was a poor but proud country gentleman who disapproved of the idea of his son becoming an artisan or artist; in his mind, there was no clear distinction. Indeed, Michelangelo was apt to be touchy on the subject. Although he served his apprenticeship in a *bottega*, he later rejected the idea that he touted for trade: "I was never a painter or a sculptor like those who set up shop for the purpose."

Michelangelo was just 18 when Lorenzo de' Medici died in 1492. Florence was plunged into chaos, because Lorenzo's son, Piero, was extravagant and unpopular, and the Florentines chased the tyrant out of the city. The artist's links with the Medici were no longer so advantageous, and so he took the road to Rome, where the Sistine Chapel awaited. Although Michelangelo is remembered as a painter and sculptor, he was also a gifted engineer and a poet of a good deal of sensitivity and insight.

anyone in Florence who dared to resist the might of the Medici. But it is indicative both of Cellini and of the enveloping atmosphere of artistic decadence that his best-known work would be the elaborate golden salt cellar crafted for François I of France.

RAPHAEL

Raphael (Raffaello) was a gentle, handsome young man who seemed to have no enemies. Born in Umbria in 1483, he received his basic training in the workshop of Perugino, working

Entombment by Raphael.

CELLINI

Michelangelo was just 25 when Benvenuto Cellini was born in 1500. Like so many of the artists of his time, Cellini was a jack of all trades – including, improbably enough, a gunner. He played a role in the tragic sack of Rome which, in effect, brought the Renaissance to an end. Acting as gunner in defence of the Vatican, he assured his supporters that the pope promised him absolution "for all the murders that I should commit".

In Florence, his most famous work is that beautiful but curiously heartless statue of *Perseus Slaying Medusa,* commissioned by Cosimo I for the statue-filled Loggia dei Lanzi on the Piazza della Signoria – a message to

on frescoes in Perugia. In 1500, at the impressionable age of 17, he came to Florence, where he absorbed the works of Leonardo da Vinci and Michelangelo. He left Florence in 1508, attracted to Rome by the fiery Pope Julius II, who was planning a series of architectural embellishments to the Vatican. There the young Raphael made a mark by painting the series of rooms known as the Stanze della Segnatura. Under the Medici Pope Leo X, he was placed in charge of archaeological excavations in Rome itself.

Thus, the last true artist of the Renaissance introduced into the mother city of Europe that passionate search for the past that had triggered the Renaissance in Florence nearly two centuries earlier.

🔍 LITERARY CLASSICS

"Florentine firsts" are not restricted to the art world – Dante, Italy's finest poet, and Machiavelli, the first political theorist, are just two names to conjure with.

In a crowded field, three towering figures provide some orientation to Tuscan literature. Dante, Petrarch and Machiavelli follow each other chronologically and, as each caused, as well as recorded, great changes, it is possible to plot the course of the region's history through them.

DANTE

Born in 1265, Dante was an exact contemporary of Giotto, whose work he admired. But where Giotto kept out of politics, Dante involved himself wholeheartedly and was exiled for his pains. *The Divine Comedy*, which deals with the great mysteries of religion, had a profound effect on Italian thought.

PETRARCH

Francesco Petrarch, though a Florentine, was born in Arezzo, where his parents had been exiled during the same feuds that caused Dante's expulsion. Petrarch was one of the first to retrieve the lost classical literature that helped to usher in the Renaissance. He travelled widely, had an enormous circle of friends and it was often through his letters that the "new learning" was disseminated. In poetry, he devised the sonnet form that took his name – Petrarchan – which was greatly to influence the poets of Elizabethan England.

MACHIAVELLI

Niccolò Machiavelli was born in 1469. Viewed from almost any angle, his life appears a failure. As a career diplomat, he never wielded real authority. As a republican, he was obliged to curry favour with the openly despotic Medici. In his political writings, the tone is ice-cold, logical, in total command. In real life, he was lecherous and adulterous. But he was, nonetheless, a realist who exposed the immorality of leaders. *The Prince* is still treated as a political manual today. Classic advice includes: "When neither their property

nor their honour is touched, the majority of men live content"; "It is better to be feared than loved, if you cannot be both" and "A prudent man should always follow in the path trodden by great men and imitate those who are most excellent."

OTHER LUMINARIES

Although innovations in literature were less spectacular than in art and architecture, there are a number of outstanding "firsts". Francesco Guicciardini wrote the first true *History of Italy*, and Giovanni Boccaccio (1313–75) produced Europe's first novel, *The Decameron*, a

Dante and the Divine Comedy in Florence's Duomo.

collection of tales told by 10 young aristocrats who retreat from the plague that struck Florence in 1348. Staying in a country house, they spend the time telling erotic stories and reciting poems, and poking fun at the clergy. All the stories demonstrate Boccaccio's well-honed skills as a storyteller.

Finally, there were the true "Renaissance men" who mastered both art and literature – as exemplified by Michelangelo's poetry and Cellini's swashbuckling *Autobiography*. Cellini, a brilliant sculptor and soldier, was also a superb writer and wrote an account of the casting of the exquisite bronze sculpture *Perseus* for the Loggia dei Lanzi. At a crucial moment, he ran out of metal and had to throw in the family pewter in order to complete the statue.

ARCHITECTURAL TREASURES

Tuscany combines a rich urban heritage with a delightful rural legacy, to create a unique architectural tableau.

Curiously, Tuscan architecture is characterised as much by diversity as it is by harmony: harmony in its aesthetic sweetness; diversity in its range of buildings, from Romanesque cathedrals to Renaissance palaces, town halls to tower-houses.

TUSCAN TOWN HALLS

Civic architecture is particularly rich. The Tuscan town hall, with accompanying bell tower, encapsulates a civic ideal. In the past, it promised a degree of democracy to the merchant guilds, the nobility and the people. The Palazzo del Comune, known by different names, has been the seat of local government since medieval times. This imposing, fortified building dominates the square today, as surely as it has always dominated the lives of local citizens. The best known is the fortress-like Palazzo Vecchio in Florence, its austerity belying its palatial interior. However, even the smallest commune has a grand town hall. In the Mugello, Palazzo Vicari in Scarperia resembles Palazzo Vecchio, with its impressive 14th-century merlons and corbels. Such public palazzi are often studded with *stemmata*, stone-carved coats of arms belonging to prominent citizens or noble clans.

In numerous cities, including San Gimignano, there is also an adjoining balcony known as the *arengo*, from which politicians would harangue the crowd. Nearby is usually a loggia, providing shelter from the sun or rain, as well as a meeting place, today often used as a small market. Thus, Tuscany's grandest buildings serve much the same purpose today as they have always done.

URBANISATION

Visually, urban Tuscany is the product of medieval and Renaissance builders, even if Roman and

The Abbazia di Monte Oliveto Maggiore.

Etruscan stones were recycled. Dismissing the Middle Ages as a period of decadence and decay does an injustice to the region's prosperity and architectural heritage. In Tuscany, the period represented a marked social rebirth, with the flowering of independent city-states in the 11th century. By 1200, most towns had become burgeoning centres with distinctive identities and a civic pride evident in the grandiose town halls and tower-houses. The medieval cathedrals and civic buildings were a testament to the citizens' refined taste, just as the ordered country estates later became a Renaissance symbol of peace and prosperity.

The medieval "skyscrapers" of San Gimignano signified the civilising effect of urban living, with the *signori* (feudal lords) encouraged to relinquish their castles for city life. The *borgo*, or fortified city, was also home to landowners and merchants, particularly with the rise of the *popolo grasso*, the wealthy middle class in the 14th century. The medieval city became a symbol of safety during the city-state conflicts.

TUSCAN ROMANESQUE

This style is less solemn, less philosophical than French, English or German Romanesque. Its hallmarks are surface decoration and space rather than sobriety and solidity, with simple the seductive decoration, including exuberant arabesques. A hallmark of the style was its talent for selecting a theatrical space: in Pisa the main buildings present a unified whole, placed on the lawn like prisms on a baize cloth.

MEDIEVAL CITYSCAPE

Given the rich Roman heritage that was available to them, Tuscans did not take to Gothic gables and sheer verticality, but preferred symmetry instead, balancing height with breadth. In great churches such as Santa Croce in Florence, naves

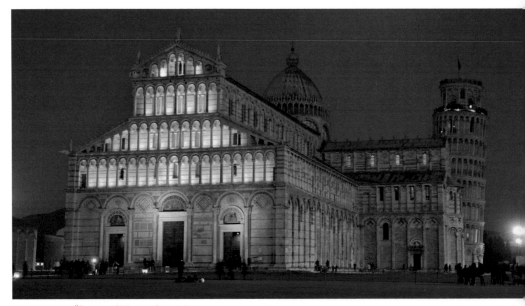

Pisa's glorious "Square of Miracles" at night.

bricks transformed by a marble veneer. The style, centred on Florence, favours contrasting patterns of dark and light marble as well as striking geometric designs. The form was first realised in the city baptistery, with its round-headed arches, classical proportions and a striving for weightlessness. The Florentine model retains a certain simplicity of form, contrasting the austerity of Romanesque with the traditional Tuscan love of polychrome marble patterns.

Pisan Romanesque is more eclectic, as befits its cosmopolitan heritage. The maritime republic of Pisa was an 11th-century power, trading with northern Europe and the Muslim world. As a result, the severe colonnaded galleries owe much to Norman models, while Sicily inspires

⊘ MARBLE CATHEDRALS

The cathedrals of Siena, Pistoia, Florence, Prato and Lucca use stripes and an interplay of light and shade. The geometry of multicoloured marble is quintessentially Tuscan, striking visitors as bold or brash, spellbinding or superfluous. The palette contrasts white marble from Carrara, rosy pink from Maremma and dark green from Prato. The predominant Pisan style combines a Tuscan taste for marble with an austere Norman Romanesque form, inspired by a Moorish Sicilian aesthetic. The Pisan Duomo was the prototype, with its contrasting bands of colour, blind arcading, colonnaded gallery and, of course, the geometry of inlaid marble.

and aisles are not vaulted, but use the open trusses favoured by Romanesque architecture.

Not that Gothic gables are a guide to a medieval atmosphere, of course. Many Tuscan towns

> In medieval Tuscan architecture, a castello was a fortified village or a castle, a rocca was a defended garrison post, and a fortezza was a fortress of strategic importance.

are authentically medieval, as is the case with Cortona, Lucca, San Gimignano and Volterra. As the largest medieval city in Europe, Siena is arguably the most authentic of them all, with strict building regulations in place since the 13th century. Certainly, its Gothic spirit is intact, from red-brick palaces to herringbone alleys, all moulded to a mystical Sienese sensibility.

TUSCAN FORTIFICATIONS

Fortifications played an important role in medieval Tuscany. Walled towns, often known as *borghi*

Piazza Salimbeni, Siena.

The Basilica of Santa Croce in Florence.

Ⓞ PERFECT PIENZA

Florence may be the most innovative Renaissance city, but Pienza is the best preserved. Built by Pius II as a papal city, Pienza brought both an echo of imperial patronage and a humanist memorial to his papacy. In 1462, the architect Rossellino grafted a monumental Renaissance core on to medieval grandiosity. All civic life revolves around one tiny square which, using a wellhead as the lynchpin, embraces an episcopal palace, a town hall with an airy loggia, and culminates with a bold tower embodying Tuscan pride. In his private palace here, the pope delighted in hanging gardens, delicate loggias and rooms for every season.

and built on hilltops, so that advancing enemies would be easily spotted, are emblematic of the Tuscan cityscape. Anghiari, Buonconvento, Monteriggioni and Montepulciano all provide proof that walls help preserve a distinct identity. The region abounds in ruined or restored examples, including castles at Poppi and Prato, and the pair of fortresses in Florence. Siena province alone boasts San Gimignano's *rocca* and watchtowers, as well as the massive *fortezza* in Siena and Montalcino, both of which have now been converted into wine-tasting centres.

Tower-houses were castle residences serving as both warehouses and fortresses, self-sufficient enclaves symbolising the wealth and influence of the feudal nobles or prosperous merchants and their scorn for civil authority. Key features of these grand buildings included a well for a constant water supply, an inner courtyard to provide light and ventilation, and an external staircase to the *piano nobile*, the grand residential first floor.

MEDIEVAL DOMESTIC ARCHITECTURE

As the great Tuscan families grew wealthy on banking and the cloth trade, their homes became more palatial and domesticated. In time, decorative details were added, notably graceful courtyards complete with sculpted wells, coats of arms, ornate arches and a loggia above. The Florentine Palazzo Davanzati preserves much of its medieval atmosphere, from its iron-bolted doors and formidable facade to an internal courtyard boasting a well with a pulley system designed to supply water to each floor. The interior presents a charming portrait of domestic life, from 15th-century frescoes and tapestries to the *cassoni*, Tuscan wedding chests, and even a privileged child's bathroom.

The fortified town of Monteriggioni.

⊘ SACRED SIGHTS

Religious architecture represents one of the highlights of Tuscany. Any tour would certainly include the cathedrals of Florence, Lucca, Pisa and Siena. Lesser-known gems include Barga's Romanesque cathedral, Montepulciano's Renaissance San Biagio and the Romanesque San Miniato al Monte in the Florentine hills. Given city rivalries, Tuscan Romanesque delights in distinctive regional variations, as in the differentiated stripes and arcading in Lucca. In San Michele, a city masterpiece, the chiselled style of the delicate colonnades emphasises the height and exuberance of the facade. In many cases, architecture is inextricably bound up with artistic wealth on the walls, as in Santa Maria Novella in Florence or Arezzo's San Francesco. However, exteriors can be austere or unfinished, a sign that patrons argued or ran out of funds.

Setting is also significant, with cathedrals usually constructed on spots hallowed since Roman or Etruscan times. Mendicant churches were often built outside city walls, with surrounding squares becoming major city markets. Abbeys and monasteries, often as large as medieval towns, were built on new sites, and blended civic and Christian concerns. Some good examples are the Romanesque abbey of Sant'Antimo the Baroque Certosa di Pisa, the Carthusian foundation of Camaldoli; and the Benedictine Monte Oliveto Maggiore, in the woods south of Siena.

RENAISSANCE PALACES

The Florentine palazzo was a direct descendant of the tower-house, but without an outmoded defensive function. In keeping with the new humanist spirit, architects designed gracious private palaces as proof of their revivalist skills, not simply as symbols of patrician pride. Foremost amongst the trailblazers was Michelozzo (1396–1472), who pursued the architectural principles of Alberti and Brunelleschi. Michelozzo designed the Florentine Palazzo Medici-Riccardi, the Medici home and bank-

built for the greatest banking dynasty. Rustication was intended to underline the Strozzi's power. Whereas Palazzo Strozzi emphasises strength and stability, homes such as Palazzo Rucellai were more harmonious, embellished with elegant loggias, classical motifs and decorative friezes.

RENAISSANCE ARCHITECTS

As the cradle of the Renaissance, Tuscany is where the profession of architect first came into its own. Imbued with a new humanist spirit,

Arezzo's stately main square.

ing headquarters, a massive mansion with an arcaded inner courtyard. He also designed Palazzo Pitti (1444), the prototype of a patrician palace, boasting strict classical proportions and a rusticated facade. Yet there are lingering traces of feudal times in the Gothic windows and heavy cornices. Built for Cosimo de' Medici, Palazzo Pitti clearly symbolises the power and prestige of the owner.

However, some nobles simply modernised their feudal seats. Palazzo Spini-Ferroni, a crenellated three-tiered fortress close to the Arno, was a 13th-century watchtower before becoming a palatial home. Just around the corner looms the grandiose Palazzo Strozzi, a rusticated stone cube of mammoth proportions

architects of the stature of Brunelleschi, Alberti, Michelozzo, Rossellino and Sangallo made their mark on churches, palaces and villas. Florence, which saw itself as the inheritor of Roman grandeur, is the Tuscan city with the greatest concentration of Renaissance monuments. Strongly influenced by Tuscan Romanesque, the buildings were models of visual restraint, dedicated to proportion, perspective and classical motifs. Brunelleschi (1377–1446), the father of Renaissance architecture, left his masterpiece on the Duomo in Florence. His spectacular dome was the fulfilment of the Renaissance ideal, an astounding feat of Florentine engineering.

Alberti (1404–72) rivalled Brunelleschi in his gift for geometry and desire to revive "the immutable laws of architecture", yet also respected the Tuscan taste for decoration. As an architectural historian, he revived Vitruvius's theories and put them into practice in Florence. The laws of proportion, perspective and the use of the classical orders all came into play in the Duomo and in the Florentine Palazzo Rucellai (1446). This landmark palace was inspired by the Colosseum and classical Rome. The Roman influence is present in the porches and panelled doors, as well as in the frieze. The magnificent Rucellai loggia was the last to be built in 15th-century Florence, such was the profligacy it engendered. Weddings and festivities in the loggia may be no more, but the family remains ensconced in the palace.

RURAL RETREATS

Tuscany's rich urban heritage risks overshadowing the delightful rural legacy of sunny villas and picturesque hilltop farmhouses. In medieval Tuscany, the traditional battlemented manor or fortified seat evolved into the gracious villa residence of Renaissance times. In the 13th century, there were two forms of rural retreat, the feudal domain – the grand preserve of the landed nobility – and the *casa da signore*, the hub of a country estate. This was a crenellated property with a watchtower, surrounded by farm buildings and cottages, and owned by the gentry or bourgeoisie.

The villa as a country retreat was a Renaissance concept, reflecting the gracious rural lifestyle cultivated by the Tuscan nobility, even today. The villas were mostly elegant but unostentatious, reflecting the cultural conservatism of the Florentine nobility. However, the grandest Medici villas, such as Cafaggiolo, designed by Michelozzo, were sumptuous princely estates. Poggio a Caiano is the model Renaissance villa, with its harmonious design and colonnaded loggia harking back to the grandeur of classical times. The rural design reflected a desire for symmetry and a rationalisation of form and function. Embellished by porticoes, the villa was built on a square plan around an inner courtyard, with a loggia on the first floor. Set in ornamental gardens and encircled by walls, the villa enjoyed superb views, often from a hilltop.

At a time when peace reigned in the Tuscan countryside, the gardens were regarded as a bucolic retreat, featuring a *giardino segreto*, a geometrical walled garden, with formal parterres and topiary, kitchen and herb gardens, lined by stately avenues of cypresses or lemon trees. The design,

> Alberti is considered the archetypal Renaissance man; a patrician playwright, humanist and philosopher, composer and lawyer, athlete and architect.

Villa Medici La Petraia, originally bought by the Brunelleschi family.

enlivened by water gardens, was set in the 16th century, when the Mannerist style acquired colonnades and statuary, grottoes and follies.

By the 17th century, the crisp geometry of the gardens was matched by formal terraces, virtuoso waterworks and sculptures of sea monsters cavorting with mythological figures. In their ease and openness, the gardens demonstrated a harmony with the house and with the patrician owner.

As the Renaissance architect Alberti declared, "Only the house of a tyrant can look like a fortress: an ideal home should be open to the world outside, beautifully adorned, delicate and finely proportioned rather than proud and stately".

WILD TUSCANY

Nature-lovers sated with the art treasures of the region will find plenty of wild refuges in which to rest or roam.

Classic Tuscany is a civilised scene of silvery olive groves, vine-cloaked hills, sunflowers shimmering in the heat and dark silhouettes of cypresses, arranged in double file along timeless avenues. The Welsh poet Dylan Thomas, who was no stranger to life on the wild side, praised the Florentine countryside – "The pine hills are endless, the cypresses at the hilltop tell one all about the length of death, the woods are deep as love and full of goats" – a seductive rural image that has attracted so many visitors to this lush region in search of their version of earthly paradise.

> The Apuan Alps are named after the Apuani Ligures tribe who lived in this region in ancient times.

Under the pines.

Given the civilisation of the landscape, "wild Tuscany" might seem a misnomer. Yet, beyond the classic chessboard of vineyards, a rugged wilderness awaits keen explorers. Tuscany is Italy's most thickly wooded region. Mountains soar, and in the northwest there are woods as thick as rainforests, while on the west coast the Maremma marshlands remain the emptiest and most ecologically pure stretch of coastline in the country. The south, meanwhile, has the unexpected primeval emptiness of the Sienese moonscape.

THE APUAN ALPS, LUNIGIANA AND GARFAGNANA

This mountain chain, with its awe-inspiring landscape, runs parallel to the coastline and the Apennine ridge. Behind the well-groomed beaches of Versilia, on the western side of the chain, lurks a rugged hinterland of marble quarries and mountain ridges, narrow gorges, deep caves and thermal springs.

Mountainous Lunigiana, north of Carrara (famous for its marble), is wedged between Emilia and Liguria. The region is crisscrossed by streams, with canoeing popular in the clear waters of the river Magra. From Aulla, a convenient base, there are organised tours of glacial moraines, karst gorges, caves and botanical gardens.

Garfagnana lies on the borders of Emilia Romagna and northern Tuscany, between the Apuan Alps and the Apennines. Parco dell'Orecchiella is the region's most spectacular park. While closely resembling the Apuan Alps, it is higher and wilder, with a mixture of woodland and pasture, picturesque clearings and mountain streams.

> *The Apennines are divided into three sections: northern (Appennino settentrionale), central (Appennino centrale) and southern (Appennino meridionale).*

THE APENNINES

While the Apuan Alps are more varied, the Apennine range of mountains has not been ravaged by quarrying. They include the range on the Emilian border, the loftiest in the northern Apennines, as well as those in the Casentino and Mugello.

The Casentino, north of Arezzo, forms a series of razor-like crests and deep woods that straddle Emilia and northeast Tuscany. Centred on Bibbiena in the Upper Arno, these ancient forests are the region's finest. While the Emilian

Hiking to San Gimignano.

⊘ HIKING FOR TUSCANY

Tuscany is beguiling walking country, with a typical hike from Volterra to San Gimignano encompassing an old Etruscan trail and the Via Francigena, the route that led medieval pilgrims from Canterbury to Rome. The dusty trail, mostly along typical Tuscan *strade bianche*, follows these unpaved roads past vineyards, sunflowers and honey-coloured hamlets. Naturally, you wind into a sleepy hilltop hamlet, such as Casole d'Elsa, in time for lunch in an arty *trattoria*, with olive-oil coated *crostini* and *panzanella* salad washed down with a crisp Vernaccia di San Gimignano. After fording a few streams and passing abandoned farmhouses, you can fall into a farm-stay for a *Fiorentina* steak and bed.

But without the right planning, the reality can shock you out of any reverie. The region is often let down by poor maps, haphazard signposting and the lack of passing help. Contrary to popular belief, Tuscany is not Chiantishire: far from being assailed by linen-clad compatriots, you may not meet a soul *en route*, apart from languid-eyed Chianina cattle. For "soft hiking", opt for a walking holiday through a specialist operator. You can still do the trails independently, but following a wonderfully detailed route-map without nasty surprises – no getting lost in the forest, or arriving at the sole *trattoria* on closing day. The walking itinerary described is available through Headwater (www.headwater.com).

side is characterised by steep bluffs and strati-fied outcrops, the Tuscan side presents a softer atmosphere and range of scenery, with pictur-esque waterfalls and streams.

The Mugello, the hilly region north of Flor-ence, resembles a landscape painted by Gio-tto, whose homeland this was. The Mugello can be explored on horseback, by following the old bridle paths between the cities of Bologna and Florence. The valleys along the Sieve, the main tributary of the Arno, are dot-ted with villages, olive groves and vineyards. The transition from valley to mountains means that olive groves give way to chestnut and oak forests before culminating in beech woods and waterfalls. Upper Mugello is a harsh, wild landscape of mountain peaks and passes, with ridges and ravines carved out by flowing rivers over the years.

CLASSIC CHIANTI

While the Florentine Chianti is devoted to wine, the Sienese side is wilder, with vineyards gradu-ally giving way to slopes covered in holm oaks, chestnuts and juniper. A 15km (9 mile) hilly hike from Greve in Chianti to Panzano covers the Via Chiantigiana and its offshoots, passing farms, cypresses and chestnut groves along the way.

In subtle Siena province, much of the land-scape is classic Tuscany, with olive groves, gently rolling hills and dark cypresses stand-ing sentinel. However, stretching from Siena to Montepulciano is a singular moonscape known as Le Crete Senesi, the strange hillocks mark-ing the Sienese badlands. Barren or virtually treeless, this is beguiling territory nonethe-less, with solitary farmhouses marooned on the crests of hills. This seemingly empty terrain is in fact home to a range of wildlife including foxes, badgers and wild boar.

Monte Amiata, the site of an extinct volcano further south, presents the province's wilder face, with a profusion of thermal springs bubbling amid the beech and chestnut groves. With its mossy banks and majestic grandeur, the mountainous setting is suitable for hiking, horse riding and skiing.

MARSHY MAREMMA

Maremma, the southern coastal strip, is a composite of natural Tuscany. The Parco della Maremma, with its soft whalebacked hills par-allel to the coast, is dotted with Spanish watch-towers, parasol pines and coastal dunes.

On La Spergolaia ranch, the legendary *but-teri*, the last of the Maremman cowboys, break in sturdy wild horses. The park can be explored on horseback or on foot from Alberese, where waymarked paths connect the shoreline and steep cliffs.

For more information on hiking in Tuscany and consult the Italian parks website, www. parks.it.

The wooded regions of Tuscany should not be overlooked.

⊘ ANIMAL MAGIC

Italian hunters' fondness for the chase means that the wildlife has taken flight. The power of the hunting lobby has depleted numbers, with the exception of wild boar. Outside designated reserves, wildlife-spotters fare less well than botanists. Hawks and golden eagles still enjoy the majesty of the mountains, but life is no idyll for deer, ravaged by hunting. But, against the odds, Apennine wolves have made a comeback in the mountains, encouraged by the profusion of their favourite dish, short-fleeced mouflons. Even so, sightings of the short-fleeced sheep or wild boar are more frequent than glimpses of the eagle owl, weasel or wildcat.

A WALK IN THE PARK

Tuscany's parks and wild places are increasingly becoming centres for rural pursuits, whether a stroll in the park with the family or a major mountain trek.

Away from the cultural crowds, nature-lovers and adrenalin junkies can indulge in hiking, skiing, horse riding, mountain biking, climbing, caving, gliding, paragliding, sailing and surfing.

Riding is very popular in Tuscan parks, with more riding stables and well-trodden mule tracks than anywhere else in Italy.

This is also a rambler's paradise. The trails are marginally better mapped than in most Italian regions, and run from relaxed to rigorous. Serious hikers can follow the long-distance trails organised by the Italian Alpine Club (CAI) (see www.cai.it for more details).

PARCO APPENNINO TOSCO-EMILIANO

The Apennine ridges that span the border between northern Tuscany and Emilia Romagna offer diverse landscapes, from moorlands and lakes to craggy summits and waterfalls. The wildlife includes golden eagles, wolves and roe deer.

The visitor centre is at Fivizzano (tel: 0585-947 200; www.parcoappennino.it).

In the Parco dell'Alto Appennino, Abetone, commanding the mountain pass separating Tuscany and Emilia, is the region's most important winter-sports resort. Fortunately, the mountain air also makes Abetone invigorating during a stifling Tuscan summer, when the cable car takes walkers up to the leafy heights.

Despite the ravages of hunting, the forest is home to roe deer, mouflons and marmots, with golden eagles swooping over the crags. One of the most rewarding stretches of the rugged long-distance path (GEA) lies between here and Cisa.

Yet Abetone is also suitable for less energetic walkers – well-marked trails in the woods are available for those who prefer to stroll.

PARCO DELLE FORESTE CASENTINESI

Home to the secluded monasteries of Camáldoli and La Verna, this corner of the Casentino lies along the ridge that divides eastern Tuscany and Emilia Romagna. Deer, golden eagles and wolves inhabit these ancient beech and chestnut woods.

The park headquarters are in Prato Vecchio (Via Brocchi 7; tel: 0575-50301; www.parcoforestecasentinesi. it), with information offices at Camaldoli (tel: 0575-556 130) and Campigna "La Villetta" (tel: 342-301 6319).

PARCO ALPI APUANE

The park extends for over 20,000 hectares (49,000 acres) between the coastal plain and the rivers Magra, Aulella and Serchio. The Apuan Alps are different from the Apennines, with deep valleys, steep slopes and mountains of glistening white marble. Forests of chestnut and beech give cover to some 300 species of bird, while marmots can be spotted on the higher slopes.

Lago di Vaglia, in the heart of the mountains, is a reservoir containing a submerged medieval village that can be seen periodically. The underground landscape is equally inspiring, with caves often as deep as the mountains are high, and notoriously long and labyrinthine.

In Fornovolasco, east of Forte dei Marmi, the Grotta del Vento has the region's most fascinating network of caverns, riddled with steep gorges and secret passages, slowly revealing stalagmites and stalactites, fossils and alabaster formations, crystal pools and echoing chambers.

The visitor centre in Castelnuovo di Garfagnana (Piazza Erbe 1; tel: 0583-644 242; www.parks.it/parco. alpi.apuane) provides help on hiking, climbing, cycling and horse riding. Park guides are available for hikes or visits to caves.

PARCO DELL'ORECCHIELLA

The mountains of the Orecchiella park in the Garfagnana region are higher than the neighbouring Apuan Alps, but the landscape is more tame and subtle, and crisscrossed by hiking trails.

The area is centred on the high broad plain of Pania di Corfino, overlooked by a dramatic limestone peak that dominates the Serchio valley. The wildlife includes deer, wild boar, mouflons, badgers, otters, weasels and wolves. San Pellegrino monastery offers fabulous views and houses a folk museum.

San Romano in Garfagnana visitor centre (tel: 0583-619 098; www.ingarfagnana.it) makes a good base for exploring.

PARCO DI MIGLIARINO, SAN ROSSORE, MASSACIUCCOLI

This park covers the coastal hinterland behind the beach resorts between Viareggio and Livorno, and includes the forest of San Rossore and Lake Massaciuccoli. Huge holm oaks and maritime pines grow right up to the beach and are home to wild boar, fallow deer and countless species of native and migratory birds. The San Rossore archaeologi-

The rugged landscape is a mixture of marsh-land, mountains and coast backed by umbrella pines, interspersed with rocky outcrops and coves. There are no human settlements, and just one access road links Alberese, the park entrance, to Marina Alberese, a virgin seaside stretch that attracts migratory birds on their journey to Africa. The dense vegetation here provides the perfect habitat for wild boar, the symbol of the Maremma, while herds of Maremman cattle and horses of the *butteri* (local cowherds) roam on its plains.

The Alberese visitor centre (Via Bersagliere 7/9; tel: 0564-407 098; www.parco-maremma.it) works with Naturalmente Toscana, which offers walking, riding and canoeing trips – as well as free food and

Poppies brighten the fields of Tuscany in springtime.

cal site, where a fleet of Roman ships was unearthed, can be visited by appointment.

There is the La Brilla visitor centre at Massarosa (Via Pietra a Padule 1181; tel: 0584-178 0676), while the Tenuta San Rossore organises walking and cycling tours (tel: 050-530 101; www.parcosanrossore. org). Boat tours of Lake Massaciuccoli depart from Torre del Lago.

PARCO DELLA MAREMMA

This beautiful, unspoilt wilderness, covering over 100 sq km (40 sq miles), stretches along the Tyrrhenian coast from Principina a Mare to Talamone. It is centred on the Monti dell'Uccellina, which rise up from the sea.

wine tastings onsite (tel: 337-106 5079; www.naturalmentetoscana.it).

PARCO DELL'ARCIPELAGO TOSCANO

This is Europe's largest marine reserve and is popular with diving enthusiasts. It covers the seven islands of the Tuscan Archipelago: Elba, Capraia, Gorgona, Pianosa, Montecristo, Giglio and Giannutri. The coastline and sea bed vary enormously from island to island, hence the variety of flora and fauna on show to curious visitors. Sea birds such as shearwaters and black-headed gulls proliferate, while dolphins, sperm whales and even the rare monk seal may also be sighted.

The marine park is based in Elba (tel: 0565-919 411; www.parks.it/parco.nazionale.arcip.toscano).

A Sienese celebratory feast during the Palio.

A TASTE OF TUSCANY

Traditional Tuscan cuisine is *cucina povera*, robust "peasant food" – but this deceptive simplicity is now valued as tasty authenticity, served straight from the land.

Tuscany has everything to offer the foodie, with dishes designed to bring out the richness of the wine. From T-bone steaks to peasant soups, wild-boar stews, truffle sauces, hearty cheeses and divine cakes, this is as far from faddish "creative" cuisine as you can get.

What is immediately striking about Tuscan food is that it is rustic, simple but robust, nourishing the soul and the spirit as much as the body. The Tuscan monks who cultivated wine and oil estates knew what they were doing and, in some cases, are still doing. The cooking is never elaborate or excessive; there are no fussy finishing touches, complex reductions of sauces or subtly blended flavours. But there is a basic earthiness about the dishes that has made them popular the world over.

Tuscany produces its own inimitable versions of Italian staples: pasta dishes with gamey wild-boar sauce; *pici* pasta with fresh ceps; and *fagioli all'Uccelletto*, beans in tomato sauce. But along with a traditional attitude to food, the region also offers distinctive delicacies and seasonal dishes, such as truffles and wild mushrooms.

BEAN-EATERS RULE

The Tuscans are known as *Toscani Mangiafagioli* – bean-eaters, because the pulse enriches so many dishes. Legumes are a mainstay in Tuscany, where *cannellini*, white kidney beans, add a smooth texture. Served in terracotta pots, thick soups and hearty bean stews are often enhanced by a trickle of olive oil added at the table. Many chefs rate Tuscan oil the world's finest but rarely agree on which area, let alone which estate, produces the very best. As the locals are never impartial, foodie visitors are left to compare the virtues of oil from Lucca, the Chianti, the Maremma and Siena.

Preparing bistecca alla Fiorentina.

Soups are made of the ubiquitous beans, and include *acquacotta*, a vegetable soup with an egg added before serving, and *pappa al pomodoro*, a thick soup of bread and tomatoes. Even more typical is the Florentine winter speciality, *ribollita* ("reboiled"), which improves the flavour of the soup.

Elsewhere, the rugged Garfagnana region favours tasty spelt soups, enriched by oil, onions and *borlotti* beans.

Coastal Livorno produces delicious *cacciucco*, a filling shellfish-and-fish soup that supposedly inspired the French *bouillabaisse*. The story goes that the soup originated in the port after a tremendous storm that left a widowed fisherman's wife desperately trying to feed her hungry brood. The children came home with handfuls of mussels, shrimps, half a fish and some fish heads – which the wily mother tossed into a pot with herbs and tomatoes to create the glorious *cacciucco*. While *zuppa di pesce* (fish soup) can be eaten all over Italy, *cacciucco* can be eaten only around Livorno, ladled over toasted, garlicky croutons.

BREAD AND CHEESE

Tuscan bread is made without salt, supposedly because salt was once reserved for "precious" foods such as salami. Dante wrote of Florentine

Picking olives, as depicted by a 15th-century artist.

bread, comparing it favourably with the salty bread he was forced to eat in exile. The importance of bread is revealed in local expressions, such as "Bread cannot be made with flour alone", or "Better stale bread at home than a roast at someone else's house". In fact, stale bread finds its way into *panzanella*, a typical peasant dish made with tomatoes, onions, cucumber and basil, drenched in olive oil. You will also sample bread in the form of *bruschetta* or *crostini*, coated with olive oil or liver-based spreads.

Tuscan cheeses are varied and plentiful. There is a delightful overspill of cheeses from neighbouring Emilia Romagna, including Parmesan, *parmigiano reggiano*, which complements Tuscany's marvellous pasta dishes and soups. Other stalwarts include pecorino, a hard, healthy ewe's-milk cheese, produced since Roman times. Although ideally suited to grating, pecorino matures well and can also be used in pasta fillings. Lesser-known cheeses include *marzolino*, a ewe's-milk cheese made in March, when milk is most plentiful in the Chianti valley; *mucchino*, cow's-milk cheese made in and around Lucca by the same procedure as pecorino; and all the local rustic *cacciotte* and ricotta made with cow's, goat's and ewe's milk. Pienza is a key centre for artisan cheeses, especially *cacio pecorino*.

HEARTY STEWS AND BARBECUES

Tuscan cooks favour rustic, outdoor cooking – a grill over an open wood fire is not uncommon behind a chic Florentine restaurant or in the garden of a rural *trattoria*. Fresh sage, rosemary and basil are used, as they grow in abundance.

The Tuscan meat dish *par excellence* is the *bistecca alla Fiorentina*, a vast, tender, succulent T-bone steak – preferably from cattle raised in Val di Chiana. With expressive eyes and long-limbed grace, the beautiful white Chianina breed was used in Roman triumphal marches, or sacrificed to the gods in Etruscan times. The meat is brushed with the purest virgin olive oil and grilled over a scented wood fire of oak or olive branches, then seasoned with salt and pepper. In good Florentine restaurants, you will be able to see the meat raw before you order.

Another famous Tuscan meat dish is *arista alla Fiorentina*, pork loin highly seasoned with rosemary and ground pepper. The dish dates back to the 15th century, when the Greek bishops were served it at a Florentine banquet and pronounced it *"aristos"*, meaning "very good" in Greek. The name stuck, and it has become a feature of Tuscan cuisine ever since.

In the Sienese countryside, the white-striped Cinta Senese breed has been producing the region's finest pork and charcuterie since Etruscan times. The odd-looking pig is even depicted in Lorenzetti's famous 14th-century fresco of *Good Government* in Siena's Town Hall.

Hunting is a popular sport, resulting in plentiful offerings of *cinghiale* (wild boar), which comes in many guises. Despite conservationists' pleas, small birds, from sparrows to quail, are also still considered fair game.

AUTUMN HARVEST

The "fruits of the forest" are particularly prized in Tuscany, especially chestnuts, mushrooms and truffles. Chestnuts are a staple, particularly in mountainous regions, where they are made into flour, pancakes, soups and sweet cakes such as *castagnaccio*, flavoured with rosemary and pine nuts. The season peaks around mid-October,

The Fruit Vendor, a 16th-century painting by Vincenzo Campi, celebrates the region's harvest.

⊘ TRUFFLE TROVE

"Truffles taste and smell of people and sweat," says chef Giorgio Locatelli. Pungent and pricey, the white truffle is a paradox; a princely treat harvested by peasants since Roman times.

Dubbed "the white diamond", it is actually a dirty yellow-brown in colour. Emperor Nero called truffles "the food of the gods", while excitable food critics wax lyrical about truffles as "the sex of the gods". Truffles are underground fungi, developing close to the roots of oaks, poplars and hazelnut trees. But the exact location of a "truffle trove" is a well-guarded secret, with truffle-hunters regarding their talented dogs, who unearth the tuber, as important members of their families.

Although the most prized white truffles come from Piedmont, Tuscany also has its share, centred on San Miniato, which hosts a truffle festival in November. The precious white truffle is available from September to December, while variants of black truffle are available all year. Connoisseurs favour simplicity in use, with shavings of white truffle grated over pasta, fried egg, salad or risotto. Black truffles suit more complex dishes, but are equally delicious grated over a *crostini* (grilled bread) coated with *stracchino* cheese.

Set in a castle in San Giovanni d'Asso, the intriguing Truffle Museum provides information on truffle fairs, tours and inns (http://museotartufo.museisenesi.org).

when chestnut lovers can travel on a restored 1920s steam train from Florence to Marradi's *Sagra delle Castagne*, or chestnut festival, to join the celebrations.

In the autumn, when the rains fall, the hills are awash with family outings. Long lines of cars park along the side of the mountain roads – particularly in the Maremma, Garfagnana and Mugello areas, where locals arm themselves with baskets and hooked knives, in search of *funghi*. The wild-mushroom season is eagerly awaited but if you want to join in, go with a local, since many types of mushroom are poisonous. Or simply purchase *funghi* from a roadside market during the August–October season. The varieties of wild mushrooms depend upon the type of tree nearby – but the most sought after are the perfect *porcini (Boletus edulis)*, ceps that grow to enormous size and thickness.

Fresh wild mushrooms are best grilled in the Tuscan way, like a steak: rub each with a slice of lemon, season with slivers of garlic and sprigs of thyme – or, even simpler, just brush with olive oil and salt. Dried *porcini* are even tastier, as the dehydration concentrates the flavour. When regener-

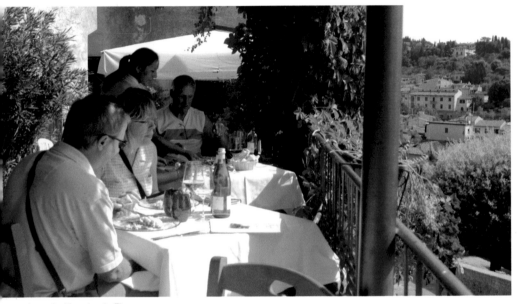

A meal with a view in Florence.

⊘ EATING ITALIAN-STYLE

Tuscans love their food. But there are "rules" to be followed if you want to "eat as the Italians do". Cappuccino in the afternoon? You'll be branded a tourist. Usually, breakfast consists of just an espresso or cappuccino, drunk on the hoof in a local bar if not at home. Traditionally, a full-blown meal begins with an *antipasto* – salami or some roasted peppers, for example. Then follows the first course, *il primo*, usually a pasta or soup. *Il secondo* is next, consisting of meat or fish and vegetables. Salad follows, cleansing the palate for *i formaggi* (cheese) and *i dolci* (dessert), often followed by an espresso. *Buon appetito!*

ated by soaking in lukewarm water, they are ideal for use in risotto or pasta sauces. Mushrooms can also be used to flavour *pici*, the typical Tuscan spaghetti. But if there is one food that provokes more excitement than wild mushrooms, it is the *tartufo*, or truffle – particularly the white variety.

Saffron is another autumn harvest, cultivated around San Gimignano for over 800 years. The valuable spice was even used as a currency, given its prestige and transportability. In 1200, the Bishop of Volterra used saffron to bribe the counsellors to the Roman Curia. Saffron only flowers for a fortnight between October and November, and must be gathered at dawn when the purplish flower is closed. Over 500 hours of work are required to produce a kilo, since the rust-coloured filaments are picked by hand, then dried and "toasted", before finding their way into risotto and sauces.

SIENESE SWEETMEATS

Siena is the most sweet-toothed city, famous for its pastries, biscuits and cakes. *Panforte*, a Sienese Christmas speciality, is unmistakable in its brightly coloured octagonal box. It is a rich, sweet cake of candied fruit, nuts, spices, honey and sugar, sandwiched between sheets of rice paper. *Ricciarelli* are delightful, diamond-shaped almond cakes, also saved for Christmas, along with the rich, golden

Santo. Castelnuovo della Garfagnana specialises in a simple chestnut cake called *torta garfagnina*, while closer to the Emilia Romagna borders, look out for a baked-apple cake, the *torta di mele*.

No visit to Florence would be complete without ice cream – the Florentines claim to have invented *gelato*. Always look for the sign *Produzione Propria* (home-made). The city produces *zuccotto*, a sponge-cake mould with a filling of almonds, hazelnuts, chocolate and cream. Once eaten, it is never forgotten. Literally translated as "small pumpkin", this dome-shaped Florentine speciality

Fresh funghi.

It is claimed that Italy's famous gelato was invented in Florence.

rice cake called *torta di riso*. Instead, *cavallucci* are hard biscuits served at the end of a meal and dipped in Vin Santo dessert wine. The local *pasticcerie* are filled with delectable varieties.

Siena faces stiff competition from the cake shops of Lucca, Pistoia, Prato and the Garfagnana. Lucca favours a plain, ring-shaped cake known as *buccellato*, and a sweet tart of spinach and chard with pine nuts. Pistoia produces the pretty *corona di San Bartolomeo* for the feast of St Bartholomew on 24 August, when mothers lead their children to church wearing this cake "necklace" to receive a blessing from the saint. *Cantuccini* are typical Tuscan biscuits: Prato's version, *biscottini di Prato*, are made from almonds, eggs, flour and sugar, and are delicious dipped in Vin

either alludes to the cathedral (Duomo) or to the clergy: in Tuscan dialect, a cardinal's skullcap is also called a *zuccotto*.

Tuscany is truly a food-lover's paradise, riddled with wine and food trails that invariably run through a patchwork of vineyards and olive groves or cornfields edged with sunflowers. The Chianti route is a chance to enjoy a T-bone steak and Chianti Classico wines. In the Tuscan capital, if you can stomach it, there is a trail that includes tripe, a Florentine delicacy. In the Garfagnana, book a tour with Sapori & Saperi to savour, or even harvest, chestnuts, salami, wild mushrooms and bread baked in a wood-fired oven (www.sapori-e-saperi.com).

Watching the crowds go by in Cortona.

Castiglione della Pescaia.

Monteriggioni in the Chianti region.

INTRODUCTION

A detailed guide to the region, with the principal sites clearly cross-referenced by number to the maps.

Pisa's famous Leaning Tower.

For many visitors, Tuscany is the true Italy – as conjured up by clichéd Merchant-Ivory film adaptations of E.M. Forster novels – a land of swaying cypress trees, olive groves and vineyards, scattered with medieval castles and Medici villas. Tuscans are more nuanced about their rural idyll. To them, Tuscany evokes the wild as well as the tamed, stretching from the Carrara-marble quarries to the Maremma wilderness, embracing the rugged coastline, rolling Chianti vineyards and the wooded slopes of Monte Amiata. Despite a deep relationship with the land, the heirs to the Etruscans recognise the tough realities of rural life. Tuscans are also innately sociable and will always prefer living in large villages or small towns to an isolated farmhouse, however idyllic.

The appeal of Tuscan towns is their timelessness, civility and sense of ease with their past. Florence, the cradle of the Renaissance, retains a huge number of the artworks created in its honour. Gazing at the skyline from Piazzale Michelangelo reveals how little the cityscape has changed since its artistic heyday. Variety underpins Tuscan townscapes: from medieval hilltop eyries to Etruscan outposts; from *fin-de-siècle* spa towns to sophisticated beach resorts; from the splendour of a Renaissance palazzo to a stark Romanesque church. Medieval Siena and Renaissance Florence may be unmissable, but spare some time for

A cypress-surrounded villa.

Etruscan Volterra, genuine Massa Marittima or cyclist-friendly Lucca. Tuscan towns are built on a human scale. As for scenery, lap up the Unesco-protected Val d'Orcia countryside, mountainous Garfagnana, and wild, coastal Maremma.

For all Tuscany's artistic and architectural riches, however, most visitors would agree that as much pleasure can be derived from lunch on the shady terrace of a rustic trattoria, as an encounter with Michelangelo's *David* and Botticelli's *Venus*. As Forster observed: "The traveller who has gone to Italy to study the tactile values of Giotto, or the corruption of the papacy, may return remembering nothing but the blue sky and the men and women who live under it."

Tuscany

0 20 km
0 20 miles

The snow-capped dome of
Florence's famous Duomo.

THE CITY OF FLORENCE

One of the world's architectural masterpieces, packed with palaces and art galleries, a revitalised Florence is an essential stop on any modern-day Grand Tour.

More than any other Italian city, Florence is defined by its artistic heritage. The city is both blessed and burdened by a civic identity bound up with the Renaissance, and basks in its reflected glory. As the birthplace of the Renaissance, the city witnessed the Florentine miracle, a flowering of the human spirit that has left a lasting artistic imprint. The churches, palaces and galleries are studded with the world's greatest concentration of Renaissance art and sculpture. In 1743, Anna Maria Lodovica, the last of the Medici line, bequeathed her property to Florence, ensuring that the Medici collections remained intact forever. As a result, Florence is still awash with many of the treasures that Vasari, the first art historian, mentions in his *Lives of the Artists* (1550).

Although artistic treasures predominate, Florence is experiencing a revival that makes it far more than a Renaissance theme park. Upon becoming the city's mayor in 2009 Matteo Renzi uttered these words: "Florence was on everyone's must-see list, and we got lazy. The sites were run for the benefit of bureaucrats. It is my duty to change this." True to his word, he pedestrianised swathes of the city, improved public transport, tackled pollution, sanctioned bicycle-friendly routes, extended museum opening times, and

introduced a combined museum and transport pass. His successor, Dario Nardella, has kept up the momentum.

Fortuitously, Florence is also experiencing a cultural resurgence, linked to the proliferation of new arts centres, theatre-dining clubs, cool bars, contemporary-art galleries and music venues, including the new opera, ballet and classical music complex **Opera di Firenze** on Viale Fratelli Rosselli.

To make the most of your stay, and to avoid the lengthy queues, either buy the three-day Firenze Card or pre-book

⊘ Main attractions

Piazza della Signoria
Galleria degli Uffizi
Bargello
Duomo and Battistero
Museo dell'Opera del
   Duomo
Cappelle Medicee
Galleria dell'Accademia
Santa Croce
Ponte Vecchio
Palazzo Pitti

Map on page 96

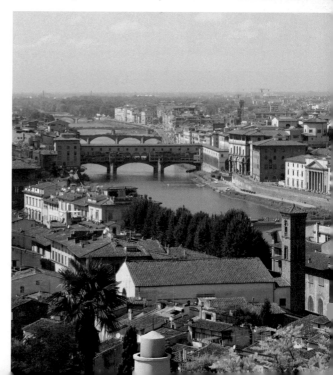

A view of the River Arno running through the centre of Florence.

the "blockbuster" museums, such as the Uffizi Gallery (www.firenzemusei.it or tel: 055-294 883; www.uffizi.it).

Viewed from the surrounding hills, Florence seems to be floating in a bowl that, at dusk, is tinged violet. The honey-coloured walls and rose-coloured roofs combine to make a unity that is dominated by a single, vast building, the Cathedral, or Duomo. It is by far the biggest building for miles around, with its roof and dome in the same subtle colour-range as the surrounding smaller buildings, above which it also seems to float like a great liner among tugs.

There are few towers or spires to be seen in Florence. Giotto's multicoloured Campanile next to the Duomo, plain in outline but intricate in detail, and the thrusting tower of the Palazzo Vecchio, elegant and sombre, soar above a low-slung skyline. The overall impression is not that of a city, but of one single, vast building, a majestic palace.

Close contact with the city can be initially disconcerting, even disappointing and claustrophobic. The streets are narrow, hemmed in by towering, plain buildings. There is no delicate filigree, as in Venice, or cheerful Baroque, as in Rome, to tempt the eye. Indeed, some of the city's buildings resemble 19th-century warehouses – grim structures that were erected at a time of social unrest, their primary function being that of fortresses. As for palaces, Florentine architectural taste runs to the monumental, macho and unembellished.

Here, the city has been grouped into four sections, starting with the area around Piazza della Signoria and the Palazzo Vecchio, followed by the Duomo area, and then by three important religious foundations (which, though physically scattered around the city, have been grouped together in this chapter). The final section is the River Arno and beyond. Many of the sights are within easy walking distance of each other – despite Florence's size, its historic centre is reasonably compact.

PIAZZA DELLA SIGNORIA: THE CIVIC CENTRE

Florence is dauntingly monumental, nowhere more so than the **Piazza della Signoria ❶**, which is an open-air museum of sculpture, starring *David*, a copy of Michelangelo's

*The courtyard of
Palazzo Vecchio.*

famed heroic boy. More than any
other square in Italy, the Piazza della
Signoria evokes the ancient world
and the overweening pride of the
Renaissance city. Even so, of all the
great city squares, Florence's is the
most perversely irregular. There is
nothing in the Piazza della Signoria
to compete with the grace of Siena's
curved Campo, or the simple majesty of Rome's Capitol. Tucked on one
side is the **Palazzo Vecchio** ❷ (www.
museicivicifiorentini.comune.fi.it; Apr–Sept
Fri–Wed 9am–11pm, Thu until 2pm,
Oct–Mar Fri–Wed 9am–7pm, Thu until
2pm), the seat of government for the
past six centuries.

The Medici administration was
based in the Palazzo Vecchio, which
remains the town hall, and which
was redesigned during the reign of
Cosimo I. The palace, under different guises, has been the emblem of
Florentine power since the 14th century. With its bold swallowtail crenel-
lations and asymmetrical bell tower,
the Palazzo is the most evocative of
city symbols.

The courtyard, with its copy of an
enchanting fountain by Verrocchio, is a
delight. Vasari's monumental staircase
leads to the frescoed **Salone dei Cinquecento**, the Hall of the Five Hundred,
where members of the Great Council
met. Cosimo I set his stamp on the
chamber by commissioning a series of
vast frescoes, painted by Vasari, which
glorified his military triumphs.

Beyond the art and the style, the palace reveals everyday Medici court life.
It also houses the "Traces of Florence"
permanent exhibition presenting the
history of Florence.

It is also one of the few museums in conservative Florence to
have moved into the 21st century
in terms of presentation. The use
of multimedia, "secret itineraries",
and a children's perspective on great
artworks has proved a resounding
success. The Associazione Mus.e
organises children's workshops with
actors who bring the history to life
and child-friendly tours of museums
including the Palazzo Vecchio and the
Museo Novecento.

The huge fountain in the centre of
the piazza is the subject of affectionate
mockery by Florentines themselves,
and no two buildings in the piazza
seem to have the same facade. With a
despot's love of order, Cosimo I tried to
impose an artificial unity on the square,
but his schemes came to nothing, leaving the piazza as a perfect illustration
of Florentine "unity in diversity".

The square has changed little over
the centuries. The **Marzocco**, the lion
symbol of the city that prisoners were
forced to kiss, can be found here,
as well as a copy of Michelangelo's
immense statue of *David* (the original
is in the Accademia), commissioned in
1501 to mark an important change in
the constitution. Nearby is a statue of
the first Medici duke, Cosimo I.

Next to the Palazzo Vecchio
stands the elegant **Loggia dei Lanzi**
❸, crammed with statues. The

loggia (named after the mercenaries employed by Cosimo) has an impressive statue of a triumphant Perseus holding the severed head of Medusa, which Cosimo commissioned from Cellini. Most stunning among the other statues in the loggia is Giambologna's *Rape of the Sabine Women* on the opposite side.

GALLERIA DEGLI UFFIZI

Adjoining the piazza are the immense galleries of the **Uffizi** ❹ (www.uffizi.it; Tue–Sun 8.15am–6.50pm; free on first Sunday of each month). Pre-booking is advisable, and you can do this through the Firenze Card, which covers all museums, www.firenzecard.it, or through www.uffizi.it.

Now Tuscany's foremost gallery, the Uffizi was the administrative nerve centre of the grand duchy, reinforcing the chain of command between the Palazzo Vecchio, the Medici power base, and the court at the Pitti Palace. Founded by the Medici, this is now the greatest art gallery in Italy. Francesco de' Medici (1541–87) decided to transform the second floor of the Uffizi into a museum, coincidentally paying tribute to the Medici's dynastic glory. For the introverted ruler, the gallery was essentially his private playground "for walking, with paintings, statues and other precious things".

On display are paintings by masters from Giotto to Botticelli, Piero della Francesca, Michelangelo, Leonardo da Vinci, Raphael, Titian and Caravaggio. Although Tuscan art reigns supreme, the panoply of Italian art is also well represented, particularly painters from Umbria, Urbino, Emilia and the Veneto. Since most visitors come to see the Early Renaissance works, the High Renaissance rooms are far more peaceful and, by the time Titian and Veronese finally make way for Caravaggio and Tiepolo, Rubens and Rembrandt, the crowds have faded away as miraculously as

a Tiepolo trompe l'oeil. By the same token, the wonderful classical and cinquecento statuary in the gallery corridors is often overlooked in the lemming stampede to see specific Renaissance paintings.

So rich is the Uffizi's collection that proposals for major expansion have been hotly debated for decades. The controversial new loggia entrance plan designed by cutting-edge architect Arata Isozaki has stalled. The focus is currently on remodelling the second floor now that new ground floor rooms have opened, see page 112 for more information on the Uffizi.

Just behind the Uffizi is the **Museo Galileo** ❺ (www.museogalileo.it; Wed–Mon 9.30am–6pm, Tue until 1pm). The museum, housed in the 14th-century Palazzo Castellani, makes a refreshing change after an overindulgence in the arts. The collection of scientific instruments shows that Renaissance Florence was pre-eminent as a centre of scientific research. Amid the museum's prized collection of Galileo's instruments, the mathematician's

Strolling among the artworks for sale.

Palazzo Vecchio at night.

middle finger of his right hand is displayed like the relic of a Christian saint.

Other rooms are devoted to astronomy, navigation, the science of warfare, and to the Medici who founded this scientific treasure trove.

THE BARGELLO

Chronologically, the Palazzo Vecchio is the second city hall of Florence. Its predecessor, the **Bargello** ❻ (www.bargellomusei.beniculturali.it; daily 8.15am–1.50pm, summer until 4.50pm; free on the first Sun of the month), was built 50 years earlier in 1250 as the seat of the chief magistrate, the *Podestà*. The Bargello was, in effect, the police headquarters, and its courtyard witnessed public executions. The building is now a wonderful museum of sculpture, with a rich collection of works by artists such as Michelangelo, Cellini, Donatello – and is not nearly as bewildering as the Uffizi. The Bargello's tantalising calling card is Donatello's coquettish *David*, a rival to Michelangelo's more virile version in the Accademia.

The Museo Galileo.

PALACES AND PIAZZAS

Just west of the Piazza della Signoria is a loosely linked cluster of buildings that span four centuries of Florentine history, from the embattled Middle Ages to the era of ducal control. The **Palazzo di Parte Guelfa** ❼ (just off Via delle Terme) was the headquarters of the all-powerful Guelf Party, which, after the defeat and expulsion of the rival Ghibellines, ruled the city.

For light relief, drop into the engagingly touristic **Mercato Nuovo** – the 16th-century covered market. Remember to stroke the *Porcellino*, the bronze boar whose snout is polished to gleaming gold: touching it supposedly guarantees your return to the city.

Also referred to as the Museo dell'Antica Casa Fiorentina, the **Palazzo Davanzati** ❽ (www.bargello musei.beniculturali.it; Mon–Fri 8.15am–1.50pm, Sat–Sun 1.15–6.50pm) is the best-preserved example of a patrician home and provides an insight into life in medieval Florence.

Built in about 1330, its painted Trecento walls serve to soften and brighten the interior, turning the fortress into a home. The great Gothic halls on the upper floors are frescoed to give the semblance of fabrics and drapery. Other striking aspects include the vaulted entrance hall and the staircase supported by flying buttresses. In style and decor, the lofty, galleried palace bridges the medieval and Renaissance eras, making Palazzo Davanzati the most illuminating example of a patrician dwelling from the period.

From Palazzo Davanzati, Via de' Sassetti leads you to the grandiose **Palazzo Strozzi** ❾ (www.palazzostrozzi. org; Fri–Wed 10am–8pm, Thu until 11pm), an important cultural hub and the setting for blockbuster art exhibitions. This bombastic building is also a testament to the overweening pride of the powerful merchant banker, Filippo Strozzi, who dared to build

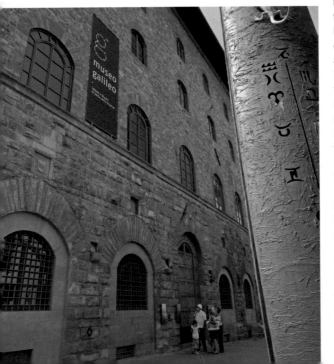

a bigger palace than the Medici's. The monumental nature of the rusticated facade is echoed by the bold inner courtyard. As the quintessential 15th-century Florentine princely palace, Palazzo Strozzi was a model for centuries to come.

Situated in the restored cellars of the Palazzo Strozzi, **La Strozzina** (www.strozzina.org) is a challenging exhibition space – which is exactly what it was until the "great flood" of 1966, when the River Arno inundated these cellars.

Worth a visit while you're in the vicinity is the Romanesque church of **Santa Trinita** (Mon–Sat 7am–noon, 4-7pm; free), which features a fresco cycle of the life of St Francis painted in 1483 by Domenico Ghirlandaio.

East of Palazzo Strozzi, **Piazza della Repubblica** ⑩ was laid out over the medieval market quarter and Ghetto, which were demolished in the 19th century. The plan to develop central Florence was conceived between 1865 and 1871, when the city was briefly the capital of Italy. The ancient and "squalid" buildings were to be swept away and replaced by broad avenues, symbolic of the new age of the United Kingdom of Italy. Thankfully, the scheme was abandoned. The self-important square, with its old-fashioned cafés, remains rather soulless, a modern intrusion into the heart of the city.

THE DUOMO: THE RELIGIOUS CENTRE

The street that links the two great monuments of the Palazzo Vecchio and the Duomo is still known as the Street of the Hosiers – Via dei Calzaiuoli – after the stocking-knitters who plied their trade here. The guilds were gathered in this area, hence the guild church of **Orsanmichele** (www.bargellomusei.beniculturali.it; church daily 10am–4pm; museum Mon 10am–4.50pm, Sat until 12.30pm; free). It is, in effect, an open-air sculpture gallery, with an array of statues displayed in individual niches in the walls.

Holding up to 20,000 people, the enormous **Duomo** ⑪ (www.

Milan may be the fashion capital, but Florence has its fair share of home-grown designers of international repute. Nearly all have their outlets at the southern end of Via de' Tornabuoni, including the shoemaker, Ferragamo.

⊘ FLORENCE FOR FAMILIES

It's a myth that the city offers little to families sated with art and culture. You can now see the city by **bicycle**, by **Segway** (www.segway.it), or by **bicycle rickshaw** (Tre Rote, tel: +39 340-329 2018; www.pedicabfirenze.it). Pick up a "normal" bike on Piazza Santa Croce or opt for a ride in a **horse-drawn carriage** (from Piazza del Duomo or Piazza della Signoria). In summer, lounge on the Lungarno **urban beach**, a sandy affair on the banks of the Arno, or cruise along the river on *barchetti*, typical boats (embarkation near Piazza Mentana). Let off steam by exploring the grotesque statues and grottoes in the **Boboli Gardens**, retreating to a **Medici villa** or cycling through the Chianti countryside.

Children will enjoy a ride on one of the horses of the antique, well-restored **carousel** in Piazza della Repubblica, near the arch. The only merry-go-round in Florence, put up by the Picci family at the beginning of the 20th century and still operated by Picci descendants, it features 20 horses and two gilded king's carriages. It runs every day May–Nov 10am–8pm, lightening up in the evening.

Children will also appreciate the street performers dotted around the square.

Child-friendly museums include the **Palazzo Vecchio**, where the Associazione Mus.e (http://musefirenze.it) organises a number of daily tours and activities for children. Little ones can dress up in historical costume, learn about life at the Medici court or explore secret passages. In the **Leonardo da Vinci Museum**, get to grips with the designer's genius by studying the wooden models of his flying machines and armoured tanks, swing bridges and robots (www.mostredileonardo.com; daily 10am–6pm, Apr–Oct until 7pm). With its chivalric mood and medieval armour, the **Stibbert Museum** is "culture lite" for kids (www.museostibbert.it; Mon–Wed 10am–2pm, Fri–Sun 10am–6pm). Jump into the cool **Palazzo Strozzi** for both arty children's tours and adult blockbusters. When all else fails, bribe the children with **ice cream** at Il Re Gelato (Piazza Strozzi), Grom (Via delle Oche) or Vivoli (Via Isola delle Stinche). As punishment, dare them to **eat tripe** ("awful offal") at San Lorenzo food market.

*Piazza della
Repubblica.*

museumflorence.com; Mon–Fri 10am–
5pm, Sat 10am–4.45pm, Sun
1.30–4.45pm; free) only serves to
emphasise the smallness of the surrounding square, and the narrowness
of the adjoining streets. At no point
can one take in the whole. But now
fully pedestrianised, the square is
yours to wander freely, possibly even
in a horse-drawn carriage, which can
be picked up in the piazza.

THE BAPTISTERY

Despite the Duomo's dominating
presence, the **Battistero** ⑫ (www.
museumflorence.com; Mon–Fri 8.15–
10.15am and 11.15am–7.30pm,
Sat 8.15am–6.30pm, Sun 8.15am–
1.30pm; combined ticket for all the
Duomo museums) easily holds its
own. The oldest building in the city, it
was built on, or reconstructed from,
a 7th-century building sometime
between 1060 and 1120 and served
as the cathedral of Florence until
1228. Dante was among the eminent
Florentines baptised there, and the
wealthy Wool Guild *(Calimala)* lavished

vast sums on the superb Venetian
mosaics decorating the cupola.

The *Calimala* then turned its attention to the three great doors, first
commissioning Andrea Pisano to
create bronze doors for the south
entrance, then initiating a competition for the other doors, which was
won by Lorenzo Ghiberti. There is no
mistaking the second pair (the east
doors, facing the Duomo) – which
took Ghiberti 27 years to create, and
which Michelangelo described as the
"Gates of Paradise". But the present
panels are copies. The original panels are in the **Museo dell'Opera del
Duomo** ⑬ on the east side of the
Piazza del Duomo (www.museumflo
rence.com; daily 9am–7pm; combined
ticket), while the competition panels
are in the Bargello.

The two doors are divided into 10
panels, each representing a scene
from the Old Testament. Round the
panels are heads of the Sibyls and
the Prophets. Seek out Ghiberti's
self-portrait, halfway down on the
right-hand side of the left-hand door:

although minuscule, it is a perfect portrait – a small, balding man peering knowingly out.

It took the Florentines over 400 years to decide on the kind of facade they wanted for the west front of the Duomo, with the present, controversial facade designed in 1887.

INSIDE THE DUOMO

After the multicoloured splendour of the exterior, the interior of **Santa Maria del Fiore** (the Duomo's official name) is muted, coming to life only at the time of religious festivals, when immense crimson banners adorn the walls. But the eye falls on two large murals high on the wall to the left of the entrance. The right-hand one is of an Englishman, John Hawkwood, a mercenary soldier (condottiero) who first attacked Florence for his paymasters and then became the city's Captain-General in 1375.

Further along the aisle is the painting of *Dante Declaiming The Divine Comedy by Michelino*. On Dante's right, Hell and Purgatory are depicted, contrasted with a contemporary view of the city's major monuments.

The Duomo's greatest treasure is Michelangelo's unfinished *Pietà*, sculpted for his own tomb in 1550, and now in the museum collection. It is entirely different from his earlier, more famous *Pietà* in St Peter's, in Rome; where that is all calm, resigned acceptance, this is simply the utter defeat of death.

THE DOME AND BELL TOWER

It is still Brunelleschi's dome that defines Florence, over 500 years after it was built. Filippo Brunelleschi created the purest Renaissance architecture, buildings striking in their simplicity and pared-down loveliness. The cupola of the Duomo, which uses rigorous geometry based on classical forms, is the perfect expression of a rational use of space. His stroke of genius was to devise a cunning system of an inner shell and outer dome to distribute the weight of the cupola, with thick walls negating the need for further buttressing. Out of respect for

The south doors of the Baptistery were the work of Andrea Pisano (c.1270–1348) – goldsmith, sculptor and architect rolled into one.

The cupola mosaics of the Battistero.

The interior of Brunelleschi's dome.

Brunelleschi's achievement, the city forbade the construction of any building taller than the Duomo – to this day, the massive dome dominates the red rooftops, rising almost higher than the surrounding hills.

If you have a head for heights, ascend to the gallery of the dome (www.museumflorence.com; Mon–Fri 8.30am–7pm, Sat 8.30am–5pm, Sun 1–4pm; combined ticket, time booking mandatory). It is not for vertigo sufferers: the gallery is narrow and the balustrade low, but only here can Brunelleschi's stupendous achievement be fully appreciated. The interior of the dome is covered in Vasari's bold allegorical frescoes, although the original plan was to cover the space with mosaics, which would have emphasised its soaring majesty. But its majesty is not in doubt.

Scarcely less tall, at 85 metres (278ft), is the **Campanile** (www.museumflorence.com; daily 8.15am–7pm; combined ticket) alongside, begun by Giotto shortly after he was appointed chief architect in 1331, and finished off after

his death in 1337 by Andrea Pisano and then Talenti. Work was eventually completed in 1359. The climb to the top is worth the effort for intimate views of the Cathedral's upper levels and the panoramic city views.

MEMORIES OF THE MEDICI

A few streets northwest of the Duomo is the heartland of Medicean Florence: the **Medici Palace** and the church of **San Lorenzo**, which is surrounded by a boisterous market. The palace – now known as the **Palazzo Medici-Riccardi** ⓮ (Thu–Tue 9am–6pm) – is dignified but not ostentatious. It still has the look of a fortress about it, particularly in the rusticated facade with its massive blocks of masonry. The Medici lived here from its completion in 1452 until 1540, when they moved into the politically symbolic Palazzo Vecchio. While much of the palace is swathed in institutional gloom, the courtyard and loggia are striking, and the Cappella dei Magi revels in the most uplifting fresco cycle in Florence.

The museum contains various mementoes of the family, including the poignant death-mask of Lorenzo, but it is the chapel that displays the brightest jewels in the Medici crown, including the *Journey of the Magi* by Benozzo Gozzoli (*c.*1460). This painting breathes the spirit of the Florentine Renaissance in its mixture of real figures of identifiable people, historical recreation and delight in colour. The immense procession, winding its way through a vividly improbable landscape, is led by a handsome, richly dressed youth on horseback – the young Lorenzo. Behind him comes his grandfather, Cosimo, soberly dressed, attended by a black servant, but look out for the painter himself, with his name inscribed on his hat. In the distance is the Medici retreat, Villa Cafaggiolo – and a couple of camels to remind the observer that the picture is set in the Middle East.

SAN LORENZO

The church of **San Lorenzo** ⑮ (www.operamedicealaurenziana.org; Mon–Sat 10am–5.30pm, Mar–Oct also Sun 1.30–5.30pm) is one of the earliest and most harmonious of all Renaissance churches, representing a break with French Gothic and a return to an older, classical style. The facade is rough and unfinished, though the Mayor has mooted a plan to complete it according to Michelangelo's designs.

The interior is outstanding, a gracious composition of the grey stone *pietra serena* and white walls. Giovanni, father of Cosimo de' Medici, commissioned Brunelleschi to design San Lorenzo in 1419, but neither lived to see it completed. Thereafter, successive members of the Medici family continued to embellish it, commissioning the greatest artists of their age to add frescoes, paintings and – ultimately – their mausoleum. Of particular note in the basilica are Donatello's pulpits with bronze reliefs of the Passion, and the Old Sacristy adorned with sculptures, also by Donatello.

THE MEDICI CHAPELS

The entrance to the **Cappelle Medicee** (www.bargellomusei.beniculturali.it; daily

The Mercato Centrale, Florence's main food market.

The church of San Lorenzo, with its unfinished facade.

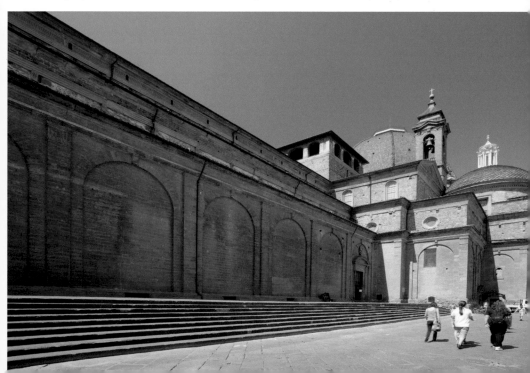

8.15am–1.50pm; free first Sun of each month) is outside the church, in the Piazza della Madonna degli Aldobrandini. You go in via the crypt, where a floor slab commemorates Anna Maria Ludovica (died 1743), the last in the Medici line. Stairs lead to the opulent **Cappella dei Principi** (the mausoleum of the Medici grand dukes) and the **New Sacristy** (the Medici tombs), the latter Michelangelo's first architectural commission, and a chilly cocoon. The two New Sacristy tombs of Giuliano (son of Lorenzo the Magnificent) and Lorenzo (his grandson) are graced with the reclining figures of *Dawn*, *Evening*, *Day* and *Night*, conveying an unforgettable feeling of uneasiness, sadness and loss.

SANTA MARIA NOVELLA, SAN MARCO AND SANTA CROCE: THREE INFLUENTIAL CHURCHES

The three great buildings of Santa Maria Novella, San Marco and Santa Croce are some distance apart – the first near the Stazione Centrale, the second in the north, and the last on the far eastern side of the city. They are grouped together here because they illustrate a truth about Florence, that religion was a driving force – probably even stronger than commerce or the desire for self-aggrandisement – a force that nearly drove the city to destruction.

SANTA MARIA NOVELLA

The church of **Santa Maria Novella** ⑯ (www.smn.it; Apr–Sept Mon–Fri 9am–7pm, Oct–Mar until 5.30pm, Sat–Sun variable hours: check online) was designed by Dominican monks in 1246. Though dignified and indeed majestic, it reflects their gloomy preoccupations: striped like a tiger, the family chapels are sombre and overwhelming, their murals little more than illustrations of sermons. The **Spanish Chapel** carries this to extremes, with its murals dedicated to the 13th-century theologian, Thomas Aquinas, who was, of course, a Dominican. The chapel now lies within the **Cloister Museum** (same hours and ticket as the church) adjoining the church, as do Uccello's frescoes. In the church itself is Masaccio's *Trinity*, and

Giotto's Crucifix in Santa Maria Novella.

the chapel is frescoed by Fra Filippino Lippi and Ghirlandaio. Although Brunelleschi's decorative touches lighten the spirit, the church feels oppressive.

At the southern end of Piazza Santa Maria Novella, the **Museo Nazionale Alinari della Fotografia** 🔢 has one of the best photographic collections in Europe. Founded in 1852, the Alinari brothers' photographic studio supplied 19th-century Grand Tourists with prints, postcards and art books. The museum is closed for renovation at the time of writing; please check www.alinarifondazione.it for information on a reopening date.

Long neglected, and once a gathering place for vagrants, **Piazza Santa Maria Novella** has returned to its former glory, prompted by renovation of the Dominican complex, with the finest facade in Florence, and by the pedestrianisation of the square. Helping to raise the tone are a cluster of chic boutique hotels, from JK Place to Palazzo dal Borgo, which overlooks the historic perfumery of the **Officina di Santa Maria Novella** (Via della Scala), where monks have been concocting precious potions since the 13th century.

SAN MARCO

The convent of **San Marco** 🔢 was almost entirely rebuilt with money provided by Cosimo de' Medici; the irony lies in the fact that San Marco became the headquarters of the friar Girolamo Savonarola, who was the greatest enemy of Cosimo's grandson, Lorenzo. Cosimo engaged his own favourite architect, Michelozzo, who had designed the Palazzo Medici, to build San Marco, and endowed it with a magnificent library.

Savonarola was Prior of San Marco from 1491 until his execution in 1498. During those years he dominated Florence, nearly succeeded in overthrowing the Medici and even presented a challenge to the papacy. The vivid portrait of him by Fra Bartolomeo, which can be seen here, shows a man with a forceful but ugly face, a great beaked nose and burning eyes.

San Marco is now a **museum** (Mon–Fri 8.15am–1.50pm, Sat–Sun until 4.50pm, closed alternate Sun/Mon). The prize exhibits are the murals of Fra Angelico, himself a Dominican, but one who brought a delicacy to his work quite at variance with the austere tenets of that order. Each of the friars' cells is graced by one of his murals, and at the head of the stairs is Fra Angelico's masterpiece, the *Annunciation*. Savonarola's cell is laid out as he knew it, complete with desk and severe-looking chair.

Just south of San Marco is the legendary **Galleria dell'Accademia** 🔢 (entrance at No. 60; Tue–Sun 8.15am–6.50pm), often identified by the enormous queues outside. Its star attraction – and the museum's raison d'être – is the colossal statue of *David*, which was carved between 1501 and 1504 from a single piece of marble, and established Michelangelo as the foremost sculptor of his time before

San Marco nuns and priest.

St Thomas Aquinas, depicted on one of the stained-glass windows of Santa Maria Novella.

Charming Ponte Vecchio.

the age of 30. The statue now standing in front of the Palazzo Vecchio is an impressive copy.

Near to the Accademia, on the Via Alfani, is the **Opificio delle Pietre Dure** (Mon–Sat 8.15am–2pm), where restoration of artistic treasures takes place. Exhibits include inlaid semi-precious stones used in *pietra dura*, as well as workbenches and instruments once used by the craftsmen.

Nearby, the **Museo Archeologico** (Tue–Fri 8.30am–7pm, Sat–Mon 8.30am–2pm) in Piazza d. S.S. Annunziata features an important collection of Greek, Egyptian, Etruscan and Roman art. The highlights include the recreation of an Etruscan tomb and bronzes of Etruscan mythological beasts.

SANTA CROCE

The great **Piazza Santa Croce** was a favoured place for processions, horse races and tournaments. *Calcio Storico*, an historic football match, is still staged here every June. The square, dominated by a statue of Dante, is also home to the fascinating Santa Croce Leather School, a testament to Florentine craftsmanship.

Although the facade of **Santa Croce** ⓴ (Mon–Sat 9.30am–5.30pm, Sun from 2pm) dates from the mid-19th century, Arnolfo di Cambio began work on the church in 1294. With the lightness and elegance associated with Franciscan churches, it is the Pantheon of Florence – and, indeed, of Italy, since this is where so many of the country's illustrious dead were laid to rest, from Galileo to Ghiberti.

The tomb of Michelangelo, designed by Vasari, invariably has a little bunch of flowers laid upon it, unlike the grave of Machiavelli, who died in 1527. Crowning the whole are the frescoes painted by Giotto and his school.

The cloisters, designed by Brunelleschi, lead to the **Cappella de'Pazzi**, which contains 12 terracotta roundels of the Apostles by Luca della Robbia.

The **Museo dell'Opera di Santa Croce** (Mon–Sat 9.30am–5.30pm, Sun opens at 2pm) houses the beguiling *Tree of the Cross* by Taddeo Gaddi and

Cimabue's iconic 13th-century *Crucifix*, which was badly damaged in the 1966 flood. It has only been partially restored since then as a poignant reminder of the city in peril.

OLTRARNO: ACROSS THE RIVER

The Florentines regard their river with mixed feelings. It has brought both wealth and disaster in its unpredictable wake. The Arno becomes a raging brown torrent in winter, although it can shrink to a trickle along a dried-up bed during summer. Recently, sun-worshippers have become fond of its enjoyable urban beach.

The **Ponte Vecchio** ㉑ was erected by Taddeo Gaddi sometime after 1345 and has become a symbol of Florence itself. Fortunately, the Germans spared it when they blew up every other Florentine bridge during World War II. It bears the same appearance that it has borne for six centuries. Even the goldsmiths and jewellers who throng it today were established there in the mid-16th century. Before the goldsmiths, the shops on the bridge were occupied by butchers and tanners, who used the river as a dumping ground until they were evicted in 1593.

It was for Ferdinando's father, Cosimo I, that Vasari built the extraordinary **Vasari Corridor** in 1565. Running from the Uffizi to the Pitti across the Ponte Vecchio, the private raised walkway made a physical as well as symbolic link between the two centres of Medicean power. In his film *Paisà*, Roberto Rossellini shot an unforgettable sequence of the fighting that took place along this gallery during the German retreat. The corridor was renovated in 2013, showcasing over 1,000 paintings and self-portraits by renowned artists. At the time of writing, it is undergoing yet more renovation and is due to reopen in 2018–19.

THE PITTI PALACE

The part of Florence south of the river, the **Oltrarno**, has a bohemian character all of its own, with its charm enhanced by the gradual pedestrianisation of this area. Yet in the 15th century, this area

⊙ Tip

Beyond the remnants of the city wall is a reminder, though a rapidly fading one, that Florence is a country town: a brisk walk along Via di San Leonardo will take you from the very heart of the city out into vineyards, olive groves and maize fields.

⊙ THE CONTEMPORARY CITY

If sleepy Florence has finally woken up, much credit is due to three Prince Charmings. Canadian James Bradburne put the city on the contemporary art map with Palazzo Strozzi and its inclusive yet international approach to culture. Not that he takes credit for it: "Florence has the highest concentration of intellectual, creative and business firepower that I have ever seen. It punches way above its weight. Here everyone from art historians to plumbers is able to carry on extraordinary conversations about art and literature. The question is, why doesn't Florence do more with this firepower?"

Mayors Matteo Renzi, between 2009 and 2014, and Dario Nardella, since 2014, have followed suit, supporting a host of creative projects, including the Nuovo Teatro del Maggio, the city's new opera house and concert hall. New festivals, art galleries and *aperitivi* bars have sprung up, along with vibrant theatre-dining clubs, such as the Teatro del Sale. Disused stations, convents and fortresses have been turned into multimedia libraries and events centres. Le Murate, a former nunnery and prison on Via Ghibellina, now offers live music, arty bars and an outdoor cinema. The Universale, once a run-down cinema, has been reborn as a designer-chic club with cinematic screens. Stazione Leopolda, a reconverted neoclassical station, now stages fashion shows, concerts and exhibitions. Symbolically, Norman Foster's avant-garde railway hub, with a view to opening in 2021, will strengthen the city's international links. Only the controversial Uffizi expansion project is on hold, considered too cutting edge for traditionalists, particularly the loggia entrance proposed by architect Arata Isozaki. Inside however, the museum's second floor rooms are being wonderfully revamped and remodelled, and numerous new ones have opened on the ground floor. Franco Zeffirelli, the Florentine-born film director, decries it as a form of "being blackmailed by progressivist culture". And many agree. But most other "grand projects" command popular support. Damien Hirst's diamond-encrusted skull has even been displayed in the Palazzo Vecchio. Bizarre, but Florence can finally claim to be about more than Renaissance art.

was the centre of opposition to the Medici, spearheaded by the Pitti family. It was they who built the **Palazzo Pitti** ㉒ (pre-booking advisable through www.uffizi.it or through the Firenze Card, www.firenzecard.it; Tue–Sun 8.15am–6.50pm; free on first Sun of each month), the most grandiose of all Florentine residences, which, by the irony of history, eventually became the seat of government for the Medici dukes themselves. Today it is home to Medici museums and art galleries, notably the **Galleria Palatina**, adorned by masterpieces by artists such as Raphael, Rubens, Van Dyck and Titian.

Adjoining the gallery are the **Appartamenti Reali** (State Apartments), lavishly decorated with impressive works of art. The palace also contains the **Galleria d'Arte Moderna** (Modern Art Museum), the **Galleria della Moda e del Costume** (Museum of Costume and Fashion) and **Il Tesoro dei Granduchi** (the Treasury of the Grand Dukes; formerly the Museo degli Argenti or Silver Museum).

An excellent antidote to the overwhelming splendours of the Pitti are the beautiful adjoining Boboli Gardens, the **Giardino di Boboli** ㉓ (daily 8.15am–sunset; closed 1st and last Mon of the month). For more details see page 116.

Also included in the Boboli ticket is the **Giardino Bardini**, accessible from Via dei Bardi 1r or Costa San Giorgio 2 (www.bardinipeyron.it; 8.15am–sunset). The park offers stunning vistas, a café and quiet spots for meditation, as well as access to the **Villa Bardini** (www.bardinipeyron.it; Tue–Sun 10am–7pm).

Once owned by antiquarian Stefano Bardini, the villa is now home to a fine restaurant and small museums dedicated to the modern artist Annigoni and fashion maestro Roberto Capucci. But Bardini's heart belonged to his Renaissance art collection down the hill in **Museo Bardini** ㉔ (Via dei Renai 37; www.museicivicifiorentini.comune.fi.it; Fri–Mon 11am–5pm). The collection mixes works by Donatello with eclectic finds, such as the original Porcellino, the wild-boar bronze created for the Mercato Nuovo.

Alternatively, from Villa Bardini, continue up Costa San Giorgio to the **Forte di Belvedere** (closed to the public; open for exhibitions only), a 16th-century fortification designed by Buontalenti for the Grand Duke Ferdinando I de' Medici. The fort, which commands breathtaking views over Florence, hosts modern-art and photography exhibitions.

THE PORTA ROMANA

The **Via Romana**, which begins just past the Palazzo Pitti in Piazza San Felice, goes to the **Porta Romana** ㉕, stretching from the city centre, via the Ponte Vecchio, to the outside world. The larger gates of Florence were, like the 14th-century Porta Romana, both a garrison and a customs post, collecting dues on all the goods that came into the city. You can now walk a section of the ramparts near Porta Romana.

The facade of San Miniato al Monte.

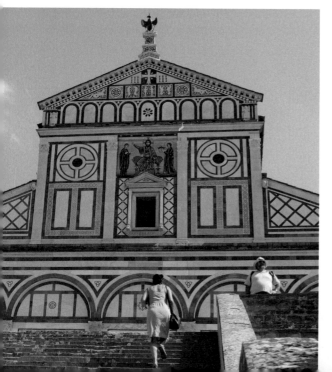

OLTRARNO CHURCHES

Several churches of note lie on this south side of the city. The first, not far from the Ponte Santa Trinità, is **Santo Spirito** (Thu–Tue 10am–12.30pm and 4–6pm; free), its modest 18th-century facade masking the harmonious interior designed by Filippo Brunelleschi.

Just west is **Santa Maria del Carmine ㉖**, which contains one of the greatest treasures of Italian painting – the **Cappella Brancacci** frescoes (www.museicivicifiorentini.comune.fi.it; Mon, Wed–Sat 10am–5pm, Sun 1–5pm; reservation required). Considered by many to rival even Michelangelo's Sistine Chapel in Rome, the work of Masolino (including *The Temptation of Adam and Eve*), Masaccio (*The Expulsion from Paradise* and *The Tribute Money*) and Filippino Lippi is truly magnificent. Unfortunately, due to the popularity of the frescoes, visitors are only allowed 15 minutes to see them.

Further east, dominating a hilltop, awaits **San Miniato al Monte ㉗** (Mon–Sat 9.30am–1pm and 3–7pm, Sun 8.15am–7pm; free). A building stood on this site as early as the 4th century, but the present complex dates from 1018 and is a fine example of Florentine Romanesque. Inside, seek out the **Cappella del Crocifisso**, a tiny vaulted temple, and the 11th-century crypt, which houses the relics of St Minias. You can hear the monks chanting here each afternoon at 5.30pm.

San Miniato towers above the **Piazzale Michelangelo**, reached from the Porta Romana along the enchanting Viale dei Colli, or else by climbing up from the river, past the Porta San Niccolò, taking the winding paths through the gardens to the piazzale.

Adorned with bronze copies of Michelangelo's various works of sculpture, this touristic terrace is a Florentine pilgrimage destination that entwined lovers feel obliged to visit. Even if the views are far lovelier from **Bellosguardo**, above Porta Romana, Piazzale Michelangelo is picture-postcard Florence – from the sheepish couples and nude *David* souvenirs to the city at sunset decked out below.

The Expulsion from Paradise by Masaccio (c.1427) in the Cappella Brancacci. They are among the most powerfully emotive figures ever painted in Western art.

View of the city from Piazzale Michelangelo.

THE UFFIZI

The greatest collection of Renaissance art to be found anywhere in the world.

THE EASTERN CORRIDOR

The two corridors from which the 45 rooms on the second floor lead off are filled with sculptures, while the strip connecting the sides allows magnificent views down the river and towards the Ponte Vecchio. Rooms 2–4 are dedicated to works from Siena and Florence during the duecento and trecento (13th and 14th centuries), exhibiting the decorative and icono-graphic pre-Renaissance style. Notable works are the interpretations of the Madonna by Giotto and Duccio, as well as that of Cimabue, Giotto's master.

Room 7 is dedicated to the early Renaissance period and its founders and leading exponents, who include Masaccio and Uccello and, later, Fra Angelico. The Filippo Lippi Room (8) holds the Franciscan monk's lovely *Madonna with Angels*, as well as a number of other celebrated works, and is worth visiting to see Piero della Francesca's portraits of the Duke and Duchess of Urbino I. Room 9 holds works by the Pol-laiuolo brothers, whose paintings display no distinc-tive style as such but are nonetheless decorative.

After a room of sculpture, the Tribuna (Room 18) is an octagonal room lit from above, with a beautiful mother-of-pearl-encrusted ceiling designed by Buon-talenti. This room's structure and decor was designed to allude to the four elements and previously exhibited the objects that were most highly prized by the Medici. It holds a collection of portraits and sculpture, as well as Rosso Fiorentino's ubiquitous *Putto che Suona*, or *Angel Musician*. The circular route visitors must take around the room unfortunately renders it somewhat difficult to either appreciate the art from a good dis-tance or to linger in front of the portraits.

The Botticelli Rooms (10–14) are the most popular in the Uffizi, containing the world's best collection of work by t artist. Here are the famous mythological paintings, which fused ideas of the spiritual and the secular: the Birth of Venus, painted around 1485, and La Primavera (Spring) painted some five years earlier. The meaning of the latt work remains a subject of fervent discussion, while Ver has overtones of the Virgin Mary.

Room 15 exhibits Leonardo da Vinci's early works – including the Annunciation (1475) and the unfinished Adoration of the Magi (1481) – and also paintings by Perugino and Signorelli.

Musical Angel, by Giovan Battista di Jacopo (aka Rosso Fiorentino), c.1522.

The Vasari Corridor, the picture-lined overhead passageway connecting the Uffizi to the Palazzo Pitti via the Ponte Vecchio, is now open to the public but you have to book your tour in advance (http://www.uffizi.com).

THE WESTERN CORRIDOR

Most rooms in this corridor, including 25–34, 41 and 43–44, are currently closed for restoration. Only the Michelangelo and the Florentines room (35), the Niobe room (42) and the room devoted to the 15th century Venetian, Umbrian and Northern European painters (45) remain open.

THE GROUND FLOOR

On the ground floor are 31 rooms, as well as the Verone sull'Arno – the bottom of the U-shaped corridor that looks over the Arno and the Piazza degli Uffizi the other side.

The Blue Rooms focus on 17th–18th century Dutch and Flemish masters; 11 Red Rooms feature among others Rosso Fiorentino and Raphael; six "Modern Manner" Rooms house *inter alia* works by Correggio and Giorgione, and there are four Caravaggesque Rooms including the Sala del Caravaggio (90), which holds three paintings by the troubled artist whose style is characterised by his realism and use of light. More new rooms are being worked on and there is also restoration work in progress on the old ones.

oms 5–6 form the International Gothic Rooms, whose intings exhibit a more conservative and less lavish proach, in keeping with the medieval mindset. Lorenzo naco's Crowning of Mary provides a good example of s by one of the main practitioners of the era.

Duke and Duchess of Urbino I, in the Eastern Corridor.

The High Renaissance continues in Room 19, which exhibits Perugino and Signorelli's work. These Umbrian artists worked during the 15th and 16th centuries, and the latter's tondo (circular painting) Holy Family is reputed to have inspired Michelangelo's version. Room 20 is a break from Italian art, with work by Dürer, including his Madonna and the Pear, and Cranach. The last few rooms on the eastern corridor hold works from the 15th and 16th centuries: the Venetian school in Room 21, followed by Holbein and other Flemish and German Realists (22) and more Italian work by Mantegna and Correggio in Room 23. Room 24 contains a collection of miniatures.

PALAZZO PITTI

The gigantic Palazzo Pitti and the Boboli Gardens were once the royal residence.

Set in a massive Renaissance palace that dominates the Oltrarno, the Pitti houses four museums, and provides access to the splendid Boboli Gardens that became a model for Italian landscaping. To appreciate the sumptuous Medici art collection and the lifestyles of the Grand Dukes, the Palatine Gallery (Galleria Palatina) and the Royal Apartments are the obvious choice. the Treasury of the Grand Dukes (Il Tesoro dei Granduchi) comes a close second, more for the magnificently decorated rooms than for the contents. In terms of art history, the Modern Art Museum (Galleria d'Arte Moderna) takes up the story where the Uffizi leaves off, and gives a sense of the lavish but somewhat dubious decorative tastes of the last residents, the rulers of the houses of Lorraine and Savoy. By comparison, the Museum of Costume and Fashion is more for connoisseurs.

On the ground floor, Il Tesoro dei Granduchi (the Treasury of the Grand Dukes) contains silverware, antique vases much loved by Lorenzo the Magnificent, baubles encrusted with semi-precious stones and jewellery. The frescoed rooms alone make a visit worthwhile – in particular the Sala di San Giovanni, which formed part of the summer apartments. The frescoes by the artist after whom the room is named depict the reign of Lorenzo de' Medici, portrayed as a great patron of the arts.

The **Galleria Palatina** (Palatine Gallery) on the first floor houses an extraordinary range of paintings collected by the Medici family. In the west wing of the building, on the same floor, are the rooms comprising the **Royal Apartments**. They are garish and ostentatious, decked out in heavy carpets, wallpapers, fabrics and furnishings, and overstuffed with treasures. Several of the rooms are named after the colour in which they are themed, and contain paintings and portraits fitting with the mood, followed by the Queen's Apartments, the King's Apartments and a ceremonial room, all filled with ponderous period furniture.

Sala di Giove ceiling detail.

The lavish Galleria Palatina.

The most important rooms, named after the planets, a frescoed by Pietro da Cortona to allegorise the stages Prince Ferdinando's education: Sala di Saturno, Sala o Giove, Sala di Marte and Sala di Venere. These contain works such as Rubens' The Consequences of War (Sal di Marte), Raphael's Portrait of a Lady (Sala di Giove). Other important paintings, such as Raphael's The Pregnant Lady (Sala dell'Iliade), Lippi's tondo of The Madonna and Child (see below; Sala di Prometeo) and Sleeping Cupid by Caravaggio (Sala dell'Educazione di Giove) are found in the smaller rooms.

The ornate Prometheus Room in the Galleria Palatina.

Modern Art

The Galleria d'Arte Moderna contains mainly Italian works from the neoclassical and Romantic movements, dating from the 18th century to the period after World War I, including *Portrait of Alaide Banti* by Michele Gordigiani. The most notable feature of the second-floor collection is its holding of paintings by the Macchiaioli, 19th-century Italian Post-Impressionists. Also situated on the second floor is the Museo della Moda e del Costume, which is an intriguing display of Italian costume and fashion, especially from the Medici to the modern period, including creations by designers such as Capucci.

Portrait of Alaide Banti by Gordigiani, in the Galleria d'Arte Moderna.

e of the finest rooms is the Sala di Apollo, in which
ng important works by Andrea del Sarto (including his
mentation of Christ, 1522–3). The Sala di Venere
:ludes works by another master of the High
naissance, Titian; notably his The Interrupted Concert
d Portrait of a Man (above).

GIARDINO DI BOBOLI

The gardens' landscaping, following the slope of the hill, provides the perfect complement to Palazzo Pitti, with longer walks leading to Forte Belvedere and the Bardini Gardens.

The gardens were commissioned by Cosimo I and created by a range of prolific figures of the day, from Vasari and Ammannati to Buontalenti. One of the most compelling characteristics of the Boboli is the shadowy dark-green colour of the cypress and box hedges that serve to highlight the statues of amorous nymphs, satyrs and statuesque deities, as well as the grottoes and fountains. The steps lead up to the terrace behind the palace and in front of Susini's fountain of 1641. The amphitheatre surrounding the fountain occupies the site of a quarry used to obtain much of the stone for the palace, and contains an Egyptian obelisk. A series of terraces leads up the hill to the Neptune Fountain, round to the Rococo Kaffeehaus and up to the statue of *Abundance*. At the summit lies the Giardino del Cavaliere, or Knight's Garden. This delightful garden – with its low hedges, rose bushes and little cherub fountain – gives open views of San Miniato to the left and the village of Arcetri to the right, rising above a valley.

The cypress-statue-lined avenue known as Il Viottolone leads to the Vasca dell'Isola (Island Pool) with its Oceanus Fountain by Giambologna, murky green water, ducks, fish, strange mythical creatures and circular hedge. The route from here to the exit leads past the Grotta di Buontalenti, named after the sculptor who created this cavern in 1583–8. Copies of Michelangelo's *Slaves* (the originals are on display in the Accademia; see page 118) are set in the four corners. Finally, on the right as one exits and nestling below the wall of the corridor, is the naked, pot-bellied statue of Pietro Barbino, Cosimo I's court dwarf, seated on a turtle. In 2013 the Boboli Gardens became a Unesco World Heritage site.

The gardens are dotted with classical and Renaissance statues.

The Pitti Palace and Boboli Gardens, painted in 1599–1602. Because of the massive size of the palace, the enterprise ruined the Pitti family; however, the Medici completed the project according to Brunelleschi's plans, with the façade enlarged to its mammoth proportions in 1620.

The Bacino di Nettuno is named after the slimy statue of Neptune who brandishes his trident at threatening sea-monsters.

The Porcelain Museum displays pottery as well as objets d'art.

Porcelain Museum

The Museo delle Porcellane (Porcelain Museum; daily 8.15am–sunset; closed 1st and last Mon of the month), which displays porcelain as well as objets d'art, is situated in the Palazzina del Cavaliere, in the exquisite Giardino del Cavaliere.

Igor Mitoraj's Tyndareus Cracked (1998), the only contemporary sculpture in the Gardens.

At the end of the Medici reign in 1737, the palazzo became the home of the Lorraines, and its elongated cubic form was further extended by the wings that curve round to frame the paved square at its front. Work on the outside was paralleled by alteration to the interior decor, which exhibits the ostentatious tastes of the period of the Lorraines and the Savoys, the next to take up occupancy within its walls. The history of the palazzo includes brief tenure by the Bourbons and the Emperor Napoleon before the last ruling monarch, Vittorio Emmanuele III, transferred the house to the public.

e Grotta di Buontalenti houses replicas of 'chelangelo's Slaves; the originals were moved to the cademia in 1908. Supervised by Vasari in the 1550s, the ly was completed by Ammannati and Buontalenti.

📷 THE ACCADEMIA

Originally the world's first school of art, the gallery is now home to Michelangelo's most famous work, *David*.

Michelangelo's *David* is the main attraction of the Galleria dell'Accademia. Most visitors dutifully come to gasp over the famous statue and then call it a day, scarcely realising that this is one of the city's finest galleries, despite its stifling intensity. The collection dates back to a school of fine arts founded by Cosimo I de' Medici in 1563. Although many treasures have moved to the Uffizi and San Marco, the remaining array of Florentine Byzantine and Gothic art justifies a visit, without the added inducement of a certain Michelangelo. The foremost sculptor of his age, or arguably of all time, is well represented by the authentic *David*, and by his magnificently unfinished *Four Slaves*. *David*, the city's most deified statue, was produced in a heroic age of sculpture. It was, in public-minded Florentine fashion, placed in front of the Palazzo Vecchio as a civic lesson. In keeping with the rulers' dissimulation of power, ostentation and self-aggrandisement were publicly frowned upon in Florence, as was the glorification of the individual. Yet the statue became both the symbol of liberty and a symbol of the artistic aspirations of the city.

   David may be the centrepiece, but the so-called *Nonfiniti* (unfinished) *Slaves* illustrate the magnitude of Michelangelo's talent and ambition. In the brooding intensity of his figures one can sense the laying bare of the innate idea, the eternal truth that his art strove to attain. More clearly than in other masterpieces, these works reveal Michelangelo's philosophy: the genesis of a sculpture is not the classic shaping of art out of chaos but the struggle to free a creature that already exists. Even if his paintings have a rare sculptural quality, only the sculpted naked body can express Michelangelo's most sublime concepts.

Botticelli's delightful Madonna and Child is in the Sale del Quattrocento Fiorentino.

Pacino di Bonaguida's Tree of Life, dating from the 14th century.

Lorenzo Monaco's Anunciation Triptych, of which only two panels are shown here, is also in the gallery.

David

As the most famous sculpture in Western art, *David* has immediate appeal, both thanks to the sculpture's recognition factor and to its accessibility. When criticising the gigantism of the work, it has to be remembered that the statue was intended for a large civic space, not designed to be cooped up in a corner of an airless museum. Michelangelo's statue was installed, with much pomp, in a specially created Tribune here, in the Accademia, in 1873.

To most modern visitors, *David* is a celebration of the nude, stripped of his original cultural and political significance. It is therefore remarkable that, even without any artistic background, the average high-school student is still awed enough to be drawn into an appreciation of Renaissance art through Michelangelo's boyish ambassador. Giorgio Vasari, Michelangelo's reluctantly admiring contemporary, concurred, praising its grace, serenity, proportion and harmony: "This figure has overshadowed every other statue, ancient or modern, Greek or Roman."

But this timeless icon of virility is under threat and may yet be on the move again. After the discovery of cracks in the 500-year-old marble, the statue has been declared at risk of toppling over. The cracks in the statue's ankles are believed to have developed after *David* spent over a century leaning forward dangerously from his proud perch on Piazza della Signoria. The weight of the marble, bearing down on *David's* left ankle, is also partly to blame, as are the vibrations from the traffic and roadworks outside the gallery and the seismic tremors the region experiences episodically. Fortunately, the experts have declared that Florence's most famous statue is not in danger of imminent collapse, but as a precaution, it will soon be getting an anti-seismic plinth. There is also perennial talk of transferring the symbolic statue to a purpose-built site on the outskirts of the city.

...mong the most notable pieces is Filippino Lippi's striking ...eposition from the Cross, which was finished by ...erugino on the former's death. Other highlights are ...hrist as a Man of Sorrows – a poignant fresco by Andrea ...el Sarto – and Fra Bartolomeo's Prophets.

David, the most famous sculpture in Western art.

📷 THE BARGELLO

The Bargello holds Florence's most important collection of sculpture from the Medici and private collections.

Unlike the Accademia, the Bargello would be a major site even without its art treasure trove. As the oldest surviving seat of government in Florence, the Bargello preceded the Palazzo Vecchio. The collection clearly shows the transition from statuary that was flaunted as public symbols to sculpture that was appreciated as private treasures.

The Bargello is also the best place in which to gain a sense of the interconnectedness of Florentine Renaissance sculpture. It provides a clear overview, with works of art by the greatest masters. Moreover, despite the virtuosity of Michelangelo, the Bargello is more of a shrine to his predecessor, Donatello, the only sculptor to lay claim to equal gifts. Unlike Michelangelo's work, Donatello's sculpture betrays little sign of creative torment and virtuosity for virtuosity's sake, which accounts, at least in part, for Donatello's less glittering reputation. However, in the Bargello at least, Donatello is the undoubted star. Those single-mindedly in pursuit of Renaissance sculpture would do well to head straight for the Donatello gallery, followed by the Verrocchio and della Robbia rooms, set on the floor above. To fully appreciate the sculpture, avoid being waylaid by the distracting displays of unrelated decorative arts.

The Bargello contains works by Andrea della Robbia, a Renaissance sculptor specialising in glazed terracotta, including Bust of a Woman.

The Bargello museum is situated in an impressive Gothic palazzo constructed in the mid-13th-century on Via del Proconsolo, in the heart of the ancient city. The building has previously been used as a barracks and a prison.

The sacrifice of Isaac, by Lorenzo Ghiberti (1401). The bronze tile was made for the competition for the portal of the Baptistery.

The Donatello and Bronze Galleries

The Salone del Consiglio Generale is often nicknamed the Donatello Gallery. Apart from *David*, other works by Donatello in the room are *Saint George*, designed for the Orsanmichele church, and *Cupid*. You can also see the bronze panels submitted by Ghiberti and Brunelleschi for the Baptistery doors here. The walls of the room feature several glazed terracotta works by Luca della Robbia, while the first floor chapel (Cappella Maddalena) features frescoes depicting Hell: look out for the figure on the right dressed in maroon thought to be a depiction of Dante. Also on the first floor is a corridor displaying an eclectic group of 5th- to 17th-century objets d'art, including ivories and Islamic treasures.

Upstairs the Verrocchio Room displays Tuscan sculpture from the late 15th century, including portrait busts of notable Florentines and an interpretation of *David* by the artist who lends his name to the room, Andrea del Verrocchio. The adjoining rooms are filled with work by members of the della Robbia family – predominantly Andrea and Giovanni – dominated by the often overbearing large reliefs coloured in yellow, green and blue.

The last major room in the museum is the Bronze Gallery. This has one of the most rewarding displays in the Bargello. The sculptures generally depict mythological tales or Greek history, in the form of both models and more functional articles such as candelabra. The model for Giambologna's *Rape of the Sabines* (on display in the Loggia dei Lanzi) stands out, as do two others of his statues: *Kneeling Nymph* and *Hercules and Antaeus*.

Completing the second floor is a collection of medals.

e museum building can be seen *the right of this* *th-century painting by* *prentine artist Giuseppe* *cchi.*

atues in the *rgello include* *natello's now* *stored David* *430–40) – a small* *onze most renowned* *being the first nude* *nce antiquity. It differs* *amatically from* *chelangelo's masterpiece* *t just in size and material,* *t also in its coyness and* *elancholy.*

Attractive villas cling to the hillsides above the city.

AROUND FLORENCE

Along with vineyards, the Unesco-listed Medici villas are one of the glories of the Florentine countryside, even if the encroaching nature of the suburbs sometimes tarnishes their allure.

Under the Medici, villa building became a form of self-exaltation and self-indulgence, allied to bucolic pleasures and property speculation. Perched on a scenic hill, the patrician villa became not just a rural estate and glorified hunting lodge, but also a place for feasting and festivities, and an escape from the summer heat. The picture of rural harmony extends to hamlets perched on steep, cypress-covered hills and to vineyards that have been producing famous wines since the Renaissance. Chianti country is close by, while, north of Florence, lies the Mugello, the fertile Apennine region bordering Tuscany and Emilia Romagna. Indulge in a little wine tasting before exploring the harsher Mugello, the Medici homeland.

HILLTOP RETREAT

The best view of the mountains is a seat in the Roman theatre of **Fiesole ①**, a delightful hill town 8km (5 miles) northeast of Florence. Fiesole was first settled by Etruscans probably in the 8th century BC. The Romans later named the place Faesulum – praising it for its freshwater springs and strategic location. During the 15th century Fiesole became a city suburb where wealthy Florentines built their villas. Today, a villa on the slopes of Fiesole's verdant hill is one of the most sought-after addresses.

The main route from the centre of Florence is the Via San Domenico (the No. 7 bus goes from Piazza Stazione or Piazza San Marco), which climbs up to Fiesole's centre. The views on the way up reveal a landscape of extraordinary beauty, dotted with Renaissance villas perched on the slope of the hill.

Everything you will want to see in Fiesole lies a short distance from the Piazza Mino da Fiesole, the main square. A lane leads north to the **Teatro Romano**, where you can buy tickets for Fiesole's **Zona Archeologica**

Main attractions
Fiesole
Mugello Valley
Castello del Trebbio
Medici Villas
Prato
San Miniato

Map on page 124

View from Sant Alessandro, Fiesole.

The Teatro Romano, with its numbered seats, could originally accommodate an audience of up to 2,000 people. It is in a remarkable state of repair, and is still used for dances and shows during the summer festival season.

(www.museidifiesole.it; daily Mar and Oct 10am–6pm, Apr–Sept 9am–7pm, Nov–Feb Wed–Mon 10am–3pm), entered from the ticket office and comprising the city's 1st-century BC Roman theatre, public baths of the same era and an Etruscan temple, built in the 4th century BC and dedicated to Minerva, goddess of wisdom and healing. Also within the complex, the **Museo Archeologico** (same hours as Zona Archeologica), built in the style of a Roman temple, is packed with finds from excavations in Fiesole. Included in the ticket is entry to the **Museo Bandini** (Fri–Sun Mar and Oct 10am–6pm, Apr–Sept 9am–7pm, Nov–Feb 10am–3pm), behind the cathedral on Via Duprè – a small art gallery with a fairly wide and representative selection of paintings from the early and middle Renaissance.

On the square, the huge **Cattedrale di San Romolo** (daily) is almost completely unadorned except for four frescoes, including a serene portrait of St Sebastian by Perugino (early 16th century). The Cathedral's jewel is the marble funerary monument to Bishop Leonardo Salutati,

by Mino da Fiesole (1429–84), with a realistic bust of the smiling bishop.

From the southwest corner of the square, Via Vecchia Fiesolana leads to the **Villa Medici** (entrance along Via Beato Angelico), a Unesco World Heritage Site since 2013, together with 11 other Tuscan villas and two gardens. Any of the downhill paths from this point can be taken to reach the hamlet of **San Domenico**, about a 15-minute walk. The church of San Domenico (1406) contains a restored *Madonna with Angels and Saints* (1430), an early work of Fra Angelico who began his monastic life here before transferring to San Marco.

Opposite, the Via della Badia dei Roccettini descends to the **Badia Fiesolana** (Mon–Fri 9am–5.30pm, Sat 9am–12.30pm; free), once a monastery and now home to the European University Institute. The unfinished brick facade of the huge church (dull inside, so don't worry if it is closed) incorporates the lovely green-and-white Romanesque facade of an earlier and smaller church. The No. 7 bus can be caught in San Domenico for the return journey to Florence.

THE MUGELLO VALLEY

Just a few kilometres north of Florence, the Apennine foothills and Sieve river basin form the Mugello region. Like the Chianti, only less well trodden, it is characterised by bluish-green hills, brooding oak and chestnut woods, silvery olive groves and well-tended vineyards. The landscape is at its most picturesque in the western Sieve valley.

The Mugello has great associations with the Medici, who originated from here and lavished a lot of attention on the region. In 1451, Cosimo il Vecchio had Michelozzo alter the old fortress of Cafaggiolo just west of **San Piero a Sieve ❷** to create a country retreat, where Lorenzo il Magnifico spent part of his childhood, and writers and artists were lavishly entertained. The palace was modified by the Borghese family, who acquired it in the 19th century. Although recently restored, this original Medici seat, known as the **Castello Mediceo di Cafaggiolo** (tel:

055-847 9396) is privately owned and closed to the public for the foreseeable future but used for weddings, events and a cookery school.

A little further south, **Castello del Trebbio** (tel: 055-830 4900; www.castellodeltrebbio.com) received similar treatment at the hands of Michelozzo, and, more than any other 15th-century Tuscan villa, retains the feudal atmosphere of a Medici villa. Deservedly popular for Chianti wine tastings, welcoming cookery classes and gourmet feasts in the vaulted cellars, this castle-like retreat is a place that celebrates all these activities in one day.

Overlooking San Piero a Sieve, high on a thickly wooded outcrop, is the **San Martino** fortress built in 1569 by Lanci and Buontalenti to enable Cosimo I to defend the Florentine state. This massive pentagonal castle is privately owned and currently being restored, although you can walk along its walls.

Just north of San Piero a Sieve is the town of **Scarperia ❸**. **Palazzo de Vicari**, in the main street, is one of the finest examples of 13th-century

Badia Fiesolana, former monastery and now home to the European University Institute. From the terrace in front of the church there are views down the Mugnone River valley back to Florence.

Fiesole in autumn.

VILLA COUNTRY

The Medici villas reflect Florentine fine taste during the Renaissance, when these retreats were a haven for philosophers, artists – and the Medici rulers themselves.

The idea of a country retreat, so popular in Tuscany today, originated with the Romans. The villas were either working farms or were planned purely for pleasure. In the 15th century, the idea of the country villa was revived by the Medici family, who commissioned magnificent residences and elaborate gardens, modelled on classical principles. In 1452, Leon Battista Alberti decreed that a truly well-appointed country retreat had to be on a slope, full of light and air, with rooms grouped round an inner hall. The villas and gardens described here are all easily accessible from Florence, but it's wise to call ahead.

The **Villa Medici** (Via Beato Angelico; tel: 055-239 8994; www.villamedicifiesole.it; Mon–Fri 9am–1pm, gardens only by prior arrangement) at Fiesole, described

Cypress avenue leading to Villa la Pietra.

as "the first true Renaissance villa", was designed by Michelozzo for Cosimo il Vecchio between 1458 and 1461. It commands a superb view of Florence.

On the outskirts of Florence, the 15th-century **Villa la Pietra** (tel: 055-500 7210; http://lapietra.nyu.edu; villa and garden guided tours Fri pm, garden tours Tue mornings; advance booking necessary) was the home of the writer Sir Harold Acton. He bequeathed the villa and his Renaissance art collection to New York University.

Another American-owned villa in the Florentine hills is the historic **Villa i Tatti** (tel: 055-603 251; www.itatti.harvard.edu; selected Tue and Wed afternoons, advance booking only; free), beside the pretty village of Settignano. Formerly the home of art collector Bernard Berenson (1865–1959), who restored the villa to house his Renaissance art collection, it is now the Harvard University Center for Renaissance Studies.

Nearby, the **Villa Gamberaia** (tel: 055-697 205; www.villagamberaia.com; gardens Mon–Sat 9am–7pm, Sun 9am–6pm; villa by group tours and reservation only) is another fine Renaissance villa whose original garden survives.

The **Villa Medicea Poggio a Caiano** is often dubbed the perfect villa. The facade was modelled by Sangallo on a Greek temple to satisfy the tastes of Lorenzo the Magnificent. In the 19th century, the gardens were converted according to the fashionable English style, with romantic temples, fountains, an aviary and a mock-Gothic ruin.

Set on a steeply sloping hill, the **Villa Medicea della Petraia** (Via della Petraia; tel: 055-452 691; daily 8.30am–sunset; villa by guided tour only on the hour from 8.30am; free) was designed by Buontalenti for Ferdinando de' Medici as an elegant villa suitable for sumptuous entertaining. The interior is marred by the pretentious taste of the house of Savoy, but the Italianate gardens are a delight.

Only the gardens of the **Villa Medicea di Castello** (Via di Castello; tel: 055-452 691; daily 8.30am–sunset; free) can be viewed. Grottoes and statuary abound.

Another villa with attractive surroundings is the **Villa Demidoff** and **Parco di Pratolino** (tel: 055-408 0741; Easter–Oct Sat–Sun 10am–8pm; free), whose Mannerist gardens were remodelled in the English Romantic style.

civil architecture in Tuscany, similar in style to Florence's Palazzo Vecchio. The outer facade, decorated with the coats of arms of local notables, carved in stone or worked in della Robbia terracotta, faces the **Oratorio della Madonna della Piazza** in the small square, which features a *Madonna and Child* by Taddeo Gaddi. At the bottom of the main street, near the entrance to the town, is the **Oratorio della Madonna dei Terremoti**, dedicated to Our Lady of Earthquakes, which contains another fresco of the *Madonna and Child*, said to be by Filippo Lippi.

Scarperia is famous as a centre of knife-making. In local workshops traditional methods are still used to fashion knives by hand. There is even a museum dedicated to the craft, the **Museo dei Ferri Taglienti** (Museum of Cutting Tools) in the Palazzo dei Vicari (Oct–May Wed–Fri 10am–1pm, Sat–Sun 10am–1pm and 2.30–6pm, June–Sept 10am–1pm and 3–7pm), and in September the town hosts an international knife exhibition.

Scarperia is also known for the racetrack on its outskirts. The scenic "Mugello" circuit is used as a Ferrari F1 test centre and hosts the Italian motorbike grand prix in June.

A turning on the left of the southern approach to Scarperia wends its way through dense woodlands to the remote **Bosco ai Frati** Franciscan convent (tel: 055-848 111; Mon–Sat 10am–noon and 6–7pm, Sun 9–10am and 6–7pm; free). This retreat retains the peace and solitude of the Franciscan ideal that places such as Assisi lack; no touring hordes, no postcard-sellers, only the peace and quiet offered by a church and its convent in a clearing in the woods. The monastic buildings were remodelled by Michelozzo around 1440 for Cosimo il Vecchio. They house a little-known, large wooden *Crucifix*, attributed to Donatello, one of the greatest masters of the Italian Renaissance.

PRATO

Prato ❹, to the northwest of Florence, is the third-largest city in Tuscany, and long-time rival of Florence. Refreshingly, Prato doesn't depend on tourism but on trade, and revels in its confident, mercantile personality. The city is renowned for its textile-manufacturing industries, with numerous factory outlets selling fine fabrics, cashmere and designer clothes. Although the trade has made contemporary Prato a rich city, it was already a leading textile town in the 12th century and its magnificent monuments are evidence of its former wealth. Amid the industrial estates, and factories dominated by Chinese immigrants, lies a compact *centro storico*, contained within medieval walls. But Prato is also a cosmopolitan city, drawn to contemporary art, as witnessed by the Henry Moore sculpture that greets most visitors.

The city possesses an extraordinary relic: in the delightful green-and-white **Duomo** (daily 10am–5pm; free) is what is believed to be the girdle of the Virgin Mary. The legends surrounding this relic

⊘ GLORIOUS GARDENS

The centrepiece of any Medici villa was the garden, which provided a harmonious link with the wild countryside beyond the walls. The enclosed medieval garden, the *giardino segreto*, survived at first, with vegetable and herb gardens planted nearby. However, Renaissance landscape gardeners embellished the concept of enclosure and, in keeping with humanistic ideals, it became a symbol of tamed nature.

The villa and garden were considered an organic whole, linked by loggias, porticoes and new perspectives. Emphasis was placed on geometrical rigour and the laws of perspective were used to create terraced gardens with straight avenues lined by cypresses or lemon trees in tubs. Semicircular ponds, adorned with sculpture, closed the line of vision.

The Mannerist era witnessed a profusion of allegorical fountains and grotesque sculpture, much of which remains. The main players were Buontalenti, who brought architectural rigour to garden design, and Il Tribolo, a pupil of Michelangelo who was responsible for the Boboli Gardens. Four of the best gardens are at: Villa Gamberaia; Villa Demidoff; Villa Medicea della Petraia; and Villa Medicea di Castello. The Pratolino gardens at Villa Demidoff became a Unesco World Heritage site in 2013.

The Pulpit of the Holy Girdle on Prato's Duomo.

Ancient San Miniato.

have been celebrated by Agnolo Gaddi, whose frescoes cover the walls of the Chapel of the Holy Girdle. Above the high altar are fresco cycles of *The Life of St Stephen* and *The Martyrdom of St John the Baptist* by Filippo Lippi. Outside the Duomo is the Pulpit of the Holy Girdle, decorated with dancing cherubs by Donatello, where, on Christmas Day and several other holy days in the year, the girdle is displayed. The **Museo dell'Opera del Duomo** (Mon, Wed–Sat 10am–1pm and 2–5pm, Sun 2–5pm) in the cloister contains paintings, sculptures and reliefs by Donatello, Fra Lippi and others.

Other notable monuments include the church of **Santa Maria delle Carceri** (daily 7am–noon and 4–7pm; free), built by Giuliano Sangallo in typical no-frills Brunelleschian style. In front of the church is the **Castello dell'Imperatore** (Wed–Mon 10am–4pm; free), built by Frederick II Hohenstaufen in the first half of the 13th century, and unique in Tuscany, taking as its model the Norman castles of Puglia. A walk along its ramparts offers a good view of Prato.

In Via Rinaldesca is the 14th-century frescoed **Palazzo Datini** (daily June–Sept 10am–1pm and 4–7pm, Oct–May 10am–1pm and 3–6pm; free), former home of Francesco Datini (1330–1410), better known as the Merchant of Prato. Datini, a successful wool merchant, died one of the richest men in Europe, leaving his money to city charities, and is commemorated in statues around the town.

For a break from Renaissance art, the **Centro per l'Arte Contemporanea Luigi Pecci** (tel: 0574-5317; www.centropecci.it) lies on the edge of town. In 2016, the museum reopened following the renovation of its original building and construction of a futuristic spaceship-shaped extension, doubling its exhibition space to 3,000 sq metres (32,300 sq ft). The complex also includes a library, cinema, bookshop, restaurant and an open-air theatre.

Outside the historic centre is the more engaging **Museo del Tessuto** (Via Santa Chiara 24; www.museodeltessuto.it; Tue–Thu 10am–3pm, Fri–Sat 10am–7pm, Sun 3–7pm), dedicated to the fine textiles that made Prato's fortune.

⊘ SAN MINIATO

The ancient town of San Miniato, which dates back to Etruscan times, is set atop three hills, equidistant from the cities of Pisa, Florence, Lucca, Pistoia, Siena and Volterra. On a fine day you can gaze as far as Volterra and the Apuan Alps. High on the hillside are the two towers of the **Rocca** (Apr–May and Sept Tue–Sun 11am–6pm, July–Aug Tue–Sun 10am–6pm, Oct–Nov Sat–Sun 10am–5pm, Dec–Mar Sat–Sun 10am–3pm), rebuilt in the 12th century by Frederick II. The older **Torre di Matilde** (Apr–Sept Mon–Fri 11am–2pm, Sat–Sun 11am–2pm and 3–6pm, Oct–Mar Sat 10am–1pm and 2–5pm, Sun 2–5pm), was converted into a bell tower when the **Duomo** (Mon–Sat 9.30am–7pm, Sun 8.15–7pm, summer until 8pm) was added. The **Museo Diocesano d'Arte Sacra** (Apr–Sept daily 9am–1pm and 2–4pm, Oct–Mar Thu 2–4pm, Fri 9am–1pm and 2–4pm, Sat–Sun 9am–1pm), in the old sacristy of the Duomo, displays art and sculpture, including works by Lippi, Verrocchio and Tiepolo. Built by the Lombards in the 8th century, the magnificent church of San Francesco (daily 9am–noon and 3–6pm) is the oldest building in San Miniato.

But to most Italians, San Miniato means one thing only: white truffles. The town produces a quarter of Tuscany's crop, which are best tasted during the November truffle fair. The Association of Trufflers of the San Miniato Hills issues a map showing where to find the aromatic fungus, which is dug out of the ground with a type of pole called a *vangheggia*.

Gorgeous masterpieces of antique cloth are on display, and the skills that led to their production are not lost, as the section on contemporary textiles clearly demonstrates.

LEONARDO COUNTRY

A gentle meander into the countryside due west of Florence takes in some lovely views, a few small towns and Leonardo's alleged birthplace of Vinci. Head west out of Florence on the SP66 (in the direction of Pistoia), and turn south at **Poggio a Caiano**, site of Lorenzo the Magnificent's favourite retreat, built by Sangallo (1480–85). It is one of the most magnificent and best preserved of Florentine rural retreats (garden daily 8.15am–sunset, free; villa by guided tour only, closed 2nd and 3rd Mon of the month).

The walled village of **Artimino ⑤**, about 11km (7 miles) from Poggio a Caiano, is a classic case of a *borgo* reborn as a villa, wine estate and medieval residential complex. It is also the setting for another huge Medicean villa (tel: 055-875 1426; www.artimino.com; open by appointment only), this one built by Bernardo Buontalenti as a hunting lodge for Ferdinando I in 1594 and curious for the number of tall chimneys on the roof. It has been beautifully restored, and converted into a distinguished hotel, complete with a restaurant specialising in dishes with Medici origins. Part of the villa is open to visitors, including a small Etruscan museum. After wandering round Artimino *borgo*, consider dining in the Biagio Pignatta in the villa stables.

A tortuous road leads through olive groves and vines from Artimino to **Vinci ⑥**, alleged birthplace of Leonardo. Here, the 13th-century castle in the centre of town is home to the **Museo Leonardiano** (tel: 0571-933 285; www.museoleonardiano.it; daily Mar–Oct 9.30am–7pm, Nov–Feb 9.30am–6pm), which has a vast selection of mechanical models built to the exact measurements of Leonardo's drawings. In neighbouring **Anchiano**, Leonardo's birthplace museum showcases the latest multimedia technology (tel: 0571-933 248; www.museoleonardiano.it).

Five kilometres (3 miles) southwest of Vinci is the hill town of **Cerreto Guidi ⑦**. Once owned by the Guidi counts, it now produces a good Chianti Putto wine and boasts yet another Medici villa, the austere **Villa di Cerreto Guidi** (Mon–Sat Oct–Mar 10am–6pm; Apr–Sept 9am–6pm, Sun 10am–7pm; closed 2nd and 3rd Mon of the month; free), built in 1564 for Cosimo I as a hunting lodge. It contains some fine portraits of the Medici family. Isabella, daughter of Cosimo I, is said to have been murdered here by her husband for her infidelities.

WEST OF FLORENCE

West of Florence, the first major stop along the superstrada is **Empoli ⑧**, a prosperous, modern market town with a small *centro storico* and a superb Romanesque church, the **Collegiata Sant'Andrea**. The

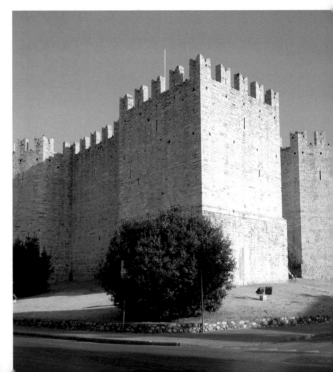

The impressive Castello dell'Imperatore.

green-and-white-striped facade is reminiscent of Florence's San Miniato, and the small **museum** (Tue–Sun 9am–noon, 4–7pm) contains a surprising amount of precious Florentine art.

A few kilometres west of Empoli is **Fucecchio**, noted for the **Padule di Fucecchio**, to the north of town. Now Italy's biggest inland marsh, covering 1,460 hectares (3,600 acres), this was a Medicean fishing ground in the 16th century, and Cosimo I had a bridge and weirs built to facilitate the sport. It is now home to rare birds and a variety of flora. The land is privately owned, but the wetland centre in **Castelmartini di Larciano** (tel: 0573-84 540) organises guided tours.

VALDARNO

East of Florence, off the SS70, a narrow pass climbs up the western slope of the Pratomagno hills to the monastery of **Vallombrosa** ❾, founded in the 11th century, but remodelled over the centuries, and its **Museo d'Arte Sacra** (late June–Aug daily 10am–noon and 3–6pm, rest of the year by appointment). The reward for making the journey is not so much the monastery itself as the splendid beech wood that surrounds it. Romanesque churches worth visiting in the vicinity include **San Pietro in Cascia** and **Sant'Agata in Arfoli**. Nearby, the tiny village of **Saltino** is handy in the winter for the ski runs of **Monte Secchieta**.

TOWARDS CHIANTI

Not far south of Florence, towards Chianti, is the town of **Impruneta** ❿ , an important sanctuary in the early medieval period when a shrine was erected here to house an image of the Virgin Mary, thought to have been the work of St Luke and believed to be capable of performing miracles. This shrine, the **Basilica di Santa Maria** (Mon–Sat 7.30–11.30am and 4.30–6.30pm, Sun 7.30–noon and 4.30–7pm, closed Wed pm), with its terracotta tabernacle by Luca della Robbia in Michelozzo's Chapel of the Cross, underwent alterations over the centuries, and was bomb-damaged in World War II.

Subsequent restoration and repair to this and to other pre-17th century buildings has meant that Impruneta has retained a great deal of its early character, though without the patina of age. Brunelleschi insisted that the tiles for the roof of the Duomo in Florence be supplied by Impruneta, which is still an important centre for terracotta production. Call into the **Tesoro**, the cathedral treasury, too (Apr–Oct Sat–Sun 9am–1pm and 4–7pm, Nov–Mar Sat–Sun 9am–1pm and 3–6pm; free).

West of Impruneta, **San Casciano in Val di Pesa** is a quiet old Chianti town, enlivened every February by carnival. The town's reputation today rests solely on the art displayed in the Collegiata church, the convent, the church of St Francis and the church of the Misericordia, including paintings by Simone Martini, Ugolino di Neri, Taddeo Gaddi and Fra Bartolomeo.

We are now in the Chianti region covered on page 193.

Impruneta, just south of Florence, is an important centre of terracotta production.

LUCCA AND PISTOIA

Take some mountains and spas, add a scattering of grand villas, blend in two underrated cities full of character, and you begin to paint a picture of Lucca and Pistoia provinces – where you can swim, ski, shop or soak in the spas to your heart's content.

Perfectly proportioned Lucca, and its harmonious, villa-studded countryside, occupy the alluring heart of this region. Lucca, like Siena, is a city built on a human scale, designed to be savoured slowly, and on foot. To the west of the walled city is the Tuscan Riviera, known as Versilia, a broad strip of land between the sea and the Apennines – and, to the north, are the steeply mountainous Garfagnana and Lunigiana regions.

Despite its charms, neighbouring Pistoia always feels marooned in a historical backwater. Pistoia province, sandwiched between Lucca and Florence, and fought over for centuries by both, has yet to make its mark. Its lower profile is partly due to its bewildering diversity. Part-fertile plain and part-mountains, the province is bordered, in the north, by the Apennines, where Abetone is Tuscany's premier ski resort. Further south, spa country rules, with Montecatini Terme playing the dowager to Grotta Giusti's laid-back younger sister.

MINIATURE CULTURAL CAPITAL

Often bypassed by fans intent on ticking off the Leaning Tower of Pisa, **Lucca ❶** is Tuscany's self-deprecating star. In spite of this, it is the only

Cycling in the sunshine in Lucca's Piazza Anfiteatro.

Tuscan city to see tourism expand exponentially in recent years. Its perfectly preserved walled heart, quiet sophistication and peaceful pace of life are all credited with winning over visitors. And that's before talking about its pinky-gold palaces, pedestrian-friendly bastions, crowd-pleasing concerts, enchanting churches, and its renowned olive oil and wine estates. To jaded urbanites, Lucca represents life as it should be led.

Sitting on a marshy plain between the Apennines and Monte Pisano,

⊘ **Main attractions**
Lucca
Casa Museo Puccini
Villa Reale
Montecatini Terme
Monsummano Terme
Cattedrale di San Zeno, Pistoia
Abetone

⊙ **Maps on pages 134, 138, 142**

A jewellery shop in Lucca.

Lucca has been inhabited since ancient times. Little remains of Etruscan Luk, but Roman Luca survives in the grid design of streets, and in the elliptical Piazza Anfiteatro, around which houses were subsequently built. As an independent city-state, 11th-century Lucca spent the next 400 years defending itself against an ever more belligerent Florence. Even though the Florentines won the title of capital of the region, Lucca never ceded its political and economic autonomy. It remained an independent republic, apart from a brief period of Pisan rule, until the Napoleonic invasion of 1796.

This graceful and prosperous provincial capital, 77km (48 miles) west of Florence on the A11, is a city of many charms, not least the walls encircling the city. They were built after 1500 to keep Lucca's enemies at bay. In 1817, the massive ramparts were planted with a double row of plane trees, which shade the broad avenue running along the top of the walls, now used by Lucca's citizens as a playground, promenade, jogging trail and cycle route.

THE CATHEDRAL SQUARE

A path from the walls leads directly to the **Duomo di San Martino** Ⓐ (mid-Mar–May and Oct Mon–Fri 9.30am–6pm, Sat until 6.45pm, Sun noon–6pm, June–Sept Mon–Fri 9.30am–7pm, Sat until 6.45pm, Sun noon–9pm, Nov–mid-Mar Mon–Fri 9.30am–5pm, Sat until 6.45pm, Sun noon–6pm). The Cathedral's striking facade is decorated with a sculpture of St Martin dividing his cloak (the original sculpture is now just inside the church). The inlaid marble designs typify Tuscan Romanesque style: hunting scenes figure large, with dogs, boars, and huntsmen on horseback. Flanking the central portal are scenes of the *Labours of the Months* and the *Miracles of St Martin*.

Inside is the octagonal *tempietto* that contains a larger-than-life *Crucifixion* in carved and painted wood. Known as the *Volto Santo* (Holy Face), the Romanesque carving was once believed to be a true portrait of Christ, carved by Nicodemus, who witnessed the Crucifixion (in fact, the highly stylised figure is probably a 13th-century copy of an 11th-century copy of an 8th-century original). Each year, on 13 September, this revered relic is paraded through the streets at dusk. Off the south aisle is the **Sacristy**. This contains the greatest treasure: Jacopo della Quercia's tomb of Ilaria del Carretto, who died in 1405. It's a tender effigy, depicting a faithful dog at her feet, waiting for his mistress to awake. As the wife of Paolo Guinigi, Lord of Lucca, Ilaria died at the age of 24, following the birth of their second child.

Across the square is the church of **Santi Giovanni e Reperata** Ⓑ (mid-Mar–Oct daily 10am–6pm, Nov–mid-Mar Mon–Fri 10am–2pm, Sat–Sun until 6pm). Originally Lucca's cathedral, the church has been excavated to reveal a wealth of Roman and Romanesque features. The earliest is a 1st-century BC mosaic floor, superseded by a 2nd-century Roman bathhouse, which itself gave way to a 5th-century baptistery, later joined by a series of churches, culminating in the present 12th-century building. Highlights include the Roman font, Romanesque pavements and the coffered ceiling.

Via del Duomo leads west of the Cathedral to Piazza del Giglio, home to the theatre and opera house. Adjoining the square is Piazza Napoleone, shaded by tall plane trees and lined by restaurant terraces.

PISAN ROMANESQUE TO PUCCINI

Heading north out of the square takes you to Piazza San Michele, ringed by Renaissance arcades. At the centre of the square, the church of **San Michele in Foro** Ⓒ (daily 7.30am–noon and 3–6pm; free), built on the site of the Roman forum, has one of the most spectacular Pisan Romanesque facades in Italy. Flanked by Lucca's loveliest bell tower, the tiered arcades are decorated with delicate motifs and allegories; hunting scenes carved in green and white marble, with creatures both exotic (bears, dragons and elephants) and domestic (a rabbit, a duck and a crow eating grapes). The church is topped by a huge gilded

Buskers in Piazza San Michele.

A variety of delicious biscotti on sale.

statue of Archangel Michael slaying the dragon, flanked by two angels.

Turning your back on the facade, take Via di Poggio, which leads to the **Casa Museo Puccini** ⓓ (www.puccinimuseum.org; Mar–Apr and Oct daily 10am–6pm, May–Sept daily until 7pm, Nov–Dec Wed–Mon 10am–1pm and 3–5pm, Jan–Feb Wed–Mon 10am–5pm), the birthplace of Lucca's celebrated composer, Giacomo Puccini.

Heading west, feel your way through Lucca's maze of medieval alleys to Palazzo Mansi, in Via Galli Tassi, which houses the **Museo e Pinacoteca Nazionale** ⓔ (www.lucca museinazionali.it; Tue–Sat 8.30am–7.30pm). Deities and allegorical figures romp across the ceilings of the splendidly furnished 17th-century home of Cardinal Spada (1659–1724). Upstairs, at the end of a sequence of rooms decorated around the theme of the Four Elements is a sumptuous bedchamber dedicated to Fire. This fire is not a destructive one, but the flame that burns when Eros strikes with his arrow. The room features a gorgeous double bed, its lovely hangings decorated with birds and flowers.

REMNANTS OF MEDIEVAL WEALTH

The wealth of Lucca, like that of Florence, was based on banking and its silk industry. As early as the 12th century, bankers were plying the Mediterranean or travelling north to Bruges, Antwerp and London, buying and selling silk and woollen cloth. Successful bankers, such as the Guinigi family, built ostentatious tower-houses, although only one of these remains, the 14th-century **Torre Guinigi** ⓕ (daily Jan–Feb and Nov–Dec 9.30am–4.30pm, Mar and Oct until 5.30pm, Apr–May until 6.30pm, June–Sept until 7.30pm). As in San Gimignano (see page 193), such fortified homes were both medieval status symbols and retreats in times of trouble. Climb the tower to admire rural views, and to make out the outline of Lucca's Roman Amphitheatre (Anfiteatro), perfectly preserved in the buildings

ⓞ GIACOMO PUCCINI

Both a giant of 19th-20th-century opera and a crowd-pleasing showman, Giacomo Puccini (1858–1924) was a musical master of erotic passion, pathos and despair. His lush operas are characterised by soft harmony, gentle orchestration and an emotional sensitivity that is very modern. Ever the populist, Puccini was the composer with the most in common with musical theatre, and conceived of opera as drama set to music.

Puccini was born into a musical family in **Lucca**, where his newly restored home is now a museum in his honour. The young Puccini womanised at **Torre del Lago**, where his villa, set between the sea and reedy **Lake Massaciuccoli**, welcomed bohemian painters, beautiful women, gamblers and hunters as keen as himself. As Puccini boasted, "I am a mighty hunter of wildfowl, beautiful women and good libretti." He was deeply attached to the lake where he went poaching as a boy and would even compose at the piano, dressed in breeches and riding boots, with a loaded gun and hunting dogs ready by his side. Here, in this villa overlooking the Luccan hills,

Puccini's jealous wife would lace her husband's wine with an aphrodisiac antidote if she felt any female guests were too alluring. The raffish playboy was reckless with women, fast cars and yachts called *Mimi*, naturally named after the heroine of *La bohème*. Puccini's music is of more lasting allure, despite his scandalous private life. "Nessun Dorma" from *Turandot* even became the theme music for the 1990 Football World Cup. Although Stravinsky dismissed *Madama Butterfly* as "treacly violin music", director Jonathan Miller disagrees: "I'm made to cry by Puccini and I never am by Verdi."

Lucca's international Puccini festival, **Puccini e la sua Lucca** (www.puccinielasualucca.com), is the only permanent festival in the world, with musical events taking place every Friday and Saturday at 7pm. Recitals, opera performances and other special concerts by renowned singers and pianists are all staged at the lovely San Giovanni Basilica right in the centre of town. And all this in honour of the greatest Luccanese of all time, much loved by his compatriots.

that were constructed against it in the Middle Ages.

For a closer look at the resulting egg-shaped piazza, turn right out of the tower, and first right in Via delle Chiavi d'Oro. Passing the Art Deco baths (now a cultural centre), keep going until you reach the curving wall of the **Anfiteatro**. Ringed by pavement cafés, restaurants and souvenir shops, the Amphitheatre is an atmospheric place in which to enjoy an ice cream or linger until the evening for dinner.

Leave through the opposite archway, following the curve of the Amphitheatre to Via Fillungo, Lucca's main shopping street and **San Frediano** Ⓖ (daily 9am–6.30pm), with its huge gold-and-blue facade mosaic of *Christ in Majesty*. The treasure of this church is its Romanesque font carved with scenes showing Moses and his entourage of camels, leading his people (dressed in medieval armour) through the divided Red Sea.

To the rear and left of the church is the **Palazzo Pfanner** Ⓗ (www.palazzo pfanner.it; Apr–Nov daily 10am–6pm), a delightful 17th-century residence. Without paying, you can catch a glimpse of the wonderful garden and external staircase at the rear by climbing on to the city walls behind San Frediano church and walking left for a short distance. Highlights inside include swathes of 17th-century Lucchese silk in the bedrooms and beer-making equipment in the cellar – the palace was used as a brewery until 1929.

The Guinigi were not the only ones to flaunt their wealth by creating towers. A picture hanging in the **Museo Nazionale Guinigi** Ⓘ (www.luccamu seinazionali.it; Tue–Sat 8.30am–7.30pm) shows that the city was once, like San Gimignano, a forest of towers, and illustrates just how wealthy medieval Lucca was. Among the artistic treasures here is a *Madonna and Child* in bas-relief by Matteo Civitalli, a contemporary of Donatello, and Lucca's most renowned sculptor.

LUCCHESI VILLAS

The area surrounding Lucca is rich in villas: the patrician Villa Torrigiani,

Bird's-eye view of Lucca and the Apuan Alps beyond.

Ornate staircases at Villa Garzoni.

the Baroque Villa Mansi and the Villa Reale at Marlia are all surrounded by beautiful parks. Most of these villas are still in appreciative private hands, but often the gardens can be visited even if the house is not open to the public. Wandering through fragrant shrubbery and cool grottoes, past whimsical statuary and fountains, is a delightful diversion on a hot summer's afternoon.

Leave Lucca on the SS12 in the direction of the Garfagnana, and after passing through Marlia, turn off at **Villa Reale** ❷ (www.parcovillareale.it; Mar–Oct daily 10am–6pm, Nov–Feb by appointment). It was built in the 17th century by the noble Orsetti family, and substantially remodelled by Elisa Bacciocchi, Napoleon's sister. There is a lush park with a lake, which surrounds the formal Italian gardens. Most wonderful of its many fine features is the *teatro verde*, an outdoor theatre surrounded by clipped yew hedges, a key setting for concerts during Lucca's summer festival.

Continue on through a fairly built-up area to Segromigno in Monte and the charming **Villa Mansi** (tel: 0583-920 234; Apr–Oct Mon–Fri 9am–4pm, Sat–Sun 2–6pm, Nov–Mar Mon–Fri 11.30am–3.30pm), with beautifully landscaped gardens. Just 2km (1.2 miles) away in Camigliano, **Villa Torrigiani** (Wed–Mon summer 10am–1pm and 3–7pm, winter 10am–noon and 3–5pm) is a fine example of Baroque architecture. Also consider **Villa Bernardini** in Vicopelago just outside Lucca (tel: 0583-164 6057; visits by appointment).

Equally splendid is the **Villa Garzoni** (www.pinocchio.it; villa houses a restaurant; gardens Mar–Oct daily 9am–sunset, Nov–Feb Sat 10am–sunset, other days open for groups by request) in the town of **Collodi** ❸, with a glorious Baroque garden full of mythical monsters modelled in terracotta, fountains and topiaried animals. The steep terraces of the 17th-century garden lead to some memorable viewing points.

If you were entranced as a child by the adventures of a wooden puppet with a remarkable nose, you may recognise the name of this town as being that of the author of *The Adventures of Pinocchio* (1881). Carlo Lorenzini adopted Collodi as his pen-name because he had fond memories of staying here as a child. The town now has **Parco di Pinocchio** (www.pinocchio. it; same hours as Villa Garzoni gardens) devoted to Pinocchio, consisting of mosaics, mazes and statues based on scenes from the story. Contemporary children, accustomed to virtual reality and adrenalin-fuelled theme parks, may find it rather tame, but there are plans to enhance the attractions at the nearby Villa Garzoni.

EN ROUTE TO THE SPA RESORTS

Where Lucca's villa country ends, Pistoia Province begins, as does the route east to the thermal-spa resorts of Montecatini Terme and Monsummano Terme. Just south of Collodi is **Pescia ❹**, cradled in the plain of the Valdinievole. Pescia is famous for its flower production and has the largest flower market outside the Netherlands. Prosperous Pescia

is surrounded by nurseries, greenhouses, olive groves and hills dotted with gracious villas. Divided by a river, the medieval town boasts several fine churches, including the cathedral and Sant'Antonio, as well as a crenellated town hall. In the hills above town is the Convento di Colleviti, a Renaissance monastery, accessible by footpath from Pescia.

Just south of Pescia are two appealing villages, notably the shabbily scenic **Uzzano**, which has a curious church on the crest of the hill, and well-tended **Buggiano**, with an interesting church and lovingly restored palazzo.

Further east awaits **Montecatini Terme ❺**, once famed throughout Europe for its elegance and luxury. It was remodelled by Grand Duke Leopold of Tuscany in the 18th century and became a destination spa resort before the term was invented. Belle Epoque nostalgia is still the order of the day, even if many foreign spa-goers feel more comfortable in the purely pampering spas. Avenues of neoclassical spa pavilions dispense

In the spring, the peach blossoms of Pescia are outstanding; every September in even-numbered years, Pescia hosts the colourful Biennale del Fiore – Festival of Flowers.

The grand Villa Torrigiani.

THE SPA RENAISSANCE

The new breed of thermal spas marks a return to Roman roots: these are both pampering and restorative spas that bathe body, mind and spirit.

AN AGE-OLD RITUAL

Taking the waters has become fashionable once more. Water cures, popular since Etruscan and Roman times, have always been part of local culture. In the 1st century AD, Emperor Augustus's physician issued a prescription to the poet Horace to visit the Tuscan spas, one of the first medical prescriptions on record. The Romans saw spas as both curative and civilising, distinguishing their citizens from the Barbarians, who didn't know how to combine warm water with warm company and well-being. Thermal spas were also recreational in the days of the Tuscan Grand-Dukes, when resorts such as Bagni di Pisa welcomed the crowned heads of Europe to wallow in the waters, gamble in the casino and dance in the ballrooms. But

The Grand Duke hammam at Saturnia Terme.

somewhere along the line, the spas languished, and lost out to "liver-boosting water cures" in echoing marble halls.

THE BEST SPAS

However, the scary white-coat brigade has been banished from the best Tuscan spas, such as Chianciano's **Terme Sensoriali** (www.termesensoriali.it), one of the most approachable yet seductive day spas. Neighbouring **Fonteverde** (www.fonteverdespa.com), floating on a sea of hills in Val d'Orcia, is a terraced spa resort clustered around a late Renaissance villa. The stylishly simple estate is dotted with thermal pools but, as a destination spa, also delivers oriental massage, skin consultations, dietary advice, yoga, spiritual healing – all presented clearly, without pushiness or psychobabble.

While not throwing the baby out with the bathwater, spas such as **Grotta Giusti** (www.grottagiustispa.com), in Monsummano Terme, manage to combine gracious 19th-century living with superb massage, thermal pools, sprawling grounds, and steamy grottoes dubbed "the eighth wonder of the world" by the composer Giuseppe Verdi. Health-seekers don bizarre boiler suits to follow the Dantesque route into "Inferno", where grottoes named Purgatory, Paradise and Hell induce a surreal detox. After sweating in Hell, there's floating under the thermal jets in the giant pool, Ayurvedic massage or sneaky golf sessions.

Set at the foot of low-slung mountains, **Bagni di Pisa** (www.bagnidipisa.com) is a delightful retreat with a view of the Leaning Tower. This romantic 18th-century resort is charmingly nostalgic, with vaulted bedrooms, a winter garden, frescoed halls, and a folly Byron was fond of. The hammam is a steamy, couples-only cavern and stone-clad pool with a 38-degree temperature conducive to chilling out, detoxing and lowering the blood pressure.

In the Maremma, **Saturnia Terme** (www.termedisaturnia.it) is a sophisticated affair, as befits a spot that has provided rest and recreation to Romans, ancient and modern. Fed by historic springs, a beguiling thermal pool is matched by an indoor recreation of Ancient Roman baths, outdoor cascades and timeless views of the Etruscan countryside.

health-giving waters to drink and offer treatments ranging from inhalation to mudbaths. With its fountains and Art Nouveau flourishes, Tettuccio is the grandest and most languid. Cast aside your wariness and dip a toe in the waters: whether sipping them in marble pavilions, strolling through the magnificent parks, or committing yourself to a complete cure.

Montecatini Alto is the original medieval fortified town above the thermal springs, and can be reached by funicular or by road. Although over-popular in high season, it is still a restful place to visit, with a shady chestnut-tree walk along the lower terrace, and panoramic views over Valdinievole, "valley of the mists". Drink something stronger than water in the main square, Piazza Giusti, and cast your eye over the ruined fortress and equally ruined Romanesque church, unfortunately marred by an ill-judged restoration.

Montecatini represents a crossroads, from where you can continue east to Pistoia, make a brief foray north, or collapse in a superb spa just south. Driving north of Montecatini along the N633, you arrive at **Marliana** via a scenic mountain road, and can meditate over views from Marliana's castle and campanile. A little further on, medieval **Vellano** makes a good lunch stop, with rustic inns overlooking the valley slopes and olive terraces. Alternatively, south of Montecatini, **Monsummano Terme** ❻ is home to an extraordinary spa, Grotta Giusti Spa Resort, where you can bathe in thermal pools or sweat it out in a bizarre steamy grotto, best savoured on an overnight stay.

Bikes for rent in Lucca.

CYCLING IN LUCCA

Lucca is full of lanes too narrow for cars, so the locals often get about by bicycle. This, combined with Lucca's reputation for culture and intellectual pursuits, has earned the city the nickname of the "Cambridge of Tuscany".

The old walls are equally popular with walkers and joggers. Every now and again, you can take the sloped exit down into the town and cycle around

Cheeky decorative tiles at Tettuccio Terme, Montecatini.

the key sites, locking the bike up to a gate when entering a museum or walking around a piazza.

You can hire a bike at Rent Bike Lucca on the square in front of the railway station (www.touristcenterlucca.com; current bike hire for a day costs from €12 per person) or at Barbetti, Via Anfiteatro 23, and Cicli Bizzarri, Piazza S. Maria 32. Cycling is also a healthy alternative to a day on the beach. Near Lucca, one leisurely coastal route runs from the Viareggio seafront to Lido di Camaiore, Marina di Pietrasanta and Forte dei Marmi. Another 20km (12.4-mile) trail links Viareggio with Torre del Lago Puccini. To book a short bike trip, or a bigger cycling holiday in Tuscany, contact Gusto Tours (www.gustocycling.com) or consult Love Italy (www.loveitaly.co.uk).

UNSUNG PISTOIA

The path most travelled from Montecatini leads east to **Pistoia** ❼. The provincial capital tends to be overshadowed by its glittering neighbour, Florence, only 37km (22 miles) distant, and is rather unfairly neglected as a result. Its historic heart is delightful, and it has a profusion of elegant shops, inns and hotels tucked away in the medieval streets. What's more, the citizens of Pistoia take great pride in their monuments and churches, and when dusk falls, the shadowy, lamp-lit streets have an authentic atmosphere. Church bells peal, Franciscan monks stride along in their unmistakable brown habits and rope belts, and the stone slabs outside the shops are laid out with goods for sale just as they might in the Middle Ages.

Pistoia was originally a Roman town, founded as a staging post on the Via Cassia. It flourished as a banking centre during its medieval heyday, but was constantly buffeted between Florence and Lucca, eventually falling under the dominion of Florence. The impressive trapezoid walls that encompass the city are part of the bastion built by the Medici during the 15th century. Much of the area around the **Piazza del Duomo**

has been pedestrianised, and, when not full of market stalls (Sat and Wed), the piazza is a peaceful place for taking stock of Pistoia's riches.

The **Cattedrale di San Zeno** (daily 8.30am–12.30pm, 3–7pm; free) originated in the 5th century, but was rebuilt in Romanesque style with a splendid Pisan-style facade of green and white marble stripes. A marble porch was added later and decorated with an exquisite blue-and-white Andrea della Robbia bas-relief.

Inside are many medieval frescoes, an impressive Crucifix (1274), Renaissance paintings and – most glorious of all – the massive, ornate silver altar in the **Chapel of Saint James** (contact the sacristan), decorated with bas-reliefs and statues over a period of two centuries by many different artists, including Brunelleschi. Next door in the Palazzo dei Vescovi (Bishops' Palace), above the helpful tourist office (tel: 0573-21622), is the **Museo della Cattedrale** (Wed–Fri, guided tours only 10am, 11.30am, 1pm, 3pm, 3.30pm, 5pm).

Beside the Duomo is the soaring **Campanile**, originally a watchtower, naturally adorned with three tiers of green-and-white Pisan arches, echoing the Duomo facade. You can climb the bell tower for magnificent views over the town (by reservation at one of the tourist offices). Opposite is the 14th-century octagonal **Battistero** of San Giovanni in Corte, designed by Andrea Pisano (June–Aug daily 10am–6pm, Sept–Easter Fri–Sun 10am–1pm and 3–6pm, Easter–May Tue–Sun 10am–1pm and 3–6pm).

The piazza is lined with Renaissance palaces, including the **Palazzo del Podestà**, still the city's law courts, with a finely decorated inner courtyard. Opposite is the **Palazzo del Comune** (Town Hall), with a harmonious facade of arches and delicately pointed windows, decorated with the ubiquitous Medici crest and a grim black-marble head. Inside is a courtyard and sweeping stairway, and sculptures by local artist Marino Marini (1901–80), many of them based on his favourite theme of riders

Detail from the entrance to the Cattedrale di San Zeno.

Della Robbia's majolica frieze above the Ospedale del Ceppo loggia.

Eat

Abetone is well supplied with mountain restaurants, which command wonderful views of the dramatic landscape and supply hearty food and restorative drinks. A local speciality is *Grappa di mirtilli*, a strong spirit made from mountain bilberries.

and horses. Upstairs in the first- and second-floor rooms is the impressive art collection of the **Museo Civico** B (Tue–Fri 10am–2pm, Sat–Sun 10am–6pm), which includes a rare 13th-century painting of St Francis.

To the north of the Duomo, in Piazza Giovanni XII, is the **Ospedale del Ceppo** C. It was founded in 1287 and still functions as a hospital. Above the loggia is a brilliantly coloured majolica frieze by Giovanni della Robbia that depicts the *Seven Works of Mercy*: worthy citizens handing out food to the poor, comforting prisoners and washing the feet of dusty travellers. The figures are realistic, often humorous, despite the gravity of their occupations.

A CONGREGATION OF CHURCHES

Pistoia's striped churches encircle the historic centre like zebras – with the Pisano pulpits the great pride of the town. **Sant'Andrea** D (8am–6pm), in the Via Sant'Andrea, has an arcaded facade and reliefs above the central door. Inside is a richly painted wooden

ceiling and narrow nave, well lit from the upper clerestory. Here is Giovanni Pisano's hexagonal pulpit (1297), modelled on the Nicola Pisano pulpit in the Pisa Duomo. The sharply carved marble reliefs border on the melodramatic in their depiction of *The Life of Jesus* and *The Last Judgement*.

San Bartolomeo in Pantano E (St Bartholomew in the Swamp; daily 8am–4pm), in the Piazza San Bartolomeo, is one of Pistoia's oldest churches, built in the 12th century with a five-bay facade. Inside there is a pulpit by Guido da Como (1250) depicting *Christ's Nativity*, with the edifice resting on the backs of men and lions carved out of marble.

In the pedestrianised *Via Cavour* is the 12th-century church of **San Giovanni Fuorcivitas** F (daily 8am–noon and 5–6pm) adorned with an almost psychedelic green-and-white striped marble facade in Pisan style. The treasures inside include a pulpit created in 1270 by Fra Guglielmo da Pisa, a pupil of Nicola Pisano, a water stoup by Giovanni Pisano, and a touchingly

Pistoia's market is set up on the pretty Piazza della Sala.

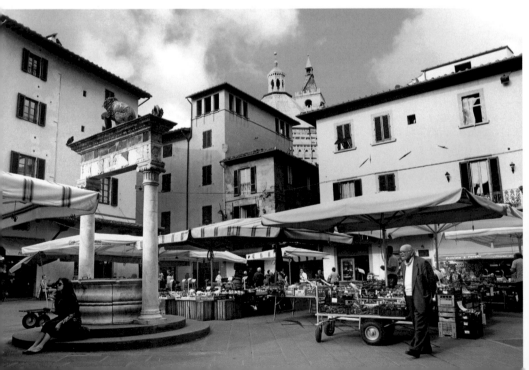

beautiful white-glazed terracotta of *The Visitation* by Luca della Robbia.

In Piazza Garibaldi, the monastery of **San Domenico** (Mon–Sat 7am–12.30pm, Sun 10am–1pm, 6.30–8pm) was insensitively restored after damage in World War II, but seek out the Renaissance tombs, cloisters and the colourful Benozzo Gozzoli fresco.

Opposite San Domenico is **Cappella del Tau** Ⓖ (Mon–Sat 8.15am–1.30pm). This former chapel is now an artistic monument, with darkly dramatic Gothic frescoes and vaulted ceilings, including a fine fresco of *The Fall*. The Palazzo del Tau is now home to the **Museo Marino Marini** (www.fondazione marinomarini.it; Tue–Sat 11am–6pm, Sun 2.30–7.30pm), named after Pistoia's most famous 20th-century son. Marino Marini (1901–80) made his native city an important bequest of his sculptures, etchings, prints and drawings based on the recurring theme of horses and riders.

Recover from an overdose of art and churches in a café on the Piazza della Sala, where the fruit-and-vegetable market is set out around an old well. At night the piazza is home to a number of lively bars. If still in need of light relief, browse the shops for embroidery, shoes, leather and jewellery on Via Cavour, Via Cino, Via Ateo Vannucci and Via d. Orafi. Ever earnest, Pistoia can even turn shopping into a dutiful museum experience. The city is famous for its embroidery, fine examples of which can be seen in the **Museo del Ricamo**, set in the Palazzo Rospigliosi (via Ripa del Sale 3; Tue–Thu 10am–1pm, Fri–Sat 10am–1pm and 3–6pm; free).

Alternatively, consider visiting **Pistoia Zoo**, which is set in a pine forest in Via Pieve a Celle about 5km (3 miles) outside town (www.zoodipistoia.it; daily 9.30am–5pm).

From Pistoia, clear your head in the mountains, going via **San Marcello Pistoiese**, the main town, traditional **Cutigliano**, and the lofty, all-year-round resort of **Abetone** Ⓗ, which is only 90 minutes' drive from Pistoia (see box).

Pistoia's Cattedrale di San Zeno and campanile, built in the 12th century.

Ⓞ MOUNTAIN PURSUITS

The drive into the mountains north of Pistoia is stunningly beautiful, especially in autumn. But winter-sports enthusiasts will prefer it with a good covering of crisp snow. The main town is **San Marcello Pistoiese**, traditionally known for the **Mongolfiera**, or hot-air balloon, launched on 8 September to mark the end of summer. Near San Marcello, at Mammiano, is a spectacular suspension footbridge, 220 metres (720ft) long, connecting to the road across the River Lima. **Cutigliano**, further down the valley, is surrounded by fir trees, but has limited skiing on its 13km (8 miles) of pistes, so serious skiers will prefer Abetone.

Abetone, set 1,400 metres (4,660ft) above sea level, is the most popular ski resort in the Apennines. It offers a wide range of pistes served by 25 ski lifts; has three ski schools and some fine new hotels, designed in "Swissified" mountain style. In the absence of good snow, the snow machines can cover 40km (25 miles) of slopes. In summer, Abetone makes an invigorating centre for climbing and walking expeditions in the surrounding pine and chestnut woods. *Rifugi*, or mountain shelters, are dotted around the area, often combining basic accommodation with an inn serving rustic fare.

VERSILIA, GARFAGNANA AND LUNIGIANA

Tuscany's northern corner is one of its wildest, loveliest, yet least explored areas – from the Versilia coast to a dramatic landscape of pine-covered mountains, craggy ravines, remote castellated villages and marble peaks. And all this with the famous beach resorts of Forte dei Marmi and Viareggio attached.

Versilia is renowned for its sociable beach resorts, which range from sophisticated Forte dei Marmi to laid-back Viareggio. But beyond the seaside bustle lies an elemental landscape that challenges popular perceptions of Chiantishire. The coastal lowlands of the Versilia give way to a dramatic hinterland of snowcapped mountains, terraced hillsides, deep gorges and mountain streams, populated by deer, wild boar, badgers, stone martens and wolves, not to mention walkers, rock climbers, cavers and canoeists. Tuscany's northernmost tip is an untamed rocky region known as the Lunigiana, bordered by the Apuan Alps in the south, Liguria in the west and Emilia to the east. Bordering it to the south is the Garfagnana, cut through by the Serchio River, which flows between the Apuan Alps and the Apennines. Together they make up one of the wildest, most beautiful, yet least explored parts of Tuscany.

VERSILIA

This coastal region lies west of Lucca, squeezed between the Apuan Alps in the east, and Lago di Massaciuccoli in the south. Michelangelo built a road from the marble quarries to transport the marble to waiting ships – and inadvertently created a summer playground. Once pine-covered, the coast

Fishing at Torre del Lago Puccini.

has succumbed to rampant development, but in the place of rustic charm it offers fine seafood restaurants, a sense of fun, and beach entertainment, Italian-style – all against the backdrop of the Apuan Alps. Whereas Forte dei Marmi is the resort for socialising and being seen, Viareggio is for everyone.

Viareggio ❶ is the oldest resort in the Versilia, and famous for its Carnival as well as for its beaches and boat-building tradition. The pre-Lent Carnival, one of the biggest and boldest in Italy, sees thematic floats spiced up with political

⊙ Main attractions

Viareggio
Torre del Lago Puccini
Pietrasanta
Forte dei Marmi
Castelnuovo di Garfagnana
Parco dell'Orecchiella
Barga
Carrara Marble Quarries
Pontrémoli

Map on page 148

satire. The resort enjoyed its heyday at the beginning of the 20th century, as testified by a handful of seafront cafés, beach clubs and historic hotels, such as the Plaza de Russie, originally built for the pre-Revolution Russian aristocracy. Today's Russian tycoons much prefer Forte dei Marmi, where their opulent villas nestle between the beaches and the Alps. Instead, unpretentious Viareggio offers pockets of genteel charm, seafood restaurants and leisurely cycle rides. The seafront boulevard, the **Passeggiata Margherita**, is at the heart of the action, especially since cycling has taken off on this stretch of the coast. For a stylish meal, seek out the Art Nouveau **Gran Caffè Margherita** (Viale Margherita 30) – Puccini's favourite.

On the downside, the beach clubs have a regimented feel: the sea can be reached only if you pay an entrance fee and wish to lie on a sunbed among rows of others, on sand carefully raked and flattened.

LAKESIDE RETREATS

An operatic pilgrimage just south of Viareggio takes you to **Torre del Lago Puccini ❷**, best reached through the deep Macchia Lucchese pine groves. Here, on **Lago di Massaciuccoli** is Giacomo Puccini's villa, where all his operas save *Turandot* were composed. This pleasant but over-popularised retreat was a peaceful backwater in Puccini's day. **Puccini's villa** (www.giacomopuccini.it; daily 10am–12.40pm and

3–6.20pm, July–Aug 10am–12.40pm and 3–8.20pm, closed Mon morning; guided tours) displays his musical instruments – as well as his guns. Puccini is buried in the nearby chapel. In August, a summer opera festival takes over the atmospheric lakeside stage beside Puccini's villa – the maestro would have approved.

The lake and neighbouring wetlands form a nature reserve and haven for birdlife – the **Parco Regionale di Migliarino-San Rossore-Massaciuccoli** (www.parcosanrossore.prg; tel: 050-539 111) is best explored on a boat trip around the lagoon.

SEASIDE RESORTS

Continuing north from Viareggio, the resorts fall into line in quick succession. **Lido di Camaiore** is slightly downmarket, but access to the beach is easier – and virtually free of pay-as-you-enter stretches of sand. From this part of the shore it is easy to reach **Camaiore** (to the Romans, Campus Maior), which is about 7km (4 miles) to the east.

Pietrasanta 3 is about 8km (5 miles) inland from the sea; its name, "Holy Stone", refers to the town's chief product, marble. This is the Tuscan centre for stone sculptors, who come here in droves to work the marble, ever since the days of Henry Moore and Joan Miró. As a result of all this artistic intensity, a fine white dust covers everything in Pietrasanta, even the wine glasses in the bars of the Piazza Carducci. Fortunately, there is some public sculpture on display, often presented to the town by the resident artists themselves.

This is the case with Colombian sculptor Fernando Botero, who lives in the resort for part of the year: "I like Pietrasanta, a beautiful town with a unique square, a cathedral worthy of a great city, and the Apuan Alps as a backdrop. What mountains, what greenery, what shade, what rivers, what fresh streams flow beneath chestnut trees and olive groves and orange orchards, all framed by marble quarries along the green." At the Enoteca Marcucci you can eat alongside sculptors and painters, feasting

Giacomo Puccini, composer of La Bohème, Tosca and Madama Butterfly, lived and died at Torre del Lago, where his villa is now a museum dedicated to his life and work.

The beach at Forte dei Marmi, with the Apuan Alps in the background.

Fresco by the 20th-century Colombian artist Botero, in Pietrasanta's church of Sant'Antonio.

on Tuscan *ribollita* soup, grilled meats and fine wines.

LUXURIOUS VILLAS

Further north, **Forte dei Marmi ❹** is the favoured retreat of Italian celebrities and captains of industry, from the Agnelli dynasty, who helped to launch this chic resort, to Giorgio Armani and celebrity tenor Andrea Bocelli. Forte *is* snooty and cosmopolitan but also charming and old-fashioned: the *dolce vita* is cultivated according to time-honoured tradition, despite the influx of a brasher set ready to pay a fortune to sit under the right beach awnings.

Forte dei Marmi grew up around a fort built in 1788 by Leopold I of Tuscany – these remains dominate the main square today. The surrounding sleek boutiques and cafés manage to combine cosmopolitan chic with a small-town atmosphere, enhanced by a lack of high-rise buildings. The parasol pines are still the tallest markers around, framing discreet villa gardens overflowing with bougainvillea.

While catering to an elite, with its exorbitantly priced beach clubs and tropical-style bars, Forte still retains something of the seductive mood that once captivated bohemian writers and artists, from Thomas Mann to Henry Moore. When the gently sloping beaches pall, today's celebrity visitors happily hop on to vintage bicycles to potter down the coast to Pietrasanta.

INTO THE MOUNTAINS

Given the mountainous nature of the interior, any inland trek along minor roads will inevitably be a leisurely trail along narrow, switchback roads, but with dramatic views and chance discoveries as compensation. This is "Slow Tuscany" so take Garfagnana and Lunigiana at a leisurely pace, ideally staying there – forays from the coast can also make a delightful diversion from the beach scene. If time is short, then bear in mind that it is quicker and easier to reach the area via Forte dei Marmi, Pietrasanta, Viareggio or Lucca than to travel as the crow flies.

⊘ TUSCANY'S BEST BEACHES

Tuscan beaches deliver both romance on the rocks and the regimented lines of beach umbrellas that most Italians consider to be beach-break heaven. In Forte dei Marmi, Versilia boasts the best-known beach resort for the chic set, while Viareggio remains the most popular big beach resort in Tuscany. The romantic, rocky cove of Cala Piccola, on Monte Argentario, arguably has the most aquamarine waters. Yachties will prefer to swim off chici Porto Santo Stefano and glitzy Porto Ercole. As for privacy and a back-to-nature remoteness, nothing beats Marina di Alberese, within the Parco della Maremma.

In the annual "beach charts", Tuscany has been triumphing for many years now. Every year Italian beaches get ranked by Green organisations, notably Legambiente's *Blue Guide*, which measures the cleanliness of the water, safety, quietness, eco-friendliness and sustainability. In 2017 a total of 342 Italian beaches passed the strict tests. Tuscany was judged to have an extremely clean coastline, with 19 beaches winning Legambiente's prestigious "blue flags", and it came second only to Liguria's 27 award-winning beaches.

In Versilia, the resorts awarded the best "blue flags" include chic Forte dei Marmi, Marina di Pietrasanta, Camaiore and bustling Viareggio. Near Pisa, family-friendly Tirrenia and Marina di Pisa are winners. Further south, on the Etruscan Riviera, the beaches do even better, with blue flags going among others to Castiglioncello, Vada, Marina di Bibbona, San Vincenzo, Cecina and Castagneto Carducci. In the Maremma, the best beaches include family-friendly Castiglione della Pescaia and most of the chic Monte Argentario peninsula's "Silver Coast".

All of the winning Tuscan beaches mentioned tend to be holidaymakers' firm favourites whose Green credentials are sound. (For more information see: www.bandierablu.org and www.legambienteturismo.it)

GARFAGNANA

Castelnuovo di Garfagnana ❺, about 64km (40 miles) north of Lucca, is a convenient stepping stone to the Garfagnana. This fortress town once controlled the route from Genoa to Lucca and Pisa, and was ruled by the Este dukes of Ferrara until Italian unification. The town suffered during World War II, even if the Duomo survived, as did the town walls, and the church of San Michele, containing a 14th-century *Madonna*.

Other highlights are the **Rocca**, or governor's palace, which is now the town hall, and the medieval fortress at the top of the hill. But beyond the sights is the sense of a Tuscany off the tourist trail. This is exemplified by Il Vecchio Mulino, an engaging Slow Food inn run by the cherubic Andrea. If you prove *"simpatico"*, Andrea will lead you through a tasting of local dishes.

SCENIC ROUTES

Northwest of Castelnuovo di Garfagnana, a scenic road runs from Poggio to Vaglia alongside the river Edron and **Lago di Vagli ❻**. The old stone houses and parish church in Vagli di Sotto are worth seeing, but the real draw is the partially submerged medieval village of **Fabbriche di Careggine**, covered by the creation of a dam in the 1940s. Sometimes seen peeking through the surface, the village is fully visible every 10 years when the lake is drained to service the dam. There are ambitious plans to construct a rope bridge over the lake and put a glass dome over the village to make it visible at all times, not only during maintenance periods.

The road winds its tortuous way through mountain scenery for about 18km (11 miles) to **San Pellegrino in Alpe ❼**, an ancient monastery housing the **Museo Etnografico Provinciale** (Apr–May Tue–Sun 10am–1pm and 2–4.30pm, June–Sept Tue–Sun 10am–1pm and 2–6.30pm, July–Aug open also Mon, Oct–Mar Tue–Sat 9.30am–1pm, Sun 10am–1pm and 2–4.30pm), whose display of peasant life is less compelling than the mountain views.

San Romano in Garfagnana offers a medieval castle and the stark peaks of the Alta Garfagnana, whose barren

◉ Tip

At almost every turn there are more medieval villages, more castles, more breathtaking views. One of the best ways to see this rich and varied region is to take the little train between Aulla and Lucca on its slow journey through the mountains.

Castelnuovo di Garfagnana.

beauty is best appreciated with a visit to the **Parco dell'Orecchiella** ❽ (see page 76), now part of the Parco-Tosco-Emiliano (www.parcoappennino.it). This wilderness, laced with waymarked trails and cycling paths, is framed by the grandiose peaks of the Apennines.

A scenic route to the coast from Castelnuovo di Garfagnana goes along the spectacular Túrrite Secca through the Parco Naturale delle Alpi Apuane, via the **Marmitte dei Giganti** ("Giants' Cooking Pots") – 23 huge hollows (20 metres/65ft in diameter) made by Ice Age glaciers – and through the Galleria del Cipollaio, a long tunnel carved out of the marble. From here the road winds down to Seravezza and Forte dei Marmi on the Versilia coast.

BARGA

To the south, pretty, arty, medieval **Barga** ❾ is by far the most beguiling town in the district. This quaint, surprisingly cosmopolitan place battles the problem of the rural exodus in its own way: many of those who left to make their fortunes abroad have returned, or keep a summer place here, including the Scots. The returning émigrés have brought a broader outlook to Barga, as seen in the kind of art galleries rarely found in a rural Tuscan outpost. The annual opera festival also brings the old town to life in July and August.

The sights, such as they are, are mostly about atmosphere, charm and stunning location, with lovely views at the very top. Leave your car outside the old city walls and head through the gate to explore the old town, with its narrow, winding streets lined with Florentine-style palazzi overlooked by the Romanesque Duomo, which commands wooded views of the Garfagnana from its hilltop position.

THE APUAN ALPS

From Barga, cross the Serchio valley to Gallicano. Just after the village, look out for signs to the 13th-century **Eremo di Calomini**, a gleaming white hermitage clinging to a rocky slope between the trees. Another 9km (5.5 miles) of steep and winding road brings

The colourful facades of Barga's backstreets.

you to **Fornovalasco** and the **Grotta del Vento** ❿ (Cave of the Wind; www.grotta delvento.com; daily 10am–6pm; guided tours only, departing on the hour), in the Apuan Alps, a labyrinthine system of tunnels, caves and secret passages full of dramatic stalactites and stalagmites, underground lakes and echoing chambers. There are guided tours of one, two and three hours, with the three-hour itinerary (10am and 2pm Apr–Oct) the most dramatic. The cave complex, one of over 1,300 in the Apuan Alps, is chilly, even in summer.

Bagni di Lucca ⓫, once a fashionable spa town, played host to Shelley, Byron and the Brownings, who all bathed in these warm, sulphurous waters. Today, the **Bagni Caldi**, the "hot baths", are scenically shabby, including an intriguing time-warp spa, with maze-like passages carved into the rock, and steam-vapour grottoes. Rugged walking country beckons, including the white-water gorge of **Orrido di Botri**, an authentic wilderness with a canyon.

From Bagni di Lucca, the road winds along the banks of the River Serchio to **Borgo a Mozzano**' and the splendid, lofty five-arched bridge of Ponte della Maddalena, also known as the **Ponte del Diavolo** – Devil's Bridge.

MASSA-CARRARA

Bordering on Liguria, the province of Massa-Carrara has only been part of Tuscany since the mid-19th century, and still feels out on a limb, particularly in Lunigiana. Many of the locals talk of "going to Tuscany" as if it were a foreign land, which it is, in some ways. While Massa-Carrara's main towns and resorts are disappointing, the marble trails make up for it, as does the jagged backdrop. Expect pine-covered mountains, craggy ravines, remote castellated villages – and the majestic marble peaks of the Apuan Alps glittering deceptively like snow in bright sunshine.

The towns of Massa and Carrara have both prospered from the marble trade, but their Faustian pact leaves them blighted by industrial eyesores. **Marina di Massa** is a popular resort, with fine wide, sandy beaches interspersed with groves of pine trees and

⊙ Fact

The impressive Ponte della Maddalena, which spans the Serchio just south of Bagni di Lucca, is also known as the Ponte del Diavolo, or Devil's Bridge. Legend has it that the bridge-builder appealed to the Devil for assistance. The Devil agreed, but in return demanded the soul of the first to cross the bridge. The shrewd builder kept his promise by sending a dog across.

⊙ SLOW FOOD IN 'SLOW TUSCANY'

Garfagnana is not just a hiking paradise. It is the domain of Slow Food. The best place to start a tasting session is in Andrea Bertucci's Osteria Il Vecchio Mulino (tel: 0583-62192), a rough-and-ready inn and a temple to Slow Food. Here, as in other welcoming Garfagnana villages, you can taste *biroldo*, the local blood sausage, and a protected Slow Food delicacy. The popularity of salami and blood sausages is also linked to the proximity of Emilia Romagna and its penchant for pork products.

The most typical ingredient is spelt *(farro)*, one of the oldest known grains, dating back to Roman times. While spelt has disappeared from most regions, it takes pride of place in Garfagnana dishes, and finds its way into spelt soup, made with sage, garlic, red wine and pork rind. Spelt is also used to make local bread, pasta and savoury tarts and pies. Whether roasted or boiled, chestnuts are also a feature of local cooking and are used in the so-called "paupers' bread". As in many mountain areas, polenta is a typical base for hearty rural dishes and is often combined with mushroom dishes. Polenta is also the base of chestnut cakes and in *castagnaccio*, the sweet local dessert. Instead, neighbouring Lunigiana specialises in *panigacci*, chestnut-flour pancakes cooked over an open fire and served with creamy cheese and home-cured meats.

To meet the cheese-makers and craftsmen, weavers and wine-makers, book a day's tour with Sapori & Saperi (tel: 339-7636 321, www.sapori-e-saperi.com). This small, local company runs food and craft adventures, introducing visitors to anything from ricotta-making to sourcing the best inns, the places that only insiders know. For instance you may engage in an exciting marzuolo truffle hunt with Riccardo and his hound and then taste the found truffles at Riccardo's house or learn how to bake potato bread in a wood-fired oven. These are culinary experiences, to meet Slow Food and wine producers and get a taste of their lives, far from the Chiantishire stereotypes.

a promenade of pretty pastel-shaded holiday villas. Ribbon development swallows up the port, from where ships carry marble all over the world.

Although somewhat lacklustre, **Massa** ⑫ has a well-preserved medieval centre, built by the dukes of Malaspina, who ruled Massa for three centuries, and were entombed in the cathedral. Massa is dominated by the magnificent Renaissance **Castello Malaspina di Massa** (Sat–Sun 3–7pm). Beyond the narrow old streets of the town, walk on up through leafy lanes past decaying villas dotted over the mountainside. The fortress walls provide marvellous views, and welded on to them is a graceful Renaissance palace, its delicate marble pillars providing a powerful contrast to the grim towers of the original castle.

The main evidence of the famous marble quarries in **Carrara** ⑬ is the river of white mud that flows through the town, which has a dusty, disaffected air about it. It is a working town, not a monument to marble; there are few fine marble statues to be seen, even in the Pisan-style Duomo.

If time is short, ignore the town centre in favour of a visit to the marble-working quarries looming above the city. From the Carrara roundabout, decorated with a lofty marble sculpture, follow signs to **Fantiscritti**. The Vara bridges signal your arrival and are a striking sight, either in full sunlight or in moonlight, when the moon intensifies the shadows and the marble glows. After your marble tour, the descent back to the coast is via hairpin bends, viaducts and gorges, and a crawl through the marble tunnel, once part of the "marble railway" linking the three main quarrying fields.

Finally, in a scruffy area off the Via Aurelia, north of Carrara, there is **Luni**, the original Roman settlement from which marble was shipped. Beyond the amphitheatre and museum, excavations have revealed columns, capitals, mosaic floors and tomb fragments.

Just over the Ligurian border is **Sarzana**, a thriving market town colonised by artists. There is a large market in the Piazza Matteotti, which is surrounded by Romanesque arcades sheltering smart little cafés.

*The Serchio River
at Bagni di Lucca.*

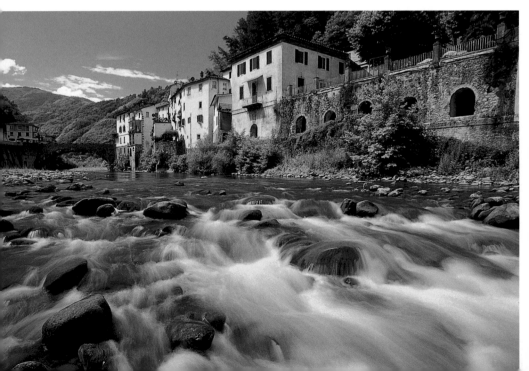

LUNIGIANA

Luni gave its name to **Lunigiana**, "the land of the moon", an inward-looking, virtually undiscovered part of Tuscany. Lunigiana has always been a main trading route, however, and its many castles were built by the powerful Malaspina family who controlled the region to extract tolls from pilgrims and merchants.

Lunigiana was in the front line of fighting at the end of World War II, and this has left its mark. Since then there has been inevitable rural depopulation, with many people emigrating to the United States. Now, an enlightened attitude to tourism promises new hope for the area, with villages and castles being restored and the roads in a good state of repair.

It is a mountainous region of steep, winding roads, deep wooded valleys and sparkling streams. On the lower slopes of the hills, vines and olives grow. Narrow valleys are dotted with tiny villages; higher up are forests of oak and the chestnut trees that have provided a staple of the local diet for centuries, and

there are deer and wild boar *(cinghiale)* in abundance. The terrain sweeps from the River Magra valley to the profound silence of deep river gorges.

The region's Romanesque churches, medieval villages and castles also attract an arty community of outsiders, with some castles taken over by eclectic sculptors, or turned into cultural centres. The inhabitants are notoriously proud and insular, in rural areas still growing most of their own food, wine and olives, and regarding other produce with suspicion. The locals will even buy in grapes from the Chianti, to make the wine themselves rather than buy a ready-made product from "foreigners".

FORTIFIED VILLAGES

From Sarzana, **Fosdinovo** ⑭ is the first fortified village en route to Aulla. Its squares are shaded by chestnut trees, and the steep streets are dominated by the magnificent 13th-century Malaspina castle. It is one of the best-preserved castles in the region, despite wartime damage. The Germans had a command post here,

⊙ Tip

In August, one of the most important Italian antique markets, "La soffitta nelle strade" (the open-air attic), is held in Sarzana, and in August the Cittadella hosts the National Antique Exhibition.

Eremo di Calomini in the Apuan Alps.

The fortress at Fosdinovo is one of the region's best-preserved castles.

A Carrara marble quarry in the Garfagnana.

exploiting its superb strategic position with views from all sides. Networks of corridors and loggias reveal beautiful frescoed walls (www.castellodifosdinovo. it; May–Sept Wed–Mon guided tours at 11am, noon, 3.30pm, 4.30pm, 5.30pm and 6.30pm, Oct–Apr Sat 3pm, 4pm and 5pm, Sun 11am, noon, 3pm, 4pm and 5pm).

Aulla itself is the gateway to Lunigiana, where the rivers Magra and Taverone meet. The brooding 15th-century fortress was restored earlier last century by Montagu Brown, the British consul in Genoa.

Fivizzano ⓖ, a few kilometres east, is an attractive market town full of elegant Renaissance palaces. Nearby is the enchantingly restored castle of **Verrucola**, a fortified settlement on the banks of the river. Red-roofed houses cluster around the castle keep, with geraniums spilling from window boxes and gardens full of courgette, beans and tomatoes crammed right down to the river's edge.

To the northwest of Fivizzano is **Licciana Nardi** ⓰, a fortified town dating

from the 11th century. Much of the town wall is still visible, with narrow passageways running through immensely thick walls into the village. In the Piazza del Municipio, the imposing 16th-century castle dominates the square, and is joined to the graceful Baroque church by a small bridge.

Comano is an important base for walking and riding, and nearby is the Castello di Comano, a ruined, malevolent-looking tower surrounded by a tiny farming community, with ducks and chickens wandering the streets, and steep steps up to the tower.

At the end of the valley is **Camporaghena**, the last outpost before the Apennines, where there is a sad war memorial in the church. When German soldiers came hunting for escaped prisoners of war and partisans, the priest rang the church bell as a warning and was summarily shot for his brave deed.

A 16km (10-mile) drive south of Fivizzano brings you to **Equi Terme** ⓱, a popular, if sulphurous, spa resort, with a lovely walk through a gorge, to the vaulted caves called **Grotte di Equi** (tel: 338-581 4482; tours mid-June–mid-Sept daily, rest of the year by appointment), where the remains of paleolithic men, dogs and even lions and leopards were found.

THE MAGRA VALLEY

A string of pretty castles and villages lines the main route (SS62) up the Magra valley between Aulla and Pontrémoli.

Bagnone ⑱ is an attractive town of Renaissance palaces, shady arcades and a honeycomb of houses, arches and passageways leading down to the river bank. Nearby **Filetto** is a symmetrical, square-walled village where almost every street is linked by covered overhead passages or bridges. Originally a defensive structure, it is now quite cosy, with cats snoozing in corners and village women passing the time of day.

Sleepy **Pontrémoli** ⑲ gives a good flavour of the Lunigiana, offering some of Italy's finest honey and mushrooms, not to mention *testaroli*, the typical pancakes, served with local pesto or cheeses. There are rich medieval town houses, and the Church of the Annunziata has a 16th-century octagonal marble temple by Sansovino. The town was once divided in two to separate the warring factions of the Guelfs and Ghibellines, and the Castruccio fortress, built in 1332, similarly divides the town.

The hulking **Castello del Piagnaro** houses the **Museo delle Statue-Stele** (www.statuestele.org; daily June–July and Sept 10am–6.30pm, Aug 10am–7.30pm, Oct–May 9.30am–5.30pm) which reopened in 2015 after thorough restoration. The multimedia museum houses prehistoric statues or menhirs found in the area, the oldest of which date from 3,000 BC.

Don't leave town before sampling the local pastries in **Antica Pasticceria degli Svizzeri** (Piazza della Repubblica), a charming Art Nouveau café serving almond cake and *spongata*, a rich and tasty honeyed nut and raisin cake. The rustic specialities are low-key, quirky, old-world and engaging – much like Lunigiana itself.

Ruins of an aqueduct near Barga.

⊘ MARBLE MOUNTAINS

The fine-grained pure white marble for which Carrara is renowned has been quarried here since Roman times. Italian medieval churches are decorated with it, and it has supplied artists from Michelangelo to Henry Moore with raw material.

Marble is formed from limestone, hardened by great pressure and heat, and Carrara is still the world's single largest and most important source of the stone. About 200 of over a thousand original quarries are still functioning. They are scattered across three steep valleys: the Colonnata, Fantiscritti and Ravaccione. Here the villages cling to the mountainside that has been sliced away like a chunk of cheese. There are extraordinary views down into the quarries, where precarious-looking staircases are strung across the sides, and massive trucks trundle across the marble surface far below.

The best way to appreciate the majesty of the marble mountains and Carrara's "white gold" is to visit a couple of quarries and do a short marble tour, ideally at the **Fantiscritti historic quarries** that Michelangelo favoured. The master-sculptor apparently spent three years looking for just the right block of marble to make Pope Julius II's tomb and found it here.

The Ravaccione section of Fantiscritti pioneered quarrying in the heart of the mountain and now runs fascinating 40-minute guided tours into the mountain (daily Jan–Oct, times vary so check online; follow signs to Fantiscritti from Carrara, via Miseglia; tel: 339-765 7470; www.marmotour.com). The main chamber in this working quarry is cavernous and genuinely feels like a "marble cathedral" so it is no surprise that it has featured in glamorous Maserati and Lamborghini advertisements. During the tour a guide describes the techniques of cutting marble and presents the used equipment. Bear in mind that the temperature inside the cave is always about 15–17°C (59–62°F) so dress accordingly and wear sturdy shoes as well.

The top of the Leaning Tower of Pisa.

PISA AND THE ETRUSCAN RIVIERA

Beyond the iconic Leaning Tower and "Field of Miracles", Pisa province has much to offer, from spa centres to family-friendly beach resorts. Further south, unsung Livorno province offers Etruscan ruins, scenic coastal stretches, forgotten hill towns and great fish restaurants – but give Livorno itself a wide berth.

With barely enough Renaissance art to enliven an overcast beach holiday, Livorno should be on the defensive. However, the province is as varied as its famed fish soup, *cacciucco*. The ingredients, a little of everything in the right proportions, apply to Livorno's seascapes. Captured in moody canvases by the Tuscan Impressionists, the rocky northern coast is as dramatic as the southern coast is soothing. The mainland stretches from wild, marshy Maremma to the rugged, hilly interior, or the Elban mountains.

Instead, Pisa province, despite its spas and beach resorts, means only one thing in the public imagination. The Leaning Tower draws tourists to Pisa like a magnet, many of them pausing to appreciate the religious architecture, others to enjoy the glorious art and history of this Tuscan city. Once a thriving Roman port, Pisa's harbour had silted up in the 15th century, and it now stands on the Arno River, 10km (6 miles) from the coast. Great sea battles were fought during the Middle Ages, with the city-state of Pisa becoming first an ally then a rival of a number of other states, including Genoa, Lucca, Venice and Florence. At its height, Pisa's power extended to Sardinia, Corsica and the Balearic Islands. Trade with Muslim Spain, North Africa and Lebanon meant that

Pisa even had a kasbah district for Arab and Turkish merchants. Arabic numerals were introduced to Europe through Pisa, and the city's major architectural monuments – the Leaning Tower, the Duomo and Baptistery – show the clear influence of Islamic architecture.

Pisa ❶ is split in two by the gently curving River Arno, its steep stone banks coloured by floating green algae. Elegant 16th-century palazzi along the banks hide the dilapidated areas in the narrow alleys behind.

Main attractions

Campo dei Miracoli, Pisa
Torre Pendente, Pisa
Borgo Stretto Quarter, Pisa
Bagni di Pisa
Certosa di Pisa
Costa degli Etruschi
Castiglioncello
Bolgheri
Suvereto
Populonia

Maps on pages 160, 166

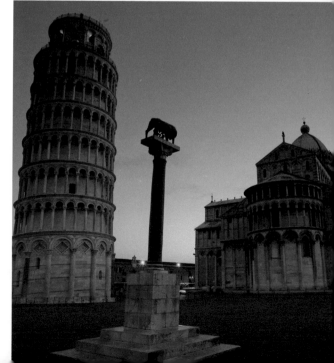

The Duomo in the "Field of Miracles".

Pisa

The city's trump card is the budget airlines' choice of Galileo Galilei airport as their regional hub; but the town doesn't want to be Tuscany's airport lounge – Pisa needs visitors to come for more than just a photo of the Tower. No city in the world is as closely associated with one single monument as Pisa is with her tower. Even during the 1990s, when the marble miracle was in architectural intensive care and out of bounds to visitors, most still failed to notice that there was life outside the Campo. But after centuries of Pisan twilight, there are signs of a resurgence, especially around the arcaded Borgo Stretto area and the Arno, an area aspiring to a Left Bank feel. Centred on the prestigious university, a large student presence brings energy to the area, as does the enthusiasm of Pisan cyclists, who are among the most dedicated in Tuscany.

Crossing the original city bridge, Ponte della Citadella, the Via Nicola Pisano leads to the **Campo dei Miracoli** (Field of Miracles), a green swathe of manicured grass in the northwestern corner of the city walls – with perhaps the most perfect assemblage of religious buildings in Tuscany. The two ticket offices at the entrances to Campo dei Miracoli (daily, 30 minutes before the sites' opening to 30 minutes before closing) sell tickets to all the sites.

THE LEANING TOWER

Visitors flock from all over the world to marvel at the phenomenon of the **Torre Pendente** Ⓐ (advance bookings www.opapisa.it; daily mid-June–Aug 8.30am–10pm, shorter hours rest of the year, hours vary greatly so check online; combined ticket; it may be possible to buy tickets on the day from the Campo dei Miracoli ticket offices; no entry to children under eight, and children between eight and 12 must be held by the hand). The best place to catch your first sight of the 12th-century Campanile is through the archway of the Porta Santa Maria, otherwise known as the Porta Nuova. When the sun is shining, the whiteness dazzles; when raining, it glistens.

Souvenir stalls near the Tower.

Ⓞ HALTING THE TILT

Pisa's Torre Pendente really does lean to a frightening degree, though less than it used to. The unstable subsoil that underlies the Piazza dei Miracoli has caused all the buildings to tilt and subside to dizzying effect. Just to the right of the entrance to the Tower is a date stone inscribed ANDMI MCLXXIII (standing for Anno Domini 1173), the year in which building work started on the Campanile. But work stopped at the third stage because the building was already collapsing. A century later, three more stages were added, deliberately constructed to tilt in the opposite direction, so the Tower has a decided kink as well as a tilt. By 1989, the Tower was leaning to such a perilous degree that it was in danger of collapse. It was promptly closed to the public, and an international team of engineers spent the next two decades in a battle to save it. During the first phase, completed in 2001, the tower was straightened by 40cms to avoid imminent collapse. In 1992 it was given a girdle of steel braces that were attached to a cunning counterweight system. A year later, the bells were silenced because of the damaging effect of vibration on the edifice. In 2011, work to stabilise the Leaning Tower was pronounced a success, and it was reopened to the public.

THE CATHEDRAL

The **Duomo** ⓑ (daily late Mar–early Oct 10am–8pm, shorter hours rest of the year, hours vary greatly so check online; free – if you only want to visit the cathedral, a free timed ticket can be collected at the ticket office), built between 1068 and 1118, is one of the major monuments of Italy. The beautiful white-marble facade, the model for the Pisan Romanesque style, is set with mosaics, inlaid marble and glass pieces.

The tomb of Buscheto, the architect of the building, is above eye level on the left of the facade, designed by Rainaldo and built in the early 12th century. The 16th-century bronze doors are surrounded by frames enlivened by animals. The main entrance to the Duomo was intended to be through the bronze transept doors of the Porta di San Ranieri, near the Tower. The work of Bonanno Pisano, dating from 1180, they are decorated with 24 New Testament vignettes, including such delightful scenes as shepherds in their conical caps playing their pipes to soothe the newborn child, and the figures of the Apostles under rows of swaying palm trees.

The rich complexity of the Cathedral interior is created by the forest of pillars rising to arches of banded white and grey stone, and the colourful mix of altar paintings and Cimabue's apsidal mosaic, from 1302. The beautiful marble pulpit by Giovanni Pisano (1301–11) is a masterpiece. Supported by figures representing prophets, sibyls and allegorical figures, its crowded and dramatic marble panels depict scenes from the *Life of Christ*.

Hanging from the westernmost arch of the great dome is Galileo's Lamp, so called because its pendulum movement is said to have inspired Galileo to discover the rotation of the Earth (in reality, the lamp wasn't here in Galileo's time).

THE BAPTISTERY

Across from the Rainaldo facade is the third building of the Duomo complex: the **Battistero** ⓒ (daily late Mar–early Oct 8am–8pm, shorter hours

Inside the Camposanto.

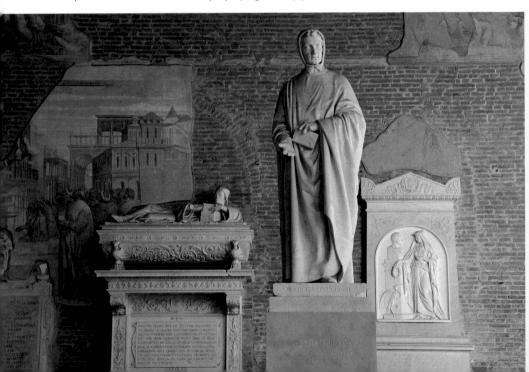

rest of the year, hours vary greatly so check online; combined ticket), the largest baptistery in Italy, with richly decorated exterior niches and statues of saints. The interior is far plainer, but it has one great treasure: Nicola Pisano's pulpit of 1260, carved with scenes from the *Life of Christ*, clearly influenced by Ancient Roman art (the source for which we shall see next, in the Camposanto). Mary, for example, has the long neck, veil and ringlets typical of middle-aged matrons in Roman portraiture. You may be lucky enough during your visit to hear one of the attendants demonstrate the Baptistery's remarkable acoustics. As four or more individual notes are sung, the long echo allows them to build up to a complete chord that rings eerily round the dome.

CAMPOSANTO

The fourth element of the Duomo group is the **Camposanto D** (daily mid-June–Aug 8.30am–10pm, shorter hours rest of the year, hours vary greatly so check online;

combined ticket), one of the world's most beautiful cemeteries. The graceful white-marble cloister is paved with the grave slabs of medieval Pisans, carved with coats of arms or tools of their trade. Roman sarcophagi, imported from the Holy Land and reused as coffins for wealthy Pisans, line the walls, carved with the mythological scenes that inspired the pulpits of Nicola and Giovanni Pisano. Frescoes damaged by incendiary bombs during World War II have been restored to their original positions. They include a grim series of images (1360–80) inspired by the Black Death, on the themes of the *Last Judgement* and the *Triumph of Death*.

On the opposite side of the Campo dei Miracoli is the **Museo delle Sinopie E** (daily late Mar–early Oct 8am–8pm, shorter hours rest of the year, hours vary greatly so check online; combined ticket), where you can learn more about the Camposanto frescoes and how they were created by laying down a sketch on the plaster

The Duomo and exterior of the Camposanto.

A relaxing way to see the city.

undercoat using red paint (called *sinopia* because the pigment came from Sinope on the Black Sea). When the final thin layer of white plaster was applied, the *sinopia* sketch showed through and guided the artists as they completed the fresco in full colour.

The fire that followed the bombing of the Camposanto destroyed some of the frescoes and left the others in so precarious a condition that it was necessary to remove them – but that was how the immense *sinopie* lying beneath the frescoes came to light and were salvaged, and are now carefully restored.

THE CATHEDRAL MUSEUM

The final piece of the jigsaw is the **Museo dell'Opera del Duomo** (closed for restoration at the time of writing) – the Cathedral Museum. Room 1 contains casts of the foundation stones of each of the buildings and a chronology, which begins in 1064 with the start of work on the Cathedral, followed by the Baptistery in 1154, the Campanile in 1173, and the Camposanto a century later, in 1277. This short burst of fireworks was followed by swift decline as the city's harbour silted up. (Recent excavations have revealed Roman and medieval boats, complete with cargoes, preserved in the water-logged silt, now exhibited in the maritime museum). By 1406, the city had been conquered by Florence and was about to be eclipsed culturally by that city's dogged determination to build even bigger and bolder monuments.

The museum is packed with 12th–15th-century sculptures and paintings: Giovanni Pisano's ivory *Virgin and Child* (1299) is one of the highlights, using the natural shape of the ivory tusk to give the Virgin her naturalistic stance. There are models to show the construction techniques used to build the domed Baptistery, and to explain the marble-inlay technique used to give all the buildings their intricate exterior decoration. Best of all, the rooms of the museum open out on to a quiet shady cloister, with a spectacular view of the Leaning Tower and the Cathedral.

⊘ THE PISAN PARADOX

Since the glory days of the "Field of Miracles", some critics feel that Pisa has rested on its laurels, overwhelmed by the burden of its great history. It is as if, after pouring all its creative genius into one square, Pisa then slumbered for the next 500 years. Nor does it help that the Leaning Tower is so iconic that most visitors to the city see virtually nothing else.

There are no easy solutions because Pisa, unlike its Tuscan rivals, has no real centre. The Field of Miracles is set on the northern edge of the city, thus distorting the geography of tourism. Pisans themselves set great store by the River Arno as a dividing line, and a defining line, between different districts. But, unfortunately, much of the river is nondescript, with the Lungarno presenting a procession of blank, ochre facades that all merge into one another, matched by an equally unappealing and muddy-coloured river.

Pisa is not picturesque, and, for outsiders, simply doesn't tug the heartstrings like many other towns and cities in Tuscany. But there is a warmer side to the city. On the north bank, Piazza delle Vettovaglie welcomes a bustling daily market, while the neighbouring arcaded Borgo Stretto is the most beguiling place for a coffee.

Visitors can best appreciate the Pisan sense of belonging at one of the heartfelt festivals held in the city, such as the Gioco del Ponte, the medieval tug-of-war fought on the Ponte di Mezzo on the last Sunday of June. During this festival, the Arno comes alive with boat races between Tramontana (north of the Arno) and Mezzogiorno (south of the river). Also in June are the celebrations in honour of St Ranieri, the city's patron saint. Known as the Luminaria, the night before the medieval regatta is a mesmerising festival that sees the banks of the Arno and the Leaning Tower bathed in candlelight.

In September the Duomo in the Piazza dei Miracoli hosts numerous events held as part of the prestigious Anima Mundi International Festival of Sacred Music. And November sees the Pisa Vini in the city's convent of Santa Croce; the festival celebrates the production of wine in the province of Pisa and features fine vintage wine and gourmet food tastings.

NEW LIFE IN THE OLD TOWN

Students often congregate on the **Piazza dei Cavalieri** , one of the most attractive squares in the city. This was the centre of activity in the Pisan Republic. It was in one of the towers of the Palazzo dell'Orologio (the building with the clock to the north of the square) – so we learn from Dante's *Inferno* – that Count Ugolino, wrongly convicted of treason in 1284, was left to starve to death with his sons.

The square is named after the order of knights *(cavalieri)* founded by Cosimo I (1561), to fight the Turks in the Mediterranean. The duke gave its members the Palazzo della Carovana, the former council chambers of the Pisan Commune. The magnificent *sgraffito* decoration (floral patterns, coats of arms, symbols) and the next-door church of **Santo Stefano dei Cavalieri** (daily, erratic opening times) were based on plans by Vasari (1511–74). In 1606 Giovanni de' Medici added the marble facade and placed the knights' emblem above the great doorway. Displayed inside are trophies and spoils of war from Pisan naval victories against the Ottomans. Just south, you can dine in an authentic early 13th-century tower-house in the **Osteria dei Cavalieri** (Via San Frediano 16; tel: 050-580 858; www.osteriacavalieri.pisa.it). This atmospheric "chivalric" inn serves hearty local dishes such as T-bone steak, cheese pie or beef with beans.

The lively warren of alleyways and shopping streets between the square and the Arno is known as the **Borgo Stretto quarter** and is the most elegant part of town. Lined with cafés and shops, the arcaded Borgo Stretto opens out at Piazza Garibaldi and the Ponte di Mezzo. Call into the **Pasticceria Federico Salza** (Borgo Stretto 46), the city's most delectable bar and pastry shop, set under the porticoes. It makes a tempting place for a light lunch, an afternoon coffee and cake, or evening cocktails.

Off the southern end of the Borgo Stretto, the arcaded **Piazza delle Vettovaglie** market area has been revamped, making it the haunt of Pisa University students who are drawn

Fact

Pisa's Museo di San Matteo displays a collection of antique armour used in the Gioco del Ponte medieval tug-of-war festival held on the last Sunday in June. The displays include breastplates, helmets and other pieces dating from the 15th and 16th centuries.

Attractive Piazza dei Cavalieri.

The Etruscan Riviera

0   5 km
0   5 miles

to the reasonably priced bars. Jus
beyond, the Arno River, with its boa
tours and festivals, is being touted a:
the Pisan "Left Bank".

BANKS OF THE ARNO

To the west, some distance along the
river, the **Museo delle Navi Antiche d**
Pisa ❶ (Museum of the Ancient Ships
of Pisa; Lungarno Simonelli; guidec
visits by advanced booking; tel: 055-
5520 407) in the Medici Arsenale, the
old Medici shipyards, houses the finds
from the excavation of Pisa's ancient
port, buried by silt in the 15th century
In 1998, workers expanding the railway
station stumbled on the site, where the
remains of 30 Ancient Roman ships
and their contents (including the skeleton of a sailor) have been unearthed
These docklands, where the sea met
the Arno, were probably composed of
marshy flatlands and lagoon, very similar to Venice. Proclaimed a "marine
Pompeii", excavations and restorations
were completed in 2016. Two of the
eight planned halls of this remarkable
museum opened in December 2016 but
the museum's construction was still in
progress at the time of writing.

On the opposite bank of the Arno,
across the Ponte Solferino, stands the
church of **Santa Maria della Spina** ❶
(open to the public only occasionally).
Don't worry if it is closed when you
visit: it is the vivacious exterior that is
the most important feature, a *tour de*
force of Gothic pinnacles and niches,
crowded with statues of saints carved
by members of the Pisano family from
1230. Back in the days when Pisa was
a port, before its harbour silted up,
seafarers came to pray here before
setting sail.

The chapel once guarded what was
believed to be a thorn (*spina*) from the
"crown" of Jesus, but that relic, plus
the original statues, is now housed
downriver, in the **Museo Nazionale**
di San Matteo ❶ (Lungarno Mediceo; Tue–Sat 8.30am–7.30pm, Sun

8.30am–1.30pm). Set in rooms around the cloister of a medieval church, the museum contains such treasures as Masaccio's *St Paul* (1426), a contemplative man with a high brow, hooked nose and patriarchal beard; Donatello's bust reliquary for San Rossore; and a whole room of glowing Renaissance paintings by artists of the calibre of Gozzoli and Ghirlandaio.

PISAN COUNTRY RETREATS

The Pisan countryside ranges from pretty to unprepossessing, with the magnificent Certosa di Pisa the main attraction, along with several charming spa resorts. Midway between Pisa and Lucca, at the foot of the Pisan mountains, is the charmingly faded spa town of **San Giuliano Terme ②**. Olives, chestnuts and pines grow in the surrounding fertile countryside, wild horses roam the hills and ruins dot the valleys. San Giuliano is renowned for the curative powers of its thermal springs. Here, the best place to try out a thermal spa treatment, or simply indulge in some pampering, is the atmospheric **Bagni di Pisa** spa resort, which, in its heyday, played host to the Romantic poets. These spa waters have been famous since Roman times, and are especially good for the treatment of rheumatism and arthritis. Montaigne, Byron and Shelley were among famous Grand Tourists.

Set in lush countryside, near Calci, 10km (6 miles) east of Pisa, stands the imposing **Certosa di Pisa ③** (Tue–Sat 8.30am–6.30pm, Sun 8.30am–12.30pm, guided tours only; part of the complex closed for restoration). The Charterhouse of Pisa was founded in 1366, but the finishing touches were only put to this Carthusian monastery in the early 18th century. The Carthusians were one of the strict new orders who believed that the increasing prosperity of the Cluniac orders was accompanied by a decline in religious observance. Their architecture reflected this stance; the monks lived in separate cells within a main enclosure. The centre of monastic life was the Great Cloister, of which the Certosa di Pisa has a particularly fine example. Work

⊙ Fact

The original spa building at Casciana Terme was designed in 1870 by Poggi, but a direct hit from a bomb in World War II left only the facade and the hall intact. In 1968 the spa was completely rebuilt around the remains of the original structure.

The Arno cuts Pisa in two.

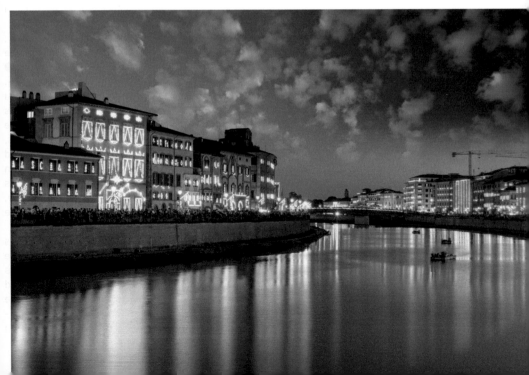

on the frescoes of the church walls began in 1701, and in 1718 workmen from Carrara carved the marble and renovated the church facade. In 1981 a part of the Charterhouse was allotted to the University of Pisa to house the **Museo della Storia Naturale** (June–Sept daily 10am–8pm, Oct–May Mon–Sat 9am–7pm, Sun 9am–8pm).

Lined with plane trees, the route to **Cascina** ❹ passes fields of sunflowers, grapevines and maize. Cascina is proud of its solid stone walls, dating from 1142, which are depicted in Vasari's energetic painting of the *Battle of Cascina*, now hanging in the Palazzo Vecchio in Florence. On Corso Matteotti, the tiny chapel of **Suore di Carmelitane di Santa Teresa**, on the left, has beautifully detailed frescoes. The nearby church of the saints Casciano and Giovanni, *c*.970, is a graceful building with a simple interior.

Casciana Terme ❺, less than 40km (25 miles) southeast from Pisa, is surrounded by vineyards, olive groves and peach orchards. The appeal of the area lies in the gentle hills, mild climate, leisurely pace of life – and the spa culture. Casciana is a dedicated spa town, with its thermal waters attracting both earnest Italians "taking the cure" and holiday-makers seeking a break. At certain times, you can even try a "spa by night" experience, including a light dinner and drinks (tel: 0587-644 61; www.termedicasciana.it).

THE PISAN COAST

The pretty road from Pisa to the coast pauses here and there at railway crossings as it follows the Arno to the sea. About 6km (4 miles) southwest of Pisa, it passes **San Piero a Grado**, a magnificent basilica that would once have overlooked the sea. Legend has it that this is the spot where St Peter first set foot on Italian soil. The fresco cycle in the nave shows scenes from the Apostle's life.

The road reaches the sea at **Bocca d'Arno**, with moody views of fishing nets. Just south, the pleasant resort of **Marina di Pisa** makes a good stop for a stroll along the café-lined

A view of Fortezza Vecchia.

promenade. On a clear day, the islands of Gorgona and Capraia can be made out in the distance.

At **Tirrenia** ❻, 5km (3 miles) further down the coast, lies a stretch of Mediterranean pine forest – the one place where building has been prohibited. The trees act as a natural barrier against the *libeccio*, a strong southwesterly wind, reducing it to a light, scented breeze of pine and juniper that cools the air on hot summer days. Despite the appeal of this patch of coast, Tirrenia is a pleasant but underwhelming resort. The seafront stretch beyond the sand dunes is currently undergoing major development, with new residential areas, restaurants and a shopping and entertainment complex all centred on **Calambrone**. While rather charmless compared with more upmarket Forte dei Marmi or Marina di Pietrasanta, this emerging holiday resort is perfect for families looking for an active holiday, centred on the beach. Reasonably priced restaurants line the main route, while golf, tennis, horse riding, fishing, windsurfing,

sailing and rowing are readily available. Each year colourful regattas and boat races are held, and the training centre for the Italian National Olympics is in Tirrenia.

LIVORNO CITY

The central coastal area of Tuscany is dominated by the busy comings and goings at the port of **Livorno** ❼, just south of Pisa. This is the Tuscan gateway to the sea and a city crossed by canals. As Italy's second-largest port after Genoa, it owes its existence to the silting up of Pisa in the 15th century; the Livornese joke that, unlike their rivals, the Pisans, they will never be so careless as to let the sea slip away from them. The rivalry between Pisans and Livornese is legendary and very much alive today. There is a saying in Livorno: *"Meglio un morto in casa che un Pisano all'uscio"* – "It is better to have a dead body in your house than a Pisan on the doorstep."

In 1421 the Florentines paid the Genoese 100,000 florins for Livorno, a vast sum for such a mosquito- and

> ⊙ **Tip**
>
> Trips to the sleepy volcanic island of Capraia are worth considering if you want to discover somewhere new. It's 64km (40 miles) off the coast of Livorno – a 2.5-hour boat ride from the port. Ferry services are run by Toremar (www.toremar.it). For more information on the seven islands of the Tuscan Archipelago, see page 179.

Early morning fish market in Livorno port.

hence malaria-plagued village. It was the enlightened Cosimo I who, in 1575, transformed Livorno into the greatest Medicean port. Cosmopolitan salons and elegant avenues made it a fashionable port of call for the Grand Tourists. But after 80 bombing raids in World War II, Livorno resembles a modern necropolis. Visitors soon realise that the city lives on commerce, not tourism. Few linger unless en route to the islands or the hills, but attractions there are. The Medicean port is unchanged. The red-brick **Fortezza Vecchia** is a patchwork of Livornese history, including Roman remains, medieval Pisan walls and a Romanesque tower. The **Fortezza Nuova**, built in 1590, completed the ambitious Medici fortifications. The murky canals encircling it once led to Pisa. Now restored, the New Fortress is landscaped as a park and is a popular spot for children's romps and summer festivals. The other main attraction is neighbouring **Piccola Venezia**, dubbed "Little Venice" for its network of quiet canals.

Rocky Castiglioncello.

The area of the port of Pisa and the **Navicelli canal**, between Pisa and Livorno, is currently undergoing a major development which will hopefully spur the revival of the Mediterranean short sea shipping. The canal through the marshes was opened in 1575 by the Medici, but fell into disuse and was partly destroyed in World War II. In the meantime, you can still do day and evening cruises on the Arno (contact Pisa tourist office, tel: 050-550 100).

THE ETRUSCAN RIVIERA

South of here is the area known as the Maremma Pisana – once a mosquito-infested swampland but now transformed – and the **Costa degli Etruschi**, the Etruscan Riviera. This is clever branding, even if it does conjure up incongruous images of beady-eyed Etruscans lounging under beach umbrellas, much as they do on their funerary urns.

Over 60 miles of coastline, Etruscan sites, medieval villages, hills, valleys and wild woods make this lesser-known part of Tuscany unique. The coast is no architectural desert: a coastline of Pisan watchtowers and Medicean fortresses hides the occasional Roman villa or Etruscan necropolis.

The high coastal road from **Ardenza** ⑧ to Castiglioncello offers some delightful scenic stretches as it hugs the cliffs' edge and dips in and out of tunnels. Ardenza, a fashionable resort flanked by palms and Art Nouveau villas, was home to what the Livornese called "Leghorn's British Factory". The sea views and the dramatic summer storms revived Shelley enough to enable him to write his famous *Ode to a Skylark*. Byron, also devoted to Ardenza, was a frequent visitor.

The coast becomes progressively more rugged, and the road winds past Medici castles, watchtowers and follies. Castello del Boccale, encircled by gulls and rocky paths to the shore, is a Medicean fort converted into a private villa. At **Calafuria**, an isolated Medicean tower and distorted rock formations provided the Italian Impressionist painters with a dramatic setting. After Romito, the coastline becomes wild and wooded. As the small resort of **Quercianella** comes into view, pine woods run down to the water's edge; small coves, shingle beaches and a narrow harbour vie for space.

Quercianella is followed by the popular rocky resort of **Castiglioncello** ⑨, which the Livornese seem to favour above the monotonous stretches of sand below Cecina. The Livornese also know that there are sandy bays tucked into the rocks. Cosimo's fort, built on the pine-clad promontory, was designed to keep pirates at bay, but since the 19th century it attracted all the great Italian Impressionists. In the 1930s, Castiglioncello was also very popular with film stars. It may not have much cachet today, but it's nice enough for a dip and a cheap lunch at one of the dockside bars.

For sightings of flamingos sheltering under umbrella pines, the **Parco Naturale di Rimigliano**, hugging the coast between San Vincenzo and Populonia, is where to head.

For a fabulous fish lunch with a sea view, this truck stop on the coastal road a few kilometres north of Quercianella is worth knowing about.

☉ TUSCANY BY TRAIN

The region abounds in scenic rail trips so do consider doing the occasional leg by train, including sampling the minor branch lines. These routes are not designed for speed but for savouring the countryside.

For arty sights and romantic scenery, the Pisa to Orvieto route is perhaps the finest introduction to the Tuscan and Umbrian landscape, which is dotted with hill towns and scenery depicted by the Renaissance masters. The route travels through the heart of Tuscany, revealing green hills striped with olive groves and vineyards, as well as historic towns studded with Renaissance art and architecture. Domesticated Tuscany melds with the hazy spirituality of Umbria's green hills. A variant on this rewarding route could take you from Pisa to Lucca, then Florence, Siena, Chiusi and possibly on to Orvieto.

Also from Pisa, you can follow the coastal route all the way to Liguria, stopping off at the oldest resort in Versilia, Viareggio, for the beach and to sip a coffee at one of the seaside cafés. And at Massa di Carrara you can visit the striking marble quarries of Fantiscritti, where Michelangelo himself came back in the day in search of the best marble for his sculptures. From Chiusi, whose cathedral bell tower rewards visitors with breathtaking views of the Val d'Orcia, there is a delightful branch line that takes you on a plucky two-carriage train to sleepy Asciano, Siena and Buonconvento, with views of sunflowers, Montalcino shimmering in the distance, and a Sienese landscape straight out of a fresco by Lorenzetti. On the Pisa–Florence railway line the major stop is Pontedera, a hub from where many smaller localities in the Pisa province can be more easily reached by bus than from Pisa. The town is home to Piaggio, makers of the famous Vespa scooters, and the Piaggio Museum is worth a visit.

Lucca also makes a lovely rail base, with good onward services to Pisa (25 minutes), Viareggio (20 minutes) and Florence (1 hour 20 minutes). From Florence, the scenic journey into Garfagnana is also recommended; its picturesque mountains and valleys are still little affected by tourism and the town itself offers a rewarding escape from the hustle and bustle of Tuscany's major cities. Welcome to Slow Tuscany. Many of the best itineraries and rail holidays can be planned through Railbookers (www.railbookers.com).

The church of Santa Maria della Pietà in the pretty inland village of Bibbona.

Beach at Golfo di Baratti, near Populonia.

RURAL HINTERLAND

But for a rewarding wine-tasting foray, leave the coast at **Cecina** and take the inland road to higgledy-piggledy **Bibbona** and wine-growing Bolgheri via **Casale Marittimo**. Quiet lanes trace through marshy countryside dotted with red farmhouses and occasional herds of placid white Maremman cattle, and spiral up into the hills.

The sun-baked hill town of Casale Marittimo offers views across the Livorno coast and out to Elba. Just south, medieval **Bolgheri** ⑩ is a pocket of the Maremma fashionable for the so-called Super Tuscans, wines such as Sassicaia, Ornellaia and Antinori Solaia. To many wine experts, this is the future of Tuscan wine-making. Continue winding south through **Castagneto Carducci**, where the flatness is broken by low farmhouses, olive trees and the village vineyards, part of the wine trail bordering the Etruscan Riviera.

Sassetta, a bird's nest of a *borgo*, with a medieval castle, waits in the hills slightly further south. From here a winding road through olive groves, oleanders and woodland leads to **Suvereto** ⑪ , another well-preserved village, with a crenellated town hall, an early Romanesque church, and a steep ascent through a rabbit warren of covered passageways. Many buildings are vividly decorated with the local red, brown or grey variegated marble, which has been quarried since medieval times. Suvereto's urban design, based on rising concentric circles, is simple but effective: each level corresponds to a street, from the church to the towering castle above. The sedate village pours on to the streets for the evening *passeggiata* and, in season, for the *sagra del cinghiale*, a wild-boar feast combining food and folklore. This area is **Val di Cornia**, an enchanting region of gently wooded hills, hot springs, lush valleys and old quarries.

The winding route south, towards the coast, leads to **Campiglia Marittima**, a hilly market and mining town known for its imposing castle and rustic cuisine based on sausages, chestnut polenta and bean soups.

POPULONIA

If the coast beckons, San Vicenzo's metallic sands and monotonous strip of beach bungalows can be sacrificed to **Populonia** ⑫, and the scenic ruins of the last of the 12 Etruscan cities to be founded, located behind the sweep of Baratti Bay (July–Aug daily 9.30am–7.30pm, Sept shorter hours). The Etruscans, very considerately, had themselves buried beside a pine-fringed beach, reason enough to visit the only Etruscan city built on the coast. The ancient city was divided into two parts: the acropolis – the religious centre clustered high around the village – and the maritime and industrial centre around the bay. The necropolises cover the slopes that sit between the two centres.

Thanks to its proximity to Elba and to the metal-bearing Campigliese hills, Populonia became a rich industrial city. While Elban iron ore was smelted and then traded within the Etruscan League, minerals from Campiglia were shipped to Corsica, Sardinia and France. In the ancient "industrial zone", excavations have uncovered a blast furnace and sophisticated metal-working equipment dating back to the 6th century BC. Foreign slave labour was used to dig water channels, operate the furnace and mint coins. In the 6th century BC, Populonia was the first Etruscan city to mint gold, silver and bronze coins. Sadly, many tombs lie buried or collapsed under the weight of ancient slag heaps. Before setting out, check the Populonia archaeological park online (www.parchivaldicornia.it) and also find time for the medieval village of Populonia. If catching a ferry to Elba from gritty Piombino, call in at the archaeological museum there, which displays the best Etruscan finds from Populonia (Piazza della Cittadella; www.parchivaldicornia.it; erratic opening hours, check the website).

From Populonia there are smoky views of **Piombino**, a grimy, gritty city, where you can catch a ferry to **Elba** (see page 175). Best seen on foot, Piombino's genteel, down-at-heel charm lingers on in quiet squares and Art Deco bars.

Relaxing on the rocky coast south of Livorno.

Fisherman with fish trap, Marciana Marina.

ISOLA D'ELBA

Every August, the beaches of "Tuscany's island" are invaded by sun-worshipping Italians. For the rest of the year, its rocky roads, wooded slopes and sandy bays belong to intrepid tourists who make the short sea crossing in search of unspoilt nature, crystal-clear waters, Napoleonic landmarks and good food and wine.

Known to the Etruscans as Ilva ("Iron") and to the Greeks as Aethalia ("Soot Island"), Elba has exploited its mineral wealth for more than 3,000 years. As the European powers occasionally took an interest in the island's attractive strategic position, waves of Romans, Pisans and Genoese were followed by Spanish, Turkish and French invasions. In 1548, the powerful and vainglorious Medici duke, Cosimo I, fortified the capital and named it Cosmopolis, after himself. His great military architect, Giovanni Camerini, designed the star-shaped defensive system and the two Medicean forts, Forte della Stella and Forte Falcone, to keep the Saracens at bay. Today, Portoferraio's horseshoe harbour, backed by a cluster of sun-baked pastel houses, is more welcoming than forbidding, as ferries, fishing boats, yachts and pleasure cruisers glide in and out of its embrace.

NAPOLEON'S ELBA

Portoferraio ❶ is inextricably linked to that other great imperialist, Napoleon Bonaparte. He made his official home in two converted windmills above the charming Forte della Stella. Under the terms of the Congress of Vienna in 1814, Elba became a principality of the fallen sovereign. Napoleon's great empire shrank to his faithful "old guard", pragmatic mother and

libertine sister Pauline. Most Elbans were proud to have him improve the administration, build new roads, develop the mines and expand the island's fleet. The foreign commissioners, however, rightly feared that the "Eagle" might spread its wings: after nine months, Napoleon flew, with the connivance of the Elbans. He escaped with no less than 1,000 troops, the Elbans' affection, his sister's diamond necklace and his mother's curt blessing: "Go and fulfil your destiny." His **Palazzina dei Mulini** (late Mar–Oct

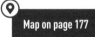

⊘ Main attractions
Palazzina dei Mulini
Marciana Marina
Marciana Alta
Monte Capanne
Capo Sant'Andrea
Capoliveri
Porto Azzurro
Rio Marina

📍 **Map on page 177**

The rugged coastline of Isola d'Elba.

Fishing boat on Elba.

Mon, Wed–Sat 8.30am–7.30pm, Sun 8.30am–1.30pm, Nov–late Mar Mon, Wed–Sun 8.30am–1.30pm) was lined with silver and books from Fontainebleau, and furniture from his sister Elisa's house in Piombino. Most of its charm lies in the period furnishings and Italianate gardens.

The 17th-century Misericordia church on the Via Napoleone, a broad stairway nearby, displays one of Napoleon's bronze death-masks.

A few kilometres inland from Portoferraio is the emperor's country residence, **San Martino** (late Mar–Oct Tue–Sat 8.30am–7.30pm, Sun 8.30am–1.30pm, Nov–late Mar Tue–Sun 8.30am–1.30pm, joint ticket with the Palazzina), purchased with one of Pauline's handy diamond necklaces. The villa's classical facade was installed in 1851 by the Russian emigré Prince Demidoff. However, after the grand cypress-lined avenue and grandiose facade, the house itself seems a spartan affair. In one room, Napoleon's Nile campaigns of 1798–9 are recalled in the Egyptian-style frescoes, painted in 1814. In another, his tiny bed is a reminder of just how short he was. Information on the emperor's life and times is thin on the ground here (though souvenir stands are not), but the fine garden, shaded by evergreen oaks and terraced vineyards, is pleasant to stroll through.

PORTOFERRAIO TO MARCIANA

The scenic drive westward from Portoferraio to Marciana Marina passes a number of popular beaches. **Le Ghiaie**, the nearest beach to the town, is noted for its multicoloured pebbles, but it's worth going the extra distance to **Capo d'Enfola** ❷. The road to the cape ends at Porto di Sansone, a tiny isthmus flanked by two small pebble beaches and a couple of restaurants. Formerly restricted for military use, the cape itself remains closed to traffic, but is popular among walkers. Viticcio is another pretty cove, but sand-seekers head for **La Biodola** ❸, considered

⊘ ELBA'S IRON HEART

Elba is a mineralogist's paradise and the island's metal heart creates a mysterious landscape that makes a lasting impression on most visitors. Its mineral wealth has been fully exploited since Etruscan times and continues to this day: the swords wielded by countless Roman legionaries were famously made from Elban iron. The very name of Elba, Ilva for the Etruscans, means "iron" and the name of the island's largest city, Portoferraio, means "iron port" in Italian.

In the Copper Age, colonisers mined copper, followed by the making of bronze and the mining of iron by Etruscan and Greek settlers. While ruling Elba, Napoleon reorganised the iron mines and was a serious steward of the island. But the last mine closed in 1984, and since then the island's economic mainstays have instead been tourism, agriculture and fishing.

To the east of Portoferraio is the scar across Elba's iron heart, where most of the mines and forges were located. In the hills around Rio nell'Elba, signs of Etruscan mining camps can still be seen. Neighbouring Rio Marina, now home to the mineralogical museum and the Parco Minerario (Mineral Park of Elba Island), was the set-off point where the cargoes of metal

were shipped overseas. At the Parco Minerario (Apr–June, Sept–Oct 9.30am–12.30pm and 3.30–6.30pm, July–Aug 9.30am–12.30pm and 4.30–7.30pm), ardent rock hunters will feel in their element. The park offers trails on foot and by mountain bike in the Valle dei Mulini, excursions to the open-cast quarries in Rio Marina and Rio Albano and guided tours in Rio Marina. Their "Cercandoi Minerali" (Mineral Hunt) tour takes in a visit to a mining site where visitors can hunt for minerals (which they can take home) and their "Trekking in Miniera" (Trekking in the Mines) excursion tours several major mining sites.

Further south, in Capoliveri, the black, iron-bearing lodestone still plays havoc with the compasses aboard passing ships. In this eastern part of the island, colourful semi-precious stones abound, from green quartz to black onyx and pink or pale-green beryl. The proper mineral name for most gem tourmalines is, in fact, "Elbaite".

In the resorts and mineralogical museums throughout the island there are ample opportunities for picking up pieces of rock or clunky jewellery that are now the last link with Elba's mining past.

the chicest beach on Elba, dominated by expensive resort complexes filled with rich bronzed Florentines in Valentino swimwear. At La Biodola and **Procchio**, a more egalitarian paradise, the rocky ocean bottom means clear, sediment-free water.

Between Procchio and Marciana Marina is "La Paolina", an islet named after Napoleon's sister, whose passion for nude sunbathing would scandalise the natives.

Marciana Marina ❹ has evolved smoothly from fishing village to elegant resort, set amidst magnolias, palms and oleanders at the end of a long valley. The thin, pastel-coloured houses in the old quarter are reminiscent of those on the Ligurian coast. On 12 August the port explodes in a firework display to honour Santa Chiara, the patron saint.

Marciana Alta ❺, perched above, is Elba's best-preserved medieval town, where chestnut woods frame red-tiled rooftops, narrow alleys and the crumbling fortress. The local "Antiquarium" displays Etruscan sacred objects, Roman oil lamps and ivory statues found in shipwrecks.

TWIN PEAKS

From the foot of Marciana, a cable car, the **Cabinovia del Monte Capanne** (mid-Apr–June, Oct–Nov 10am–1pm and 2.20–5pm, July–Sept until 5.30pm) lurches over crags and chasms up to the summit of **Monte Capanne ❻**. When not misty, the views are all-encompassing. Even in high summer, this wooded mountain area is wonderfully quiet and breezy. Depending on the season, patches of orchids, snapdragons and helianthemums are as common as the cedars and chestnuts. Even the coastal vegetation is more exotic than in the east: eucalyptus and magnolia rather than vines or maquis.

The high road from Marciana to the south side of the island winds past the quiet, neglected village of **Poggio** to Monte Perone nature reserve (for a scenic walk on the mountain, stop off at Poggio and follow the waymarked trail), vineyards and the plains behind

Forno beach, on the Biodola Bay.

Cloud-covered Poggio.

Marina di Campo, the only part of the island flat enough for an airport.

THE "OTHER ELBA"

The northwestern corner of Elba is a protected area of wild, natural beauty, with granite cliffs, thick holm-oak and chestnut woods, and dense maquis. Dubbed the "Other Elba", this craggy corner attracts the active and eco-conscious. The sea here is ideal for snorkelling, diving and kayaking, while the mountains are exploited by mountain bikers, birdwatchers, trekkers and climbers. A long, winding road leads down past houses and hotels to **Capo Sant'Andrea ❼**, a tight bay with a small port protected from westerly winds by the surrounding cliffs. This is an ideal base for exploring the area, starting with the walk from Capo Sant'Andrea to the next bay at Cotoncello.

The coastal road from Sant'Andrea to Marina di Campo clings to the edge of the island, an exhilarating and occasionally heart-stopping drive. Wherever you see a cluster of parked cars, chances are there's a rocky cove

The pretty resort of Marciana Marina.

below, where those in the know gather to swim and sunbathe. This section of the coast is good for diving and snorkelling; most of the diving schools can be found in and around Pomonte.

As you round the southwestern corner, the first visible stretch of sand at **Fetovaia** comes into view – a pretty, child-friendly sweep of beach, edged by trees, that gets very crowded in summer. Between Fetovaia and Cavoli, another small, pleasant enough resort, the low rocks make perfect sunbathing platforms.

THE SOUTH

With its expanse of golden sand, **Marina di Campo ❽**, in the south, is the largest, most buzzing resort on the island. While often overrun by German package tours in summer, it is still a good springboard to the medieval hamlets in the hills behind. Fortified by the Pisans in the 12th century, the hamlets of **San Piero in Campo** and San Ilario conceal Romanesque churches and hermitages.

Capoliveri ❾ is a traditional inland village, with a Roman and medieval past as dramatic as its location high on the southern promontory. Carved into the iron mountain of Monte Calamita, Capoliveri is also an ancient mining village, where the mineral-rich soil is ideal for the production of sweet red Aleatico, reputedly the favourite wine of Napoleon Bonaparte. Often independent, Capoliveri was the only village to reject Napoleon in 1814. The story is that only the intercession of a local beauty saved the village. It soon became part of Napoleon's hunting estate, and to this day is noted for its dishes of woodcock, pheasant and hare.

The hills are covered with heath, fern and juniper; the scent of thyme and rosemary are never far away. Roads from the hills to the sea often turn into cart tracks but are worth pursuing unless specifically marked *strada privata*; this is often the only access to the loveliest beaches.

Innamorata is a sandy inlet linked to the romance between a nymph and a fisherman. Believing her lover drowned in a shipwreck, the nymph drowned herself; he survived and asked the gods to turn him into a seagull so he could seek her out.

FROM THE EAST TO THE INTERIOR

Capoliveri also surveys fashionable **Porto Azzurro** ⑩, the main town on the east coast of Elba and once part of the Spanish protectorate. The vast Forte Longone, constructed in 1603 as a Spanish naval base, is now a top-security prison. Forte Focardo, its sister fortress across the bay, has uninviting ramparts running down a sheer cliff. By day, Porto Azzurro has a rather uninspiring seafront. In the evening, however, it comes to life with a leisurely promenade (the famous *passeggiata*), designer shopping and people-watching. It is also a top place for sampling seafood, including *cacciucco*, a seafood soup of octopus, scorpion fish, prawns and *riso nero* or "black rice" (risotto with dark cuttlefish ink), perhaps followed by *schiaccia briaca* ("drunken cake"), made with hazelnuts and Aleatico wine. After enough Elban wine, one's impressions of Porto Azzurro are

⊘ Tip

Capo Sant'Andrea makes a good base for hiking, mountain biking, birdwatching, sea kayaking, snorkelling and other outdoor activities in the northwest of the island. For more information, go to www.visitelba.com, a useful website run by the owner/manager of the Hotel Ilio, who is a keen promoter of eco-tourism on the island.

Portoferraio Lighthouse.

⊘ ARCHIPELAGO

Elba is the largest island in a chain of seven between the Ligurian and Tyrrhenian seas, all loosely protected as part of the Arcipelago Toscano marine park. On a clear day, Pianosa, Gorgona, Montecristo and Capraia are visible from the island's highest reaches. Pianosa, just 14km (9 miles) from Elba, was a maximum-security prison until 1997 but is now a marine reserve. Gorgona, the smallest and most northerly island in the archipelago, is still a prison. Montecristo, 34km (21 miles) away, is a nature reserve, uninhabited but for its four guardians. So as not to disturb the fragile ecosystem, visitor numbers are restricted, but day trips are available from Porto Azzurro on Elba. Capraia, a miniature Elba without its history or architecture, is a two-hour ferry ride from Livorno and draws divers and those wishing to explore the marine grottoes.

Giglio, the second-largest island, and Giannutri are the southernmost islands. Giglio is popular with weekending Romans and divers. Both can be reached from Porto Santo Stefano on the Argentario peninsula. Frequent hydrofoils to Elba run from Piombino, on the mainland, to Rio Marina (45 minutes) to Portoferraio (1 hour). See Toremar ferries at www.toremar.it.

Divers heading to sea.

Smooth rocky platforms attract sunbathers.

of harbour lights, cheerful bustle and gently bobbing boats.

Behind Porto Azzurro is the most mystical spot on the island, the remote sanctuary of **Madonna di Monserrato** (daily June–Sept 9.30am–12.30pm and 3–7pm, shorter hours rest of the year; free). It was built in the Toledan style by a Spanish governor, Ponce de León, in 1606. A steep, rocky track leads high up the mountain to the tiny red-domed church precariously balanced among the crags. Despite mountain goats cavorting on impossible ledges, the place has great solemnity and few visitors, and is the most important shrine on Elba. The Spanish facade and bell tower find echoes in the *Black Madonna* inside, which is a copy of an early Spanish painting. Every September, an Elban pilgrimage celebrates the Festa della Madonna with a walk past ravines and isolated grottoes to the church.

East of Portoferraio, the workaday town of **Rio Marina** was once the centre of the mining activity. Surrounded by hills rich in ferrous oxide, the whole port has a pinkish hue, including the octagonal Pisan watchtower overlooking the harbour. More than 700 mineral exhibits are on display in the **Museo Mineralogico** (daily Apr–June, Sept–Oct 9.30am–12.30pm and 3.30–6.30pm, July–Aug 9.30am–12.30pm and 4.30–7.30pm). Only dedicated rock-hunters will continue to the **Parco Minerario**, set in a disused mine, where you can book a train tour or a hunt for minerals.

Inland, **Rio nell'Elba** is a strange, rather wild village perched on a couple of ledges among desolate mountain slopes and scattered remains of mines. A few kilometres west, on the road to Portoferraio, a steep road leads uphill to Volterraio and the ruins of an 11th-century Pisan fortress, perched on a rock.

From Rio nell'Elba to the small beach resort of **Cavo** in the northeast, the picturesque road cuts through woods and moorland. Paths trail through gorse, heather and the wild flowers of the maquis. Like the northwestern corner of the island, Elba's northeastern tip has quiet, unspoilt stretches of coast. Just north of Cavo, the remains of a Roman villa can be seen at Capo Castello.

VOLTERRA AND MASSA MARITTIMA

Perched on a windy plateau overlooking the Sienese hills, Volterra remains the most Etruscan of cities. The scenery sweeps from dry and desolate crags to the dense, eerie forests of the "Metal-bearing Mountains" – south to engaging Massa Marittima, the gateway to the Maremma.

One of the most important towns in Tuscany is **Volterra** ❶, which has a richly layered history with abundant evidence of its 3,000 years of civilisation. It commands a majestic, windswept position on a steep ridge 545 metres (1,780ft) above sea level. Walking round the ancient fortifications is an excellent way to view the medieval town, the Roman and Etruscan walls, and the wide sweep of countryside below.

Volterra was the Etruscan city-state of Velathri, one of the confederation of 12 city-states that made up Etruria. It became an important Roman municipality (Volterrae) when Rome annexed Etruria in 351 BC. It followed the new faith of Christianity, and at the fall of the Roman Empire, AD 476, it was already the centre of a vast diocese.

The modern city of Volterra sits within the walls of a much larger Etruscan predecessor. Wherever archaeologists dig in the city, they turn up new treasures. Sometimes they do not even need to dig, since parts of the city, built on tufa and undermined by subterranean springs, have been slipping slowly down the hillside for centuries, revealing the remains of an extensive necropolis.

EXPLORING VOLTERRA

The **Porta all'Arco** (the Arch Gate) is the best-preserved Etruscan gateway in Italy, dating from the 4th century BC

(though partly rebuilt by the Romans in the 1st century BC), with sides of huge rectangular stone blocks and three mysterious carved basalt heads above the gateway, thought to represent Etruscan gods.

From the arch, a pretty road winds its way uphill to the **Piazza dei Priori.** Evidence of the Middle Ages is to be found both in Volterra's urban structure and in its buildings, the most important of which are clustered around the main square. It is dominated by the tall **Palazzo dei Priori**

◉ Main attractions

Piazza dei Priori, Volterra
Palazzo Incontri-Viti, Volterra
Museo Etrusco, Volterra
Teatro Romano, Volterra
Le Balze
Piazza Garibaldi and
  Duomo, Massa Marittima
Citta Nuova, Massa
  Marittima
Museo della Miniera,
  Massa Marittima
Abbazia di San Galgano

Map on page 185

Porta all'Arco.

Walk along the remains of Volterra's Etruscan walls, at the northwestern edge of town, for lovely views at sunset.

Piazza dei Priori.

(1208), the oldest town hall in Tuscany, and said to be the model for Florence's Palazzo Vecchio. Across the square is the 13th-century **Palazzo Pretorio**, with its crenellated Torre del Porcellino (Tower of the Little Pig), named after its decorative relief of a boar. On the square, call into the wonderfully helpful tourist office (tel: 0588-87257) to pick up the Volterra audioguide. It is a model of its kind, providing judicious background on all the main sights, visited at your own pace.

To the south of the square, Via Turrazza leads to the 12th-century **Duomo** (Piazza San Giovanni; closed for restoration at the time of writing), which boasts works of art from the Middle Ages to the Renaissance. The sculpture of *The Deposition* is an extremely rare Romanesque woodcarving, simple in execution but bursting with pathos and drama.

The bishop's palace next door is now the **Museo d'Arte Sacra** (Via Roma; closed until further notice), a collection of gold reliquaries, church bells, illuminated manuscripts and some 13th-century sculptures of the Sienese school. The octagonal **Baptistery** opposite has an elegant marble doorway with a fine baptismal font sculpted by Sansovino.

As you head back towards the square, take Via Roma to Via Buonparenti and the Pisan-style **Casa Torre Buonparenti**, a pair of Gothic tower-houses.

At the top of Via Buonparenti, the **Pinacoteca e Museo Civico** in Palazzo Minucci-Solaini (www.volterratur.it; daily mid-Mar–Oct 9am–7pm, Nov–mid-Mar 10am–4.30pm) displays valuable paintings of the Sienese and Florentine schools, including an *Annunciation* by Signorelli and *Christ in Glory* by Ghirlandaio. The most famous painting in the collection is a masterly *Deposition from the Cross* by Rosso Fiorentino (1495–1540).

The **Palazzo Incontri-Viti**, on Via dei Sarti (www.palazzoviti.it; Apr–Oct 10am–1pm, 2.30–6pm, Nov–Mar by appointment only), is an impressive mansion whose facade is attributed to Ammannati, who worked on the Palazzo Pitti in Florence. Each salon is grander than the one before, adorned with art, porcelain and alabaster objects, a reminder that the palace once belonged to an alabaster merchant, whose heirs still live here. Renaissance buildings like these blend in surprisingly gracefully with the medieval Volterran houses. After exploring the patrician palaces, retreat to **Le Cantine**, the ancient cellars below Palazzo Incontri-Viti, for a drink in a cavern-like bar that contains a Roman cistern.

THE ETRUSCAN MUSEUM AND ROMAN THEATRE

The best of the city's ancient treasures are displayed in the **Museo Etrusco Guarnacci** (Via Don Minzoni; www.volterratur.it; daily mid-Mar–Oct 9am–7pm, Nov–mid-Mar 10am–4.30pm). This is packed with ancient Etruscan funerary urns, proof that Volterra has some of the best Etruscan art outside Rome. The alabaster sarcophagi run the gamut of Etruscan demonology and Greek mythology, featuring sea monsters, Greek gods, griffins and sirens. *The Married Couple* urn is a masterpiece of realistic portraiture, but even more stunning is the bronze statuette known as *L'Ombra della Sera (The Shadow of the Evening)*. Resembling a Giacometti sculpture but cast in the 5th century BC, this enigmatic elongated figure does indeed resemble the shadow of a boy thrown by the low beams of the setting sun. It blurs immortality and mortality in true Etruscan fashion.

After focusing so much on death, it's definitely a case of *carpe diem*: feast on Tuscan dishes in **Del Duca**. Naturally, the restaurant terrace is built below the walls of the Etruscan acropolis. The spirit of the enigmatic Etruscans will accompany you throughout your stay in Volterra. Like the mystical *Shadow of the Evening* sculpture, the Etruscans knew how to live as well as how to die.

Volterra is dominated at its highest point by the **Fortezza Medicea**, a magnificent example of Renaissance military architecture – today it serves as a top-security prison. Intriguingly, the prisoners perform plays of a professional standard every summer but, to watch them, visitors need a certificate stating that they have no criminal record, which is not easily come by.

Nearby, on the site of the former Etruscan acropolis, the **Parco Archeologico** (mid-Mar–Oct daily 10am–5.30pm, Nov–mid-Mar Mon–Fri 10am–4.30pm) is an ideal spot for a picnic.

On the north side of town, just below the city walls, is the excavated **Teatro Romano** (mid-Mar–Oct 10am–5.30pm, Nov–mid-Mar 10am–4.30pm), the impressive remains of a complex built during the reign of Augustus, behind which lie the ruins of a 3rd-century Roman bathhouse. One of the loveliest walks runs along the city walls, from Porta Fiorentina to Piazza Minucci, and affords compelling views of the theatre below.

Medieval Volterra.

LE BALZE

The countryside around Volterra is one of gentle, undulating hills, interrupted in the west by the wild and awe-inspiring spectacle of abrupt crevasses known as **Le Balze** (The Crags). Over the centuries, these deep gullies, created by the continual erosion of layers of sand and clay, have swallowed up churches and settlements along with Etruscan and early Christian remains. Today, an 11th-century abbey, the Badia, sits on a precipice, awaiting its inevitable fate. For the perfect view of this dramatic landscape, exit through the western San Francesco Gate, passing the Borgo San Giusto and its remains until you reach Le Balze campsite (a 20-minute walk).

METAL MOUNTAINS

The terrain south of Volterra goes from the crags of Le Balze to the dense, eerie forests of the "Metal-bearing Mountains". The wide vistas of the dry, desolate terrain just south of town seem a world away from the cosy green hills of Chianti. In a remote area without significant sights, it is the journey that counts, an elemental voyage through a disconcertingly untamed Tuscany of gullies, mining gashes and belching fumaroles. Geothermic geeks will be in their element, but so, too, will open-minded adventurers. Fortunately, at either end of this surreal journey, whether Volterra or Massa Marittima, the cities are as beguiling and warmly welcoming as any in Tuscany.

At Saline di Volterra, an industrial suburb that developed around its salt mine, the SS439 leads south to Massa Marittima and the coast, cutting through the **Colline Metallifere**, or Metal-bearing Hills. Beyond the Upper Cecina valley, dense forests of chestnut, beech and oak are punctuated by fumaroles, cooling towers and gleaming silver pipelines, making for a strange and distinctly un-Tuscan picture.

The first noteworthy town on this surreal route is **Pomarance ❷**, which retains vestiges of its prosperous past, including medieval town gates and the Romanesque church of San

⊙ ALABASTER WORKSHOPS

Like everything in Volterra, alabaster carving is an Etruscan legacy. It is one of the many gifts the Etruscans have passed on to their descendants in this most Etruscan of cities. The ancient craftsmen made great use of alabaster from the 5th century BC onwards, primarily for their beautifully sculpted funerary urns.

Visit the Etruscan Museum before looking at alabaster objets d'art *in situ*, beginning with the grand collection created by Giuseppe Viti, the city's foremost alabaster merchant in the 19th century. Viti travelled the world to present his wares and, in India, sold his alabaster to the local rajah and, bizarrely, was then made Emir of Nepal. **Palazzo Incontri-Viti** displays superb pieces, including the grand candelabra in the ballroom, made for Emperor Maximilian, who was shot in 1867 before he could collect them. Admire the palazzo's floor, all white tesserae of hardened alabaster, and some decorative tables are adorned with alabaster mosaics.

Alabaster is sold in Volterra's workshops, as well as being exported. One of the most respected alabaster-crafting firms is the family-run **Ali, Alabastri Lavorati**

Italiani (Ali, Piazza Martiri della Liberta; tel: 0588-86078; www.alialabastro.it). Its showroom is the most elegant in town. Choose from lamps, sculpture, figurines, chess pieces, table tops, picture frames: so much can be carved from alabaster. Prices depend on the type, colour and veining of the alabaster, with colours ranging from creamy white to murky yellow. Visit one of the last remaining traditional alabaster craftsmen in his cramped workshop; **Giuliano Ducceschi** (Via Porta all'Arco 59) has been carving owls and fish, his favourite subjects, since the 1950s, and will continue until he drops.

Also call in at the alabaster museum, the **Ecomuseo dell'Alabastro** (Piazzetta Minucci, daily mid-Mar–Oct 9.30am–7pm, Nov–mid-Mar 10.30am–4.30pm). The museum tells the story of the alabaster craft, from the excavation of the stone to its artistic production and trade – from the Etruscan to the present times. On display are over 300 alabaster art works, mainly from the 18th and19th centuries, including female busts beautifully carved by Giuseppe Bessi.

Giovanni. A short walk away, Via Roncalli is home to the **Bicocchi Museum** (May–Sept Sat–Sun guided tours at 4, 5 and 6pm and by appointment), a lavish early 19th-century home, whose decorations evoke the lifestyle of the wealthy mine-owning families. A little further along the road is the hamlet of **San Dalmazio**, and a short but steep walk (2km/1.25 miles) that culminates in commanding views from the ruins of the 11th-century castle, **Rocca di Sillana**.

Across the valley, the medieval hamlet of **Montecastelli Pisano** ❸ is dominated by the Torre dei Pannocchieschi. Like the Rocca Sillana, this fortified settlement was a pawn on the Tuscan chessboard, finally won by the Florentines in the 16th century. Follow the signs to **Castelnuovo Val di Cecina** and the "Buca delle Fate", a small but well-preserved 6th-century BC Etruscan tomb, just outside the village.

The road south from Montecastelli Pisano offers the best views of the medieval village of Castelnuovo Val di Cecina, which commands a steep ridge surrounded by woodland. A short walk east of the village leads through chestnut groves and down to the River Pavone, where you can swim in the rock pools, overlooked by two medieval bridges.

STEAMING FUMAROLES

At the heart of this vast geothermic area, the industrial village of **Larderello** has been valued for its healing spring waters for centuries. But unless you're into industrial archaeology, move swiftly on to see geothermal activity in its more elemental form.

South along a back road from Larderello lie the hamlets of **Leccia** and **Sasso Pisano**, the latter of which commands a rocky outcrop above the Cornia River. The hamlets are linked by a narrow, winding route that cuts through a landscape of steaming fumaroles. Just outside Leccia are the ancient baths of **Bagnone**, a vast Etruscan-Roman complex from the 3rd century BC. The craggy medieval village of **Sasso Pisano** is a strangely appealing place, often shrouded in

⊙ Tip

A memorable experience – and a lot easier to see than Siena's Palio – is the traditional Balestro del Girifalco, every last Sunday in May and every second Sunday in August. The *terzieri* of Massa (old city, new city and the outer Borgo) hold a shooting contest using mechanical falcons with ancient crossbows.

The ruins of the Roman theatre.

*The Romanesque
Cappella di Montesiepi.*

*Larderello, at the
centre of geothermic
activity.*

clouds of steam from the surrounding fumaroles, and the air is heavy with the smell of sulphur. The road through the village leads back to the SS439.

As the main road winds south towards Massa Marittima, it climbs up steeply wooded hillsides to the summits of the Colline Metallifere. It is an area of outstanding natural beauty, with dense forest and large open views across to Maremma and the Gulf of Follonica; on a fine day, the islands of Elba and Corsica can be clearly seen.

MASSA MARITTIMA

Massa Marittima ❹ is about 24km (15 miles) inland, despite its maritime name. It is one of the most astounding Tuscan cities, perched on top of a high hill on the edge of the Colline Metallifere. Although its relative remoteness from "picture-postcard Tuscany" has resulted in far fewer visitors than it deserves, Massa Marittima is finally coming into its own. This underrated gem

has preserved its gorgeous medieval core as well as gracious palaces, authentic regional restaurants, and a clutch of fine museums.

Massa Marittima grew up in the 10th century, after the decline of ancient Populonia, which was too exposed to coastal malaria and plundering by pirates.

Massa, once the second city of the Sienese Republic, prospered from copper and silver mines exploited since Etruscan times. Although the proud city spiralled into centuries of decline when the mines failed and malaria returned, its stagnation has proved a joy for visitors today. Massa feels authentic, harmonious, a picture of urban refinement.

The city's old republican pride is reflected in the concentration of public buildings around the cathedral. In the main square – the spectacular **Piazza Garibaldi**, one of the finest squares in Tuscany – are Palazzo Vescovile (seat of the bishop); Palazzo del Podestà (seat of the governor, now an archaeological museum); Palazzo del Comune (town hall); Zecca Cittadina (the mint); Fonte Pub-blica (public fountain); and Palazzo dell'Abbondanza (the public granary). Set on a pedestal, the Pisan-Roman-esque **Duomo** boasts Gothic windows and marvellous reliefs of the *Madonna delle Grazie*, ascribed to Duccio di Buoninsegna (1316), as well as the *Arca di San Cerbone* (St Cerbone's Ark), a Sienese sculptural master-piece. Return to the theatrical square in the evening, when you can drink or dine while admiring the cathedral facade by moonlight.

Leave the old **Citta Vecchia** area around the Cathedral for the so-called **Citta Nuova**, hardly new despite its name. The quaint **Via Moncini** climbs to this Gothic quarter clustered behind Sienese fortifications, and ends in Piazza Matteotti, beside the medieval clock tower, the **Torre del Candaliere**. Nearby, on Corso Diaz, is the **Museo di Arte Sacra** (Apr–Oct Tue–Sun 10am–1pm and 3–6pm, Nov–Mar Tue–Sun 11am–1pm and 3–5pm). This delight-ful museum of sacred art is in the

equally lovely complex of San Pietro all'Orta, a frescoed Romanesque-Gothic monastery. The art reflects Massa's period of medieval glory, with the highlight being Lorenzetti's *Maesta*, the Madonna in Glory. Sculp-tures taken from the cathedral facade are also on display here. Virtually next door is the intimate church of **San Agostino** and the **Museo Santa Cecilia** (Wed–Sun summer 10.30am–1pm and 3.30–7pm, winter 10.30am–12.30pm and 3–6pm), which is more engaging for its mood and architecture than for its treasures on display.

There are two mining-related museums in town, with the best being the **Museo della Miniera** in Via Corridoni (tel: 0588-31026; open-ing times are variable so call ahead; guided tours only), a short walk from the cathedral. Set in natural galler-ies and medieval mineshafts, this atmospheric mining museum saw service as an air-raid shelter in World War II. The child-friendly tour passes wagons, pneumatic drills and munitions stores as it burrows

Houses in Massa Marittima.

Abbazia di San Galgano.

⊘ THE "TWILIGHT" TOUR

Ever since Stephanie Meyer set her bestselling vampire novel in Volterra, droves of "vampire-ologists" have been visiting. The *Twilight* saga has sold millions of copies worldwide and *New Moon*, the second in the series, depicts the fictional home of the Volturi, a coven of elite vampires. Even if neighbouring Montepulciano was chosen for the filming (it has a larger main square), Volterra was the inspiration for the melodrama. Wildly popular vampire tours now visit the Piazza dei Priori where the heroine, Bella, rushes to save Edward, her vampire love. With its stern clock tower, the vampires' den can seem suitably chilling after dark.

The tour is not just for impressionable teenage girls, but is also a surreal way of discovering the dark side of Volterra, including candlelit caverns where you come face to face with cloaked vampires. In a secret wine bar with an Etruscan well you can drink local red wine masquerading as blood. Even if Volterra is probably vampire-free, a particular bronze in the Etruscan Museum would suggest otherwise – *The Shadow of the Evening* is reminiscent of the long shadow cast by a person at twilight.

(Book a vampire tour through the tourist office or tel: 0588-86099, 0588-87257; www.newmoonofficialtour.com).

deeper into the rock. The small display of minerals is a reminder that medieval Massa grew prosperous thanks to the discovery of silver and copper deposits nearby, followed by the mining of pyrites, found in veins of quartz.

GOTHIC RUIN

Heading east from Massa Marittima along the Siena road leads to the Gothic ruins of **Abbazia di San Galgano** 5 (daily 9am–5.30pm), best seen when the setting sun sends shafts of light through its windows. This roofless abbey, with grass for a nave and fragments of frescoes clinging to crumbling walls, feels a mystical spot. Once the finest French Gothic abbey in Tuscany, San Galgano is now a noble ruin, albeit one tended by Olivetan nuns, who allow concerts to be staged here in summer. Consecrated in 1288, the abbey of San Galgano was the Cistercian mother abbey that held sway over central Italy. Its abbot arbitrated in disputes between city-states, while its monks oversaw the building of

Siena Cathedral. In the mid-14th century, the abbey was ransacked by the English mercenary Sir John Hawkwood – an attack sanctioned by the Pope, who was fearful of the Order's influence. Decline set in and by 1576, San Galgano was occupied by one solitary monk "who didn't even wear a robe". A lightning strike during Mass in 1778 saw the collapse of the campanile and signalled the last service at San Galgano. Although it sounded the death knell for the abbey, San Galgano, like its mystical founder, never gives up the ghost.

On the neighbouring hillock is the circular Romanesque **Cappella di Montesiepi**, built on the spot where St Galgano had a vision and renounced soldiering to become a hermit, thrusting his sword into a rock. The sword remains in the church, protruding from the rock. The bizarre event is illustrated by the frescoes of Ambrogio Lorenzetti that adorn the adjoining chapel walls.

Siena is about 35km (22 miles) distant on the SS73.

The landscape around Volterra.

Vampire-friendly Volterra.

San Gimignano's towers.

SAN GIMIGNANO

This is quintessential Tuscany, taking in the medieval "skyscrapers" of San Gimignano, the quaint hill town of Certaldo, and the rolling hills between Siena and Florence – the harmonious vineyards, villas and wine estates dotted along the Chianti trail.

Famous for the sculptural quality of its skyline, **San Gimignano** ➊ is a spectacular sight. It may be a cliché to call this hill town a "Medieval Manhattan", but the famous towers do resemble miniature skyscrapers. Seen from inside, it is the unspoilt townscape that bowls you over: almost nothing seems to have changed since the Middle Ages. In its heyday, the city had a total of 76 towers, only 14 of which remain. After San Gimignano fell under Florentine control, it became an economic backwater, bypassed by the Renaissance – for which we are eternally grateful.

EXPLORING SAN GIMIGNANO

The towers are concentrated around the **Piazza del Duomo** and **Piazza della Cisterna**, which is teeming with tourists all year round. The towers alone make a visit here worthwhile, but the town abounds in quirky sights, even if staying overnight is the only way to appreciate this medieval time capsule in peace.

The Romanesque **Collegiata** (www.duomosangimignano.it; Apr–Oct Mon–Fri 10am–7.30pm, Sat 10am–5.30pm, Sun 12.30–7.30pm, Jan 1–15, Feb–Mar, Nov 1–15, Dec Mon–Sat 10am–5pm, Sun 12.30–5pm but no visits during Mass; combined ticket for most town attractions – San Gimignano Pass) will detain you longest, as every inch of wall space

Chiesa di Sant'Agostino, San Gimignano.

is covered in frescoes. The north aisle has Bartolo di Fredi's dramatic scenes from the Old Testament (1367), while the opposite aisle has Lippo Memmi's *Life of Christ* (1333–41) and the nave the *Last Judgement* by Taddeo di Bartolo (1393–6). Contrast these Gothic-style narrative paintings with Ghirlandaio's lyrical Renaissance frescoes (1475) on the life of a local saint, in the chapel of Santa Fina.

FOUR MUSEUMS

Next to the Collegiata, the **Museo d'Arte Sacra** (www.sangimignano.com;

Main attractions

San Gimignano Cityscape
Collegiata, San Gimignano
Museo Civico, San Gimignano
Certaldo
Monteriggioni
Greve
Radda in Chianti
Badia a Coltibuono
Gaiole in Chianti
Castello di Brolio

Map on page 195

⊘ Tip

To see San Gimignano at its best, stay overnight in one of the characteristic hotels. Then you can savour the peaceful beauty of the town in the evening and early morning, after the coach-trippers have gone.

same hours as Collegiata; combined ticket) contains a variety of sacred art from the 13th to the 15th century.

Alongside is the **Museo Civico** (www.sangimignano.com; daily Apr–Sept 10am–7.30pm, Oct–Mar 11am–5.30pm; combined ticket), housed in the Palazzo del Popolo, a forbidding fortress that served as the town hall. Completed in 1311, its tower, the **Torre Grossa** (www.sangimignano.com; same hours as Museo Civico; combined ticket), is the tallest in the town (54 metres/175ft) and the only one you can climb; the views of the Val d'Elsa from the top are spectacular. Among the museum's many good paintings is a set of early 14th-century frescoes by Memmo di Filippucci – rare in that they depict secular rather than religious scenes. Known as the *Wedding Frescoes*, they show a young bride and groom sharing a bath and climbing into their nuptial bed – an intimate glimpse into the private life of medieval Italy.

On Via Folgore, the former convent of Santa Chiara is now home to the **Museo Archeologico** (www.sangimignano. com; same hours as Museo Civico; combined ticket). Fascinating exhibits range from Etruscan finds to a 16th-century pharmacy displaying ceramic and glass vessels designed for herbal remedies and healing lotions and potions.

The nearby **Piazza della Cisterna** is a lovely triangular space with a 13th-century well and medieval palazzi. East of the square, on Via di Castello, is the **Museo della Tortura** (www.torturemuseum.it; daily 10am–7pm), with a gruesome collection of medieval instruments of torture.

Every church in San Gimignano offers some reward, but perhaps the best is **Sant'Agostino** (www.sangimig-nano.com; Apr–Oct daily 10am–noon and 3–7pm, Nov–Dec daily until 6pm, Jan–Mar Mon 4–6pm, Tue–Sun 10am–noon and 3–6pm; free) to the north of the town (near Porta San Matteo). Here, in Gozzoli's faded frescoes on the *Life of St Augustine* (1465), you will find the same love of colour, rich clothing and exact portraiture as in Gozzoli's other frescoes, notably in

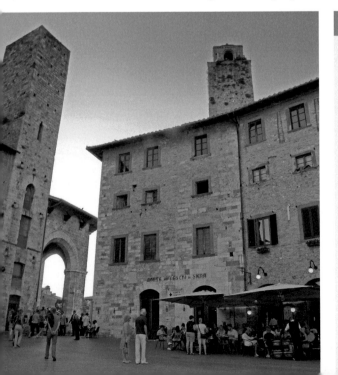

Piazza del Duomo at dusk.

⊘ MEDIEVAL MANHATTAN

San Gimignano's towers were built in the 12th and 13th centuries by the *magnati*, or nobles, during the Guelf-Ghibelline conflicts. As well as defending the city, they served as status symbols: the higher the tower, the richer and more powerful its owner. The local 14th-century poet Folgore described the "earthly pleasures" he encountered in the city, including "silk sheets, sugared nuts, sweets and sparkling wine". The arrival of the Black Death in 1348 put an end to silk sheets in San Gimignano until the 20th century. While more civilised cities were exchanging towers for palazzi, this medieval backwater destroyed nothing and built nothing. The city's misfortune has made it the best-preserved medieval city in Tuscany.

The Journey of the Magi in the Palazzo Medici Riccardi in Florence.

On Via Costarella, call into the **Museo SanGimignano1300** (www.sangimig nano1300.com; Jan–Feb 10am–5pm, May–Nov until 6pm). The museum seeks to show how the city was in its 13th-century heyday, with reconstructions of the 72 tower-houses, fortifications, churches and convents. But what is remarkable is how much of this medieval cityscape remains in San Gimignano today.

A short walk along the city walls to the 14th-century fortress before leaving is worthwhile. This semi-derelict **Rocca** has views over tiered gardens and olive groves winding down to the Vernaccia vineyards, which produce the famous white wine that was even mentioned in Dante's *The Divine Comedy*. Just beyond the fortress, **Vernaccia di San Gimignano Wine Experience** (www. sangimignanomuseovernaccia.com; daily 11.30am–7.30pm; free) is the place to sample a range of local wines and participate in a multimedia tour focusing on wine.

THE VAL D'ELSA

A few kilometres north of San Gimignano, the windswept medieval hill town of **Certaldo** ❷ straddles the summit of a steep hill. To reach it, park in the unprepossessing lower town, Certaldo Basso, and take the funicular up the steep slope to the delightful upper town, which is closed to traffic. Certaldo Alto is a literary landmark as it was the home of Giovanni Boccaccio (1313–75), author of *The Decameron*, who died here in 1375. What is thought to have been his home was restored in 1823, bombed during World War II, and has now been rebuilt as the **Casa di Boccaccio** (Apr–Oct daily 9.30am–1.30pm and 2.30–7pm, Nov–Mar Wed–Mon, closes at 4.30pm). An allegorical garden, inspired by *The Decameron*, has recently been created here. Featuring a marble fountain, and dotted with references to Boccaccio, the garden is used for concerts and film screenings.

The red-brick town is crowned by the castellated **Palazzo Pretorio**, whose 15th-century facade is studded with terracotta coats of arms. Any

One of five circular towers along San Gimignano's city walls.

THE NECTAR OF THE GODS

Delightfully torn between tradition and creativity – like the contradictory Tuscans themselves – the wine scene allows for a duality between provenance and personality.

The know-how in the vineyards today compared with even a decade ago, is phenomenal," claims Lamberto Frescobaldi, whose Florentine family has been in the wine business for 700 years. For all its history, Tuscany remains at the forefront of the wine industry, which is still dominated by many of the original noble families. Wine-growing dates back to Etruscan times, as evidenced by the goblet found in an Etruscan tomb at Castellina in Chianti, and surviving Etruscan frescoes that depict Bacchus, the Roman god of wine. Medieval monasteries established viticulture here – where Badia a

Vineyard below San Gimignano.

Coltibuono and Antinori's Badia a Passignano remain beguiling wine estates today.

In the mid-19th-century, Barone Bettino Ricasoli capitalised on improvements in production and spearheaded the modernisation of wine-making, with the establishment of the Chianti Classico brand. Since then, a consortium, the Consorzio Chianti Classico, controls production, with the *gallo nero* (black cockerel) emblem guaranteeing quality. (Try Barone Ricasoli Castello di Brolio Chianti Classico 2006.)

To some outsiders, Tuscany is still synonymous with Chianti – to the chagrin of the region's other fine red-wine producers. Situated between Florence and Siena, the Chianti Classico heartland includes Barberino Val d'Elsa, Castellina, Greve, Gaiole, and San Casciano. However, the top Tuscan red is arguably Brunello di Montalcino, made from Sangiovese grapes grown on hillsides south of Siena. Brunello is a powerful yet refined red that ages superbly, with Rosso di Montalcino its more approachable younger sister, and the "princely" Vino Nobile di Montepulciano, loved by princes and popes since Medici times.

The wines of the Maremma are increasingly fashionable, and mostly made with Bordeaux varieties such as Cabernet Sauvignon, Franc and Merlot. These elegant wines have a crispness rarely found in New World Cabernets or Merlots. Around Bolgheri, look out for great names such as Sassicaia and Ornellaia. Antinori Solaia, Frescobaldi Giramonte, Sette Ponti Oreno and d'Alessandro Syrah are other superb "Super-Tuscans". Detractors claim that Super Tuscans lack a sense of place and are overpriced. Fans retort that these wines express the true creativity of the wine maker. The debate between native and French varieties pits provenance against personality, a sense of place against the creativity of the wine maker.

Follow your nose: if Bordeaux blends don't appeal, there is ample choice among native grape varieties. That's without mentioning Vernaccia di San Gimignano, the characteristic white wine – crisp, full-bodied, golden-hued, and popular since Dante's day. Or dipping almond cantuccini biscuits into Vin Santo, Tuscany's amber-hued dessert wine: nectar of the gods indeed.

wandering will reveal impressive medieval gateways that lead down to steep, narrow-approach lanes. If hungry, stop at the **Osteria del Vicario** (Wed–Fri 4.30am–10.30pm, Sun 12.30–10.30pm). This frescoed, former monastery is now a delightful hotel and a good restaurant. Also be sure to drop into **Giuseppina** (Via del Castello 34, tel: 0348-003 4869; www.cucinagiuseppina. com) to sample and buy local produce. It's worth booking a taster class in the eponymous owner's authentic cookery school, where you can learn how to make *ribollita* soup, *Sienese pici* pasta or crunchy almond cantuccini biscuits. The chef, Giuseppina herself, is helped by her wine-specialist son, who guides tastings at local vineyards or sets up truffle-hunting experiences for interested visitors.

South of San Gimignano, **Colle di Val d'Elsa** ❸ is split between two sites. The lower "new" town is a busy, haphazard sprawl, whose centre of activity is the crystal factory – Colle is Italy's largest producer of crystal and fine glass, and there are plenty of shops selling it. The **Museo del Cristallo** (www.museodelcristallo.it; Via dei Fossi; Tue–Sun May–Sept 10am–6pm, Oct–Apr until 5pm) tells its story. Follow the signs up to the ancient upper town. Here the main street is lined with 16th-century palazzi of unusual refinement, and, at one point, the stately procession of buildings is interrupted by a viaduct from which there are splendid views of the surrounding landscape.

More spectacular sights await in nearby **Monteriggioni** ❹, just off the N2 to Siena. The fortified town, encircled by walls and 14 towers, was built in 1213 to guard northern Sienese territory. Like Montepulciano, this little hill village is emblematic of the Tuscan landscape. It is seen at its best first thing in the morning, when you can enjoy a coffee on the main square before the coach parties arrive.

THE CHIANTIGIANA

Spanning the hills between Florence and Siena, "Chiantishire" is a gentle vision of cypresses, vineyards and Medicean villa gardens. The rolling

> **⊘ Fact**
>
> In 1716, a decree issued by the Grand Duke of Tuscany defined the boundaries of the Chianti area and established the laws governing the production and sale of wine. Today, this region is the world's oldest wine-producing league. The Chianti Classico area includes the communes of Barberino Val d'Elsa, Castellina, Greve, Gaiole, San Casciano and Tavernelle Val di Pesa.

Fortified Monteriggioni.

⊙ **Tip**

Cycling is an immensely popular way of touring Chianti country, and countless companies organise group or family holidays for people of all ages and abilities. You can also organise bike rental by the day or week through any of the Chianti tourist offices.

slopes are planted with olive groves that shimmer dark green and dusty silver. The Chianti is a spiritual rather than a geographical location. Its shifting borders reflect the fluctuations in Florentine and Sienese power, but, although it lies in Siena province, its soul remains where it has always been: on Florentine soil. It is a place whose turbulent history has shaped a scene of utter tranquillity, a harmony of tame hills and gentle people. In a place where nothing is essential viewing, everywhere is a glorious detour.

The SS222, known as **the Chiantigiana**, or Chianti Way, winds its picturesque way from Florence to Siena, through the heart of the region, offering archetypal scenes of cypress trees, olive groves and vineyards. First stop is the market town of **Greve in Chianti** ❺, with an impressive arcaded square, Piazza Matteotti, topped with wrought-iron balconies dripping with geraniums. The shops under the arcades are crammed with the usual assortment of local foods, crafts and wines. The annual September Mostra Mercato del Chianti draws a large crowd.

Driving the Chiantigiana.

An oft-missed jewel just five minutes' drive west of Greve is the tiny medieval walled town of **Montefioralle**, which was originally built as a feudal castle. Its narrow streets, stone houses and underpassages are beautifully preserved and splendid views are to be had from the various trattorias in the town.

Next on the SS222 is **Castellina in Chianti** ❻. Castellina overlooks symmetrical vineyards and wooded groves, a landscape dotted with low stone houses and Renaissance villas. New wine estates have been built from the remains of medieval castles. Villas have lazily domesticated the original castle or tower, but names like "La Rocca" or "La Torre" reveal the original function.

Castellina's name also reveals its medieval function as a Florentine outpost. In the late 13th century it was the first site of the Chianti League, a group of three Florentine feudal castles, each responsible for a third of the territory. The castle is now a fortified town hall hiding a small Etruscan museum and a warren of atmospheric backstreets with half-glimpsed views of the Chianti hills.

RADDA IN CHIANTI

East of Castellina, **Radda in Chianti**
❼ retains its medieval street plan and
imposing town hall. As in Castellina, the
spontaneous rural architecture is more
rewarding. Classical Medici villas with
16th-century windows and wells compete with romantic villas, constructed
from castles or Etruscan ruins. One
17th-century masterpiece is Villa Vis-
tarenni, a white beacon of sophistication. The elegant loggias and the
openness of the architecture symbolise
the increasing wealth of the countryside
and its proximity to urban Florence. In
the tranquil Chianti, the country is
richer and more civilised than the town.

From Radda a tortuous road climbs
to **Volpaia** ❽, a pretty medieval village
with a ruined castle and Brunelleschi-
style church. If Chianti villages and
towns have little sense of identity and
few artistic treasures, it is because
they came into being with fully fledged
Florentine and Sienese identities, while
military outposts such as Radda had
no time to develop artistically. Only the
Chianti abbeys, which were endowed
separately, had the independence to
shape their own culture.

ABBEY OF THE GOOD HARVEST

Between Radda and Gaiole is the aptly
named **Badia a Coltibuono** ❾ (www.col
tibuono.com; Abbey of the Good Harvest;
www.coltibuono.com; tastings Apr–Oct
daily), set among pines, oaks, chestnut
trees and vines. Since the Dissolution
of the Monasteries in 1810, this medieval abbey has belonged to one family. The lovely 15th-century cloisters,
chapel and frescoed ceilings can be
viewed as a guest of the cookery school
or the bed and breakfast, while the
12th-century walls and bell tower are
open to all. The cellars are filled with
Chianti Classico, the abbey's traditional
living. No less famous are the aromatic
chestnut honey and olive oil, which can
be bought on the premises.

CHIANTI CASTLES

Gaiole in Chianti ❿ is a newer river-
side settlement in a wooded valley. It
is a popular summer escape for hot

*A wine maker promotes
his produce at the
Chianti wine festival
held in Greve in Chianti
every September.*

*A fountain in Radda
in Chianti.*

The famous Chianti flask is no longer mass-produced for export. However, the nostalgic will be pleased to find rustic wicker fiaschi for sale throughout the region.

San Gimignano through the early morning mist.

Florentines in search of family-run hotels, home cooking and the familiar *gallo nero* (black cockerel) wine symbol. History lies in wait at Meleto and Vertine, unusual castles, and Barbischio, a medieval village, is nearby. Tempting footpaths marked Sentieri del Chianti lead all the way to Siena. With vineyards rising up gentle slopes, tranquil Gaiole and sleepy Greve are traditional Chianti.

The countryside from Gaiole south to Siena and east to Arezzo is higher, wilder and wetter. The wooded peaks are green and fresh, with scents of thyme, rosemary and pine. Deep chestnut woods provide ideal cover for wild boar, recently reintroduced.

Of the many Florentine castles in the woods, **Castello di Brolio** ⑪ (www.baronericasoli.com; Apr–late-Oct daily 10am–7pm) is the most impressive – not least because of its views over the original Chianti vineyards stretching as far as Siena and Monte Amiata. On the medieval chessboard, every Florentine castle faced its Sienese shadow. If the surviving castles are

Florentine, it is because Siena lost the match and all its pieces. While Sienese Cereto and Cettamura are small heaps, Florentine Brolio and Meleto are resplendent. As a Florentine outpost, Castello di Brolio's past spans Guelf-Ghibelline conflicts, sacking by the Sienese in 1529, and German occupation and Allied bombing in World War II. The medieval walls are the castle's most striking feature, along with the 14th-century chapel. Brolio has long been controlled by the Ricasoli, Chianti landowners since the 8th century. Baron Bettino Ricasoli, Italian premier in 1861, founded the modern Chianti wine industry, a business continued by the present family. (To visit the cellars, tour the estate, taste the wines, and see the family museum, tel: 0577-730 220; www.baronericasoli.com).

The Chianti is a place for pottering and chance encounters, one of which could be tiny **Campi di San Gusmé** ⑫, just south of Brolio. A short climb leads to a Romanesque church and views of tumbledown castles and vineyards.

The view of the Chianti vineyards from Castello di Brolio.

THE CHIANTI WINE TRAIL

The Chianti Classico wine trail explores some of the most ancient and imposing wine estates, an experience combining countryside, castles, cuisine – and wine.

The Chianti covers an enormous region, spanning seven different wine "zones". At its heart, in the hills between Florence and Siena, is Chianti Classico, with the remainder – the Colli Fiorentini, Colli Senesi, Colline Pisane, Colli Aretini, Rufina and Montalbano – spread out over central Tuscany. The main centres in Chianti Classico are Greve, Panzano, Castellina, Gaiole, Fonterutoli and Radda. Easily accessible off the picturesque route SS222, the grandest, castle-like estates have often been run by the same families since medieval times, as is the case with the aristocratic Antinori, Frescobaldi, Mazzei and Ricasoli dynasties. Their vaulted castles, rolling vineyards and gastronomic restaurants encourage you to linger.

Contact the Chianti Classico consortium (tel: 055-82285; www.chianticlassico.com) for links to their producers. For a memorable experience, book a tasting (degustazione) combined with a tour of the vineyards and cellars.

The distinctive black cockerel logo of Chianti Classico.

The smaller barrels used to store the wine produced in the Chianti region are known as barriques; the larger barrels are known as botti.

The hills of Chianti are blanketed with vineyards; many of the wine estates are hundreds of years old and have been run by the same families for generations.

Chianti grapes.

Recommended Wine Estates

Badia a Coltibuono
Gaiole in Chianti; tel: 0577-746 110; www.coltibuono.com
This wine estate, run by the Stucchi Prinetti family, markets itself as a "wine resort" – stay overnight; dine in the stables; do a cookery course – within the former Romanesque abbey. Guided tours May–Sept daily 2.30pm, 3.30pm, 4.30pm, 5.30pm and 6.30pm, late Mar–Apr and Oct 2.30, 3.30, 4.30pm and 5.30pm; tastings Apr–Oct Tue, Wed and Fri 11am or by appointment.

Badia a Passignano
Tavarnelle Val di Pesa; tel: 055-807 1278; www.osteriadipassignano.com
Book a tour at this estate and sample iconic Antinori wines, such as Tignanello, Guado al Tasso and Solaia, as well as Chianti Classico Riserva Badia a Passignano. After the cellar visit, enjoy an oil tasting, followed by lunch in the Michelin-starred Osteria.

Castello di Brolio
Gaiole in Chianti; tel: 0577-730 220; www.baronericasoli.com
Baron Ricasoli, whose descendants now run the castle (mid-Mar–late Oct daily 10am–6.30pm/7pm), first designated the grape mixes to be used in Chianti wine. Explore the castle gardens and cellars before a tasting and lunch (best to book).

Castello di Fonterutoli
Castellina in Chianti; tel: 0577-741 385; www.mazzei.it
Owned by the Mazzei family since 1435, Fonterutoli's award-winning wines are matched by their grappa, olive oil and Tuscan cuisine. Wine tours several times a day, reservations are recommended.

though chestnut was the traditional wood of the region, hianti normale is now usually kept in oak barrels for veral months to mature.

state owners are usually proud to show off their wines nd explain their particular methods of wine-making.

A bottle of Castello di Brolio Chianti.

SIENA

Siena is a classic case of a city that Italians call *"a misura d'uomo"* – meaning a city "made to the measure of man". Siena is, indeed, a Gothic city built on a human scale, and is effortlessly civilised, harmonious and at ease with itself.

From its striped marble Cathedral to its tunnelled alleys, brilliant Campo and black-and-white city emblem, Siena is a chiaroscuro city. In its surging towers it is truly Gothic. Where Florence is boldly horizontal, Siena is soaringly vertical; where Florence has large squares and masculine statues, Siena has hidden gardens and romantic wells. Florentine art is perspective and innovation, while Sienese art is sensitivity and conservatism. Siena is often considered the feminine foil to Florentine masculinity.

For such a feminine and beautiful city, Siena has a decidedly warlike reputation, nourished by sieges, city-state rivalry and Palio battles. The pale theatricality in Sienese painting is not representative of the city or its inhabitants: the average Sienese is no ethereal Botticelli nymph, but dark, stocky and swarthy.

A BRIEF HISTORY

In keeping with Sienese mystique, the city's origins are shrouded in myths of wolves and martyred saints. According to legend, the city was founded by Senius, son of Remus, hence the she-wolf symbols you will encounter throughout the city. St Ansano brought Christianity to Roman Siena and, although he was promptly tossed into a vat of hot tar and beheaded, he has left a legacy of mysticism traced through

St Catherine and St Bernardino to the present-day cult of the Madonna. The power of the Church came to an end when the populace rose up against the Ecclesiastical Council and established an independent republic in 1147. The 12th century was marked by rivalry in which the Florentine Guelfs usually triumphed over the Sienese Ghibellines.

In 1260, the battle of Montaperti routed the Florentines and won the Sienese 10 years of cultural supremacy, which saw the foundation of the University and the charitable

Main attractions

Il Campo
Palazzo Pubblico
Duomo
Museo dell'Opera
  Metropolitana
Santa Maria Della Scala
Pinacoteca Nazionale
Fortezza Medicea

Map on page 206

A Sienese backstreet café.

"fraternities". The Council of the Twenty-Four – a form of power-sharing between nobles and the working class – was followed by the Council of Nine, an oligarchy of merchants that ruled until 1335. Modern historians judge the Nine self-seeking and profligate, but under their rule the finest works of art were either commissioned or completed, including the famous amphitheatre-shaped Campo, the Palazzo Pubblico and Duccio's *Maestà*.

The ancient republic survived until 1529, when the reconciliation between the pope and the emperor ended the Guelf-Ghibelline feud. The occupying Spanish demolished the city towers, symbols of freedom and fratricide, and used the masonry to build the present

fortress. The final blow to the republic was the long siege of Siena by Emperor Charles V and Cosimo I in 1554.

After the Sienese defeat, the city of Siena became absorbed into the Tuscan dukedom. As an untrusted member of the Tuscan Empire, impoverished Siena turned in on itself until the 20th century. Still today, Siena's tumultuous history as arch-rivals of Florence is written in the streets and squares, and resonates in the passionate souls of the Sienese. Of all Tuscans, the Sienese have the longest memories and there are local aristocrats who still disdain to visit Florence.

Change is anathema to the city: traditional landowning, financial speculation, trade and tourism are more appealing than the introduction of new technology or industry. Siena has made a virtue of conservatism; stringent medieval building regulations protect the fabric of the city; tourism is decidedly low-key; old family firms such as Nannini, Siena's most famous café, do a roaring trade with locals (and also produced Gianna Nannini, one of Italy's best-known female singers). Siena is Italy's last surviving city-state, a city with the psychology of a village and the grandeur of a nation.

IL CAMPO

All roads lead to **Il Campo Ⓐ**, the huge main central square, shaped like an amphitheatre – the Sienese say that it is shaped like the protecting cloak of the Virgin, who, with St Catherine of Siena, is the city's patron saint. From the comfort of a pavement café on the curved side of the Campo, you can note the division of the paved surface into nine segments, commemorating the beneficent rule of the "Noveschi" – the Council of Nine that governed Siena from the mid-13th century to the early 14th, a period of stability and

prosperity when most of the city's main public monuments were built.

The Campo is tipped with the Renaissance **Fonte Gaia** (Fountain of Joy). The marble carvings are copies of the original sculptures by Iacopo della Quercia, which are on display in Santa Maria della Scala. Beneath the fountain lies one of Siena's best-kept secrets – a labyrinth of medieval tunnels extending for 25km (15.5 miles), constructed to channel water from the surrounding hills into the city. The underground aqueduct has two main tunnels: one leads to the Fonte Gaia and the other to the Fonte Branda, the best preserved of Siena's many fountains. Parts of this subterranean system can be visited and explored on a guided tour (enquire at the tourist office for more information).

At the square's base is the **Palazzo Pubblico Ⓑ**, the dignified Town Hall with its crenellated facade and waving banners, surmounted by the tall and slender tower. The Town Hall, which has been the home of the commune since it was completed in 1310, is a Gothic masterpiece of rose-coloured brick and

Chiocciola contrada; traditionally, its residents worked as terracotta makers.

Romulus, Remus and the she-wolf: Remus' son is said to have founded Siena.

silver-grey travertine. Each ogival arch is crowned by the *balzana*, Siena's black-and-white emblem representing the mystery and purity of the Madonna's life.

The distinctive **Torre del Mangia** (daily Mar–mid-Oct 10am–7pm, mid-Oct–Feb until 4pm) – named after the first bell-ringer, Mangiaguadagni, the "spend-thrift" – is 87 metres (285ft) high, and it's a 500-step climb to the top to enjoy glorious views of the pink piazza and Siena's rooftops. At the bottom of the tower, the Cappella in Piazza (Chapel in the Square) was erected in 1378 in thanksgiving for the end of the plague.

THE CITY MUSEUM

Although bureaucrats still toil in parts of the **Palazzo Pubblico**, as they have for some seven centuries, much of the complex is now dedicated to the **Museo Civico** (daily mid-Mar–Oct 10am–7pm, Nov–mid-Mar until 6pm), which displays some of the city's greatest treasures.

Siena's city council once met in the vast **Sala del Mappamondo**, although the huge map that then graced the

Contrada procession in the Campo, by Vincenzo Rustici.

walls has disappeared. What remains are two frescoes attributed to the medieval master Simone Martini: the majestic mounted figure of *Guidoriccio da Fogliano* and the *Maestà*. Martini's *Maestà*, a poetic evocation of the Madonna seated on a filigree throne, has a rich, tapestry-like quality. The muted blues, reds and ivory add a gauzy softness. Martini echoes Giotto's conception of perspective, yet clothes his Madonna in diaphanous robes, enhancing her spirituality in dazzling decoration.

Opposite is the iconic *Guidoriccio*, the haughty diamond-spangled *condottiero* (mercenary) reproduced on calendars and *panforte* boxes. But in recent years, despite Sienese denials, doubts have been cast on the authenticity of the fresco. Art historians maintain that a smaller painting uncovered below the huge panel is Martini's original, and the Guidoriccio we see was executed long after the artist's death.

In the next room is a genuine civic masterpiece, Ambrogio Lorenzetti's *Effects of Good and Bad Government*, painted in 1338 as an idealised tribute to the Council of the Nine. Its narrative realism and the vivid facial expressions used on this impressive painting give the allegory emotional resonance to observers. A wise old man symbolises the common good, while a patchwork of neat fields, tame boar and busy hoers suggests order and prosperity. By contrast, *Bad Government* is a desolate place, razed to the ground by a diabolical tyrant, the Sienese she-wolf at his feet.

THE CATHEDRAL

Exiting the Campo, turn left and head up the hill via one of the winding streets to the Piazza del Duomo. The **Duomo** 🅲 (www.operaduomo.siena.it; Mar–Oct Mon–Sat 10.30am–7pm, Sun 1.30–6pm, Nov–Feb 10.30am–5.30pm, Sun 1.30–5.30pm; combined ticket) is Siena's most controversial monument, either a symphony in black-and-white marble, or a tasteless iced cake, depending on your point of view. It began in 1220 as a round-arched Romanesque church, but soon

acquired a Gothic façade festooned with pinnacles. Bands of black, white and green Tuscan marble were inlaid with pink stone and topped by Giovanni Pisano's naturalistic statues.

The Cathedral interior is creativity run riot – oriental abstraction, Byzantine formality, Gothic flight and Romanesque austerity. A giddy chiaroscuro effect is created by the black-and-white walls reaching up to the starry blue vaults.

The inlaid floor is even more inspiring, and the Duomo is at its best between August and October when the intricate marble-inlaid paving is on display. Outside these times, to preserve the well-restored floor, many of the most captivating scenes are hidden. Major Sienese craftsmen worked on the marble *pavimentazione* between 1372 and 1562. The finest scenes are Matteo di Giovanni's pensive sibyls and the marble mosaics by Beccafumi. Giorgio Vasari called these "the most beautiful pavements ever made".

Nicola Pisano's octagonal marble pulpit is a Gothic masterpiece: built

The interior of the Duomo, a magnificent Gothic structure of banded black-and-white stone, with a superb floor of inlaid marble depicting biblical and pagan themes.

The fan-shaped Campo.

in 1226, it is a dramatic and fluid progression from his solemn pulpit in Pisa Cathedral. Off the north aisle is the decorative **Libreria Piccolomini** (www.operaduomo.siena.it; Mar–Oct 10.30am–7pm, Nov–Feb until 5.30pm; combined ticket), built in 1495 to house the personal papers and books of Pope Pius II. The frescoes by Pinturicchio (1509) show scenes from the life of the influential Renaissance pope, a member of the noble Sienese Piccolomini family and founder of the town of Pienza.

The **Crypt** is an extraordinary discovery, with recently revealed frescoes attributed to Duccio's school. Because the frescoes were perfectly concealed for so long, the intensity of the colours shines through in a vivid array of blue, gold and red. Given that the frescoes date from 1280, the "modern" expressiveness is all the more remarkable.

In the unfinished eastern section of the Cathedral is the **Museo dell'Opera Metropolitana �D** (www.operaduomo.siena.it; times as for the Libreria Piccolomini; combined ticket)

A backstreet leading towards the Duomo.

and Pisano's original statues for the facade. In a dramatically lit room above is Duccio's *Maestà*, the Virgin Enthroned, which graced the High Altar until 1506. Siena's best-loved work, the largest known medieval panel painting ever, was escorted from the artist's workshop to the Duomo in a torch-lit procession in 1311. The biggest panel depicts the Madonna enthroned among saints and angels, and, since the separation of the painting, facing scenes from the Passion. Although Byzantine Gothic in style, the *Maestà* is suffused with melancholy charm. The delicate gold and red colouring is matched by Duccio's grace of line, which influenced Sienese painting for the next two centuries. The Sienese believe that Giotto copied Duccio but sacrificed beauty to naturalism. The small panels do reveal some of Giotto's truthfulness and sense of perspective.

AROUND THE CATHEDRAL

Opposite the cathedral on the piazza, **Santa Maria della Scala ⊖** (www.santamariadellascala.com; times vary greatly so call 0577-534 504) is often described as a city within a city. It began as a hospital a thousand years ago and continued as one until its reincarnation as a museum in the year 2000. The far-sighted foundation originally functioned as a pilgrims' hostel, a poorhouse, an orphanage and a hospital, but is now a magnificent museum complex, embracing frescoed churches, granaries and an archaeological museum. Symbolically, the hospital door never had a key, demonstrating its role as a sanctuary to all-comers. The Pilgrims Hall, depicting care for the sick, is frescoed by Siena's finest 15th-century artists. The scenes portrayed, of wet-nurses, alms-giving and abandoned children, reveal a human side of the city absent from the luminous sacred art. The complex is also a venue for major medieval and Renaissance art exhibitions.

The city's **Museo Archeologico** (www.operaduomo.siena.it; mid-Mar–mid-Oct Sat–Thu 10am–7pm, Fri until 10pm, mid-Oct–mid-Mar Mon, Wed–Thu 10am–5pm, Fri until 10pm, Sat–Sun until 7pm; combined ticket) is also here, with its significant collection of Etruscan and Roman remains. The vaulted, former granaries make a moody setting for the display of Etruscan treasures, including funerary urns and sarcophagi from Sarteano.

A set of steps behind the Duomo leads down to Piazza San Giovanni, a small square dominated by the **Battistero di San Giovanni** (www.operaduomo.siena.it; times as for the Libreria Piccolomini; combined ticket), built beneath part of the Cathedral. Inside are frescoes and a beautiful baptismal font by Jacopo della Quercia.

ART MUSEUM AND CITY VISTAS

The **Pinacoteca Nazionale** Ⓕ (Via San Pietro 29; Tue–Sat 8.15am–7.15pm, Mon–Sun 9am–1pm) contains the finest collection of Sienese "Primitives" in the suitably Gothic Palazzo Buonsignori close to the Cathedral complex. The early rooms are full of Madonnas, apple-cheeked, pale, remote or warmly human. Matteo di Giovanni's stylised Madonnas shift to Lorenzetti's affectionate *Annunciation* and Ugolino di Neri's radiant *Madonna*. Neroccio di Bartolomeo's *Madonna* is as truthful as a Masaccio.

As a variant, the grisly deaths of obscure saints compete with a huge medieval crucifix with a naturalistic spurt of blood. The famous landscapes and surreal Persian city attributed to Lorenzetti were probably painted by Sassetta around a century later. But his *Madonna dei Carmelitani* is a sweeping cavalcade of vibrant Sienese life.

Those who want to enjoy a breathtaking view of Siena can visit the **Palazzo delle Papesse** (Via di Città 126), which offers a 360-degree view of the city from its loggia. Nearby, next to the Museo dell'Opera Metropolitana, another place to enjoy an extraordinary panorama of Siena is the **Facciatone**

Siena's ornate cathedral.

⊘ TURF WARS

The Palio horse race is the symbol of the Sienese's attachment to their city, and outsiders challenge it at their peril. One of the piazza's tight turns, the Curva di San Martino, set at a 95-degree angle, has often been the cause of fatalities among horses. Animal-rights activists have long protested against the event and Michela Brambilla, when she was Minister for Tourism in 2009–11, refused to allow the race to be put forward for Unesco World Heritage status. She said: "The shame of 48 horse deaths since 1970 marks the Palio of Siena, and a current investigation will shed light on accusations of doping in some horses. This damages the image of one of the most beautiful cities in the world." The Sienese beg to differ.

Statue of Sallustio Bandini, founder of Siena's library, on Piazza Salimbeni.

Strolling the walls of Fortezza Medicea.

or the "Duomo Nuovo," the facade of what was supposed to become the new cathedral but was never finished (http:///www.operaduomo.siena.it; times as for the Libreria Piccolomini; combined ticket with the Duomo).

For some outdoor space and greenery, turn left out of the gallery and head south to the **Orto Botanico** Ⓖ (Via P.A. Mattioli 4; Mar–mid-June, mid-Sept– mid-Oct daily 9.30am–5pm, mid-June– mid-Sept until 6.30pm, mid-Oct–Feb until 4.30pm), a small botanical garden just inside the city walls. Opposite the Orto Tolomei is another little garden, with a lovely view over the countryside and a sculpture that – although not obvious at first glance – outlines the shape of the city.

ST CATHERINE TRAIL

Slightly outside the historic centre, on Vicolo del Tiratoio, is the **Casa di Santa Caterina da Siena** Ⓗ (Costa di Sant' Antonio; daily 9.30am–7pm; free), the home of Catherine Benincase (1347–80), canonised in the 15th century by Pope Pius II and proclaimed Italy's patron saint in 1939, along with St Francis of Assisi. The house, garden and her father's dye-works now form the "Sanctuary of St Catherine". Although never taking holy orders, Catherine was an ascetic, and lived like a hermit in a cell, reputedly sleeping with a stone as her pillow. If it didn't sound too smug, the Sienese would admit to spiritual superiority. Apart from producing two saints and fine religious art, the city still venerates the Virgin.

Inside the nearby **Basilica di San Domenico** Ⓘ (www.basilicacateriniana. com; Mar–Oct 7am–6.30pm, Nov–Feb 9am–6pm; free) – a huge fortress-like church founded by the Dominicans – a reliquary containing the saint's head is kept in the Cappella Santa Caterina. The chapel is decorated with frescoes depicting events in the saint's life, the majority completed by Il Sodoma in the early 16th century. The view from outside the Basilica across to the Duomo is spectacular.

THE FORTRESS

From here it's a short walk to the Forte di Santa Barbara, also known as the **Fortezza Medicea** Ⓙ, built by Cosimo I after his defeat of Siena in 1560. The red-brick fortress now houses an open-air theatre, provides glorious views of the countryside and contains the **Enoteca Italiana** (www. enoteca-italiana.it; Wed–Sat 3–8pm). The latter, a wine exhibition and shop, allows for guided tastings from a wide range of Tuscan wines. This is also the best place to study and savour Sienese wines, from Chianti Classico to Vino Nobile di Montepulciano, Brunello di Montalcino and Vernaccia di San Gimignano.

Via Banchi di Sopra, lined with fine medieval palazzi, is one of the three main arteries of the city centre (the other two being Via Banchi di Sotto and Via di Città). It links the Campo with the splendid **Piazza Salimbeni** Ⓚ

at its northern end. The grand palazzi flanking the square are the head office of the Monte dei Paschi di Siena, one of the oldest banks in the world. Founded in 1472 and still an important employer, it is known as "the city father".

BASILICA OF ST FRANCIS

From the square, Via dei Rossi leads east to the **Basilica di San Francesco** **❶** (7.30am–noon, 3.30–7pm; free). Now housing part of the University, the vast church exhibits fragments of frescoes by Pietro and Ambrogio Lorenzetti. Next door, the 15th-century **Oratorio di San Bernardino** (www. operaduomo.siena.it; Mar–June and mid-Aug–Oct 1.30–7pm, July–mid-Aug 1.30–4.30pm), dedicated to Siena's great preacher, contains frescoes by the artists Il Sodoma and Beccafumi.

Here, as at all its far reaches, the city has well-preserved walls and gateways. Siena's compactness makes these easy to explore, inviting you to wind through the sinuous medieval streets and stumble across secret courtyards, fountains and surprisingly rural views. This perfect, pink-tinged city is a delight to discover on foot, from the shell-shaped Campo to the galleries full of soft-eyed Sienese madonnas. In the backstreets, the city history is laid out before you, with noble coats of arms above doorways, or *contrada* animal symbols defining where their citizens belong. Everywhere leads back to the Campo, at its most theatrical in the late afternoon, after a day spent in the shadows of the city walls and inner courtyards.

But to escape the crowds, walk along the walls, or take the countrified lane of **Via del Fosso di Sant'Ansano**, which runs behind Santa Maria della Scala. Or stroll to **Santa Maria dei Servi** to lap up equally lovely views en route to a sublime church.

Given its impossibly narrow alleys threading between tall rose-brick palaces, Siena is mostly pedestrianised. Although the city is closed to traffic, visitors with hotel reservations are generally allowed to drive in, if only to park in a designated spot.

Sienese panforte.

Shopping for sweet treats in a deli.

⊘ SIENESE SWEETS

Sienese pastries are so renowned that they even have their own saint watching over them, San Lorenzo. Exotic spices reached Siena along the Via Francigena pilgrimage route, and many find their way into the medieval recipes still used today. *Panforte*, a rich, filling cake, dates back to 1205, and is often eaten with sweet Vin Santo. The intense flavours are created by a mix of honey, almonds, hazelnuts, candied orange peel, and a secret blend of spices such as cinnamon and nutmeg. *Panpepato*, a spicier version, predates it. The delicacy was originally the preserve of Sienese nuns, who guarded their secret recipes, which were also a source of revenue. Such was *panforte's* popularity that even in the 14th century, it was being exported. Originally a festive treat, *panforte* is now eaten all year round. *Ricciarelli*, small almond biscuits, are also typically Sienese, and far lighter.

The most famous place for *panforte* is **Nannini** (Banchi di Sopra 24; www.pasticcerienannini.it), a bar and pastry shop, but **Pasticceria Bini** (Via Stalloreggi 91) is even more illustrious, occupying what was supposedly Duccio's workshop. Carved into the former stables of a patrician palace, **Antica Drogheria Manganelli** (Via di Citta 71) is another exotic shop for Sienese delights.

📷 THE PASSION OF THE PALIO

In little more than a minute, the Campo is filled with unbearable happiness and irrational despair as centuries-old loyalties are put to the test.

It is strange how a race that lasts just 90 seconds can require 12 months' planning, a lifetime's patience and the involvement of an entire city. But Siena's famous Palio does just that, as it has done since the 13th century, when an August Palio made its debut. At that time, the contest took the form of a bareback race the length of the city. The bareback race around Siena's main square, the Piazza del Campo, was introduced in the 17th century. Today the Palio is held twice a year, in early July and mid-August. The Palio, which has been run in times of war, famine and plague, stops for nothing. In the 1300s, criminals were released from jail to celebrate the festival. When the Fascists were gaining ground in 1919, Siena postponed council elections until after the Palio. In 1943, British soldiers in a Tunisian prisoner-of-war camp feared a riot when they banned Sienese prisoners from staging a Palio; Sienese fervour triumphed.

Although, as the Sienese say, *"Il Palio corre tutto l'anno"* ("The Palio runs all year"), the final preparations boil down to three days, during which there is the drawing by lots of the horse for each competing ward *(contrada)*, the choice of the "jockeys" and then the six trial races – the last of which is held on the morning of the Palio itself.

The ruthless race lurches around the Campo three times. If a riderless horse wins, the animal is almost deified: it given the place of honour in the victory banquet and has its hooves painted gold.

A highlight of the Palio pageantry is the spectacular display of the flag-wavers, famous throughout Italy for their elaborate manoeuvres.

Palio band.

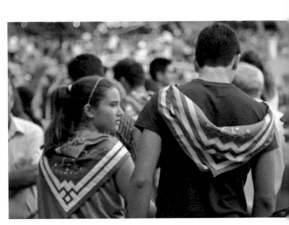

Proud members of the Oca (goose) contrada.

The Power of the Contrade

In Siena the *contrada* rules: ask a Sienese where he is from and he will say, *"Ma sono della Lupa"* ("But I'm from the Wolf *contrada*"). The first loyalty is to the city in the head, not to the city on the map.

Ten out of Siena's 17 *contrade* take part in each Palio: the seven who did not run in the previous race and three more who are selected by lot. Each *contrada* appoints a captain and two lieutenants to run their Palio campaign. In the Palio, the illegal becomes legal: bribery, kidnapping, plots and the doping of horses are all common occurrences.

Each *contrade* has its own standard, many of which are displayed around the city during the Palio and play an important role in the ceremonial aspect of the event.

Flags, or standards, are a central theme of the Palio event. In fact, the *palio* itself – the trophy of victory for which everyone is striving – is a standard: a silk flag emblazoned with the image of the Madonna and the coats of arms of the city, ironically referred to by the Sienese as the *cencio*, or rag. The *contrada* that wins the event retains possession of the prized *palio* standard until the next race takes place.

The Historical Parade, which is staged in the run-up to the main race, retraces Siena's centuries of struggle against Florence, from the glorious victory against its rival in 1260 to the ghastly defeat in 1560.

...ena's Campo becomes extremely crowded during the ...ce so TV screens are set up in the contrada squares. ...fter the race, feasts are held to celebrate, or to ...mmiserate, the result.

The words "C'è terra in piazza" ("There's earth in the Campo") are the signal to remove the colourful costumes from Siena's museums to feature in the great Historical Parade.

SOUTH OF SIENA

The route through the dramatic Crete region delivers you to the heart and soul of Tuscany. Pienza, Montalcino and Montepulciano are must-sees, but countless other lesser-known towns await discovery, while the hidden beauty of the Val d'Orcia river valley and the tortuous roads of Monte Amiata beckon the intrepid.

Main attractions
Abbazia Monte Oliveto
  Marriore
Pienza
Montepulciano
Val d'Orcia
Bagno Vignoni
Chiusi
Monte Amiata
Montalcino
Sant'Antimo

Map on page 219

The area just south of Siena is a primeval landscape of stark beauty. Appropriately called **Le Crete**, it is a moonscape of interlocking pale-clay hummocks and treeless gullies. In winter it is cold, bleak and even more crater-like. In summer the curvaceous terrain is softened by a deep green blanket. Sienese city-dwellers love this barren landscape and are successfully discouraging local farmers from accepting European Union funds to flatten the land and grow wheat.

There is an extraordinary range of wildlife in the area: by day, wild deer roam beside the Ombrone River; by night, porcupines and foxes are about in the woods. If intrepid walkers venture out on a late autumn evening they may meet a strange character with a couple of dogs, a torch and a harness. He is a truffle hunter, sniffing out truffles in the dampest ditches. More legal are the Sardinian peasants selling cheese. Unlike many Tuscans, Sardinians are prepared to live in remote, infertile places.

The best route through the Crete is the SS438 to Asciano, and the SP451 to Monte Oliveto Maggiore – empty roads through a barren landscape, dotted with striking hilltop farmhouses and lone cypresses. Known as the Accona Desert in medieval times, it retains its spiritual remoteness.

MONTE OLIVETO MAGGIORE

After so much pale, undulating land, the red abbey of **Monte Oliveto Maggiore ❶** (daily 9.15am–noon, 3.15–6pm, winter until 5pm; free) is glimpsed through a wood of pines, oaks and olive trees. If the land appears to fall away from the abbey, it is not far from the truth: land erosion and frequent landslides provide a natural defence to the abbey's mystical centre. In 1313 Tolomei, a wealthy Sienese, abandoned the law for a life of prayer

A timeless Tuscan landscape.

in the wilderness, taking with him two fellow hermits. After a vision of white-robed monks, Tolomei established an Olivetan Order under Benedictine rule. The monks followed St Benedict's precept that "a real monk is one who lives by his own labour". Fortunately, a meagre diet, fervent prayer and lack of conversation stimulated the monks to artistic endeavour in the form of wood-carving, sculpture and manuscript design. As a noted artistic centre, the abbey invited Luca Signorelli and Il Sodoma to decorate the cloisters with scenes from St Benedict's life.

The excitement of Il Sodoma aside, Monte Oliveto is a spiritual retreat. The austere refectory, the library cluttered with ancient manuscripts and books, the exquisite marquetry work of the choir stalls are as peaceful as the hidden walks deep into the woods. Today, there is a restaurant, and a lovely shop selling honey, oil and liqueurs made by the monks, as well as wine tasting in vaulted cellars. The former monastic cells are also available for overnight visitors (tel: 0577-707 611; closed in winter).

Situated on a plain in the heart of the Crete, **Buonconvento** is worth a brief stop, if only to admire the imposing red 14th-century walls and massive medieval city gates of iron-bound wood. In 1366 Siena rebuilt the walls because, as a Sienese outpost, Buonconvento had been devastated. Today, the town is essentially a place for a leisurely introduction to truffles or game, or for a summer picnic in the peaceful gardens beside the town walls.

PIENZA

Pienza ❷ is an exquisite Renaissance showpiece, slightly suffering from its over-popularity. Although created by a humanist pope, Pius II, Pienza is almost too perfect to be human and too precious to be spiritual. Every fountain, piazza and painting is harmonious. Model citizens walk through streets as romantic as their names – Via dell'Amore, Via del Bacio, Via della Fortuna – streets of "love", "kiss" and "fortune".

Pienza's origins date back to 1458. When E.S. Piccolomini was elected pope, he could not resist playing God

A view of Pienza.

⊙ Tip

The pretty walled village of Monticchiello offers fine views of Pienza, just 4km (2.4 miles) away. It is also renowned for the Teatro Povero – an annual play written and starring the villagers about life in rural Tuscany.

in his home village, Corsignano. He chose the noted Florentine architect Bernardo Rossellino to ennoble the hamlet in accordance with humanist principles. When the first masterpiece in modern town planning emerged late and over budget, the Pope reduced his fraudulent architect to tears with his words, "You did well, Bernardo, in lying to us about the expense involved in the work... Your deceit has built these glorious structures; which are praised by all except the few consumed with envy."

Bernardo Rossellino was rewarded with a scarlet robe, 100 ducats and some new commissions. The decision to build a cathedral enabled the pope to rechristen Corsignano the village as Pienza the city. The result is what locals call a *città d'autore*, a city inspired by one vision. After Pienza, other cities in Tuscany or elsewhere are liable to look chaotic.

Much of the symmetry lies in the cathedral square, **Piazza Pio II**, and the slightly listing Duomo adds to the charm. Despite a Renaissance facade, the interior is late Gothic and decorated with mystical paintings from the Sienese school. In one central alcove is a chilling *Assumption* by Vecchietta, in which St Agatha holds a cup containing her breasts, torn off by the executioner. The Duomo's facade, the gracious arches, the well and the Palazzo Piccolomini, the pope's home, are just as Pius left them when he set off to fight the Crusades, never to return.

Palazzo Piccolomini (Tue–Sun mid-Oct–mid-Mar 10am–4.30pm, mid-Mar–mid-Oct until 6.30pm; guided tours only), now a museum, is lined with both grand and homely treasures, including a library and arms collection. In the pope's bedroom, the intriguing book-holder, as cumbersome as a church lectern, is proof that the pope did not read in bed. The library opens on to a tranquil loggia with Etruscan urns, hanging gardens and a panorama stretching across the Orcia valley as far as Monte Amiata.

On the opposite side of the square, the **Museo Diocesano** (mid-Mar–Oct Wed–Mon 10am–1.30pm and 2.30–6pm, Nov–mid-Mar Sat–Sun

Chapel in a golden field outside Pienza.

10am–1pm and 2–5pm) has a rich collection of medieval paintings, tapestries, and ornate gold- and silverware.

Just outside Pienza is the **Pieve di Corsignano**, a simple but coherent Romanesque church where Pope Pius II was baptised.

MONTEPULCIANO

The winding road from Pienza up to **Montepulciano ❸** – visible for miles around, with houses clustered on the sides of the hump of a hill on which it is built – is lined with *vendita diretta* signs, offering pecorino and wine. After Pienza, Montepulciano's asymmetrical design and spontaneous development give it the architectural tension that the earlier city lacks. If Pienza belongs to

Rossellino, Montepulciano is Antonio da Sangallo's masterpiece.

Just outside and below the city walls, at the end of a long line of cypresses, lies Sangallo's **San Biagio**, the Renaissance church most at ease with its setting. The building's isolation focuses attention on the honey-coloured travertine, the Greek Cross design, the dome and the purity of the line. Sangallo's design skills rival Bramante's, not just in the church, the elegant well and the porticoed Canon's House, but elsewhere in the city. The airy interior has a deeply classical feel, more akin to the Roman Pantheon than to a small Tuscan church.

Traffic is banned within the city walls, but you can park outside San Biagio, from where it's a short but steepish

The Chiesa San Biagio in Montepulciano.

walk into town. Alternatively, park in one of the many car parks at Montepulciano's eastern end and enter through the Porta al Prato. Here, Piazza Savonarola is guarded by a statue of the Marzocco lion, the symbol of Florentine power. From here the princely Via di Gracciano nel Corso leads up to the main square. Its lower end is lined with noble palaces. The Renaissance **Palazzo Bucelli**, at no. 73, is decorated with a mosaic of Etruscan urns and pots, a reminder of the city's ancient origins. The road continues upwards to Piazza Grande, both the highest part of town and the highpoint culturally.

Florentine design has shaped the grand facades on Piazza Grande, but earlier Sienese Gothic touches are present in the interiors, double arches and doorways. Both styles reflect Montepulciano's buffeting between the two city-states and the eventual supremacy of Florence. On one side, the 15th-century **Palazzo Comunale** (Town Hall) has a Florentine Michelozzo facade adorning Sienese turrets. The **Tower** (Apr–Oct daily 10am–1pm, 2–6pm),

modelled on that of Florence's Palazzo Vecchio, surveys the whole province: from Monte Amiata to Siena and across to Lake Trasimeno in Umbria.

Sangallo's **Palazzo Contucci**, on the other side of the square, still belongs to the aristocratic Contucci family, who produce Vino Nobile. In the **Cantine Contucci** (wine cellars; www.contucci.it; Mon–Fri 9.30am–12.30pm, 2.30–6.30pm), Ginevra Contucci will be delighted to expand on the noble wine heritage of her family, the virtues of their silky *Riserva*, and the maze of secret tunnels underneath the palace. Vino Nobile, a smooth red wine with a hint of violets, was "ennobled" in 1549 when Pope Paul III's sommelier proclaimed it "a most perfect wine, a wine for lords".

Between the two grand palazzi, at the top of wide steps, stands the **Duomo** (daily 8.30am–6.30pm), which contains a masterpiece of the Siena school: the huge *Assumption* triptych by Taddeo di Bartolo (1401) shines out above the high altar in the vast, gloomy nave. If you need cheering up, call into the labyrinthine cellars of **Cantine del**

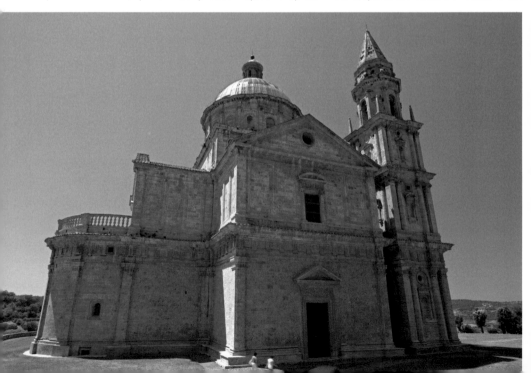

Redi (Via Ricci), where part of the *Twilight* vampire series was filmed (see page 189).

A CIRCULAR TOUR

Scattered among the rolling landscape of Siena province are some beautiful villages, each with a separate identity and architectural treasures espied almost incidentally over the brow of a hill. A circular itinerary from Montepulciano unites a group of tiny villages once ruled by the Cacciaconti barons.

Montefollonico ❹, 8km (5 miles) northwest of Montepulciano, has a 13th-century frescoed church and one of the best restaurants in Italy, La Chiusa.

Petroio ❺, set on a rocky, wooded promontory, is a grand fortified village on an old pilgrim route. In recent years it has been undergoing a revival thanks to its terracotta – examples of which adorn the city walls, Palazzo Pretorio and the medieval towers. Look out for the Canon's House, which contains a remarkable *Madonna and Child* by Taddio di Bartolo. Near the village is the intact **Abbadia a Sicille**, built by the Knights Templar as a refuge for knights on the way to the Holy Land. The adjoining Romanesque church is decorated with two Maltese crosses, but an Olivetan coat of arms marks the abolition of the Templars.

Set among farmland and woods, **Castelmuzio** is a medieval village wrapped up in itself, its Museum of Sacred Art and its direct line to San Bernardo. Narrow shops in winding streets sell honey, salami and cheese made by an ageing population of churchgoers.

Once a Cacciaconti fortress, aristocratic **Montisi ❻** commands a view over two valleys, a view that is even more stirring when seen from the basket of a hot-air balloon (www.ballooningintuscany.com). Even discounting the ballooning base in the village, Montisi offers lofty views, intriguing alleys, earthy inns, and two tiny Romanesque churches, one featuring a Scuola di Duccio crucifix. A few apparently stark, uninviting farmhouses conceal wonderful frescoes and the occasional private chapel so are worth investigating.

One can return to Montepulciano via **Sinalunga**, a dual-personality town

One of the more spiritual aspects of the St Benedict frescoes.

⊘ IL SODOMA'S FRESCOES

The main cloister of Monte Oliveto Maggiore is covered in frescoes dedicated to the *Life of St Benedict*, begun by Luca Signorelli in 1495 and completed by Il Sodoma from 1505. Of the two contemporaries, Signorelli had the more spiritual approach, but his loveliest work is a domestic scene portraying two monks being served by girls at an inn. In 1497, after only nine frescoes were completed, Signorelli left the rest for Il Sodoma to execute. Vasari adored Signorelli's spirituality as much as he loathed Il Sodoma's exuberance, hedonistic lifestyle and "licentious" fondness for "boys and beardless youths", which earned him his name. In one scene Il Sodoma portrays himself with his pet badgers looking like a pair of well-trained dogs. Il Sodoma's love of what Vasari called his Noah's Ark of "badgers, squirrels, apes, dwarf asses and Elba ponies" is often present, but his landscapes only come to life with the temptations of the flesh. His gaze rarely focuses on the main subject, but is deflected by the turn of an attractive leg, a mischievous smile, a perky badger or a soldier's buttocks. Needless to say, the inhibited monks preferred Signorelli's work to that of the man they labelled "Il Mataccio", the imbecile or madman.

The entrance to Chianciano Terme.

Montepulciano's Etruscan origins are evident everywhere.

with a hideous "low town" but a pleasant "old town". Its original name, Asinalunga, echoes its shape, "the long donkey". But in the lively market, pigs, not donkeys, are in evidence in the form of *porchetta*, the local speciality of roast pig flavoured with rosemary.

VAL D'ORCIA

The **Val d'Orcia** is a beguiling rural area south of Le Crete, but within sight of hulking Monte Amiata. Although these villages suffered from depopulation in the 1950s, today they are reaping the benefits of an intact urban and rural landscape. **San Quirico d'Orcia** ❼ is a dignified valley town still waiting for its heyday. It survived both an attack by Cesare Borgia's troops in 1502 and a World War II bombardment.

The Romanesque **Collegiata**, made from sandstone and local travertine, has three remarkable portals and columns supported by two stony lionesses. The lovely park, the **Horti Leonini**, is a model 16th-century Italian garden, complete with geometric beds. Stern, 17th-century **Palazzo Chigi** has now

opened its frescoed rooms for inspection (daily 8am–6.30pm), and, round the corner, a bijou boutique hotel is flourishing. It seems that San Quirico might well be enjoying a belated renaissance.

Just south of San Quirico, off the SS2, **Bagno Vignoni** ❽ is a tiny but lively spa station, at its most evocative at dusk. The steam rises from the hot springs, and the yellowish light of the lanterns dimly illuminates the stone facades of the buildings lining the square, which is in fact a stone pool of sulphurous water, where both Lorenzo de' Medici and St Catherine once bathed. The hot springs were used by the Romans but became public baths in medieval times. Bathing is now forbidden, but the baths of Hotel Posta Marcucci are open to non-residents for a fee, and are also open at night on summer weekends.

From the relaxation of the pool, all senses are fulfilled at once: outside the pool of light, the sound of sheep and crickets reverberates; the softness of the hot, chalky water dissolves tiredness; and the smell of sulphur evaporates into the night air. After a swim, a

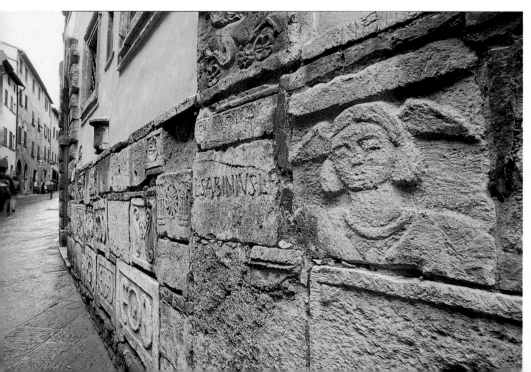

short *passeggiata* around the old baths shows the well-restored square at its most romantic.

In the vicinity are three medieval fortresses – Ripa d'Orcia, Rocca d'Orcia and Castiglione d'Orcia. After the turning to Bagno Vignoni, **Ripa d'Orcia**, an enchanted castle (now a hotel; tel: 0577-897 376; www.castelloripadorcia.com) set among cypress groves, comes into view.

Rocca d'Orcia ❾, a fortified village once owned by the warring Salimbeni clan, has an impressive castle open to visitors. **Castiglione d'Orcia** offers more of the same: an atmospheric, cobblestoned centre, a ruined fortress and wonderful views. The abbey of Sant'Antimo can be reached from here. The mountain roads in the area are tortuous but beautiful, as are the walks.

CHIUSI

Although set among attractive low hills, **Chiusi** ❿ comes across as a rather unprepossessing town, somewhat devoid of Renaissance charm. The "low town" is a commercial centre and the shabby "high town" is endearing but overwhelmed by its glorious Etruscan past.

Then, as now, the Chiusini were farmers, merchants and craftsmen, a spirit that predominates over artistry. Yet, with a little Etruscan knowledge and much curiosity, the town is as fascinating as any in Tuscany. It boasts a complete underground city; an unrivalled collection of female cinerary urns; and the only tomb paintings in their original setting in all of Tuscany.

As one of the greatest city-states in the Etruscan League, Chiusi, or "Kamars", controlled the area from Lago di Trasimeno to Monte Amiata. After reaching its zenith as a trading centre in the 7th century BC, Etruscan Kamars became submerged by Roman Clusium and then by medieval Chiusi. The old city now survives on three levels of civilisation: the Etruscan necropolis beneath the city hills; the Roman street-grid system below the Cathedral; and the medieval city above it.

The **Museo Archeologico Nazionale** (daily 9am–8pm) has one of the finest collections of its kind in Italy, which

⏹ Eat

On the main square of Bagno Vignone you can sample the spa and Tuscan trattoria at Albergo Le Terme (www.albergoleterme.it; tel: 0577-887 150). The hotel, setting and food are better than at the Posta Marcucci, even if the latter has a far more romantic spa pool. A hard call.

Montepulciano is bathed in a russet glow at sunset.

VAL D'ORCIA

The Val d'Orcia combines the most crowd-pleasing elements in one small valley: castles and country walks; spas and superb inns; iconic scenery and intoxicating settings.

The valley's prime location on the Via Francigena pilgrim route partially explains the surprisingly noble architecture and grandiose Romanesque churches; medieval insecurity accounts for the cluster of castles built to watch over the Orcia valley. But nothing quite explains why these elements come together so well.

A SPECIAL BOND WITH THE LAND

Landscaped since time immemorial, the Val d'Orcia represents quintessential Tuscany: clusters of cypresses, ribbons of plane trees, sloping vineyards and farms perched on limestone ridges. But it was not this alone that won the area Unesco World Heritage status in 2004. It was as much to do with the harmonious relationship between the custodians and their landscape, a bond that has survived to the present day, leaving the countryside cultivated but unscathed. This

Vineyards below Sant'Antimo.

harmony extends to the hilltop hamlets, the Romanesque churches, the isolated farmhouses and the contemplative abbeys. All entities are anchored in this mystical yet pragmatic patchwork: they serve a purpose yet transcend it. This happy partnership has produced an idealised landscape that is at once the continuation of the natural order and the best that man and nature can achieve in unison.

Partly boosted by its Unesco recognition, Pienza, in particular, has become very popular, almost as much for its superb pecorino cheeses as for its perfect architecture and splendid views of Monte Amiata.

But it's not a case of the valley selling its soul. If spas can be mystical, then Bagno Vignoni comes close, not just because St Catherine of Siena bathed there. The ancient abbey of Sant'Antimo continues to inspire visitors: the Romanesque church reels you in with its carved capitals, its Gregorian chant, its Cistercian spirit.

ORCIA TRAILS

This soft mysticism extends to the landscape, where the rambles around Sant'Antimo are among the loveliest in Tuscany. A waymarked trail links the abbey with Montalcino on a gentle, 9.5km (6-mile) walk that unravels views over Monte Amiata and the whole of Val d'Orcia. A far more challenging 18km (11-mile) trail connects the abbey with Bagno Vignoni, via the medieval fortress of Ripa d'Orcia. En route are views of the Brunello vineyards, the soft hills around Pienza and the looming presence of Monte Amiata.

TRAIN TRAVEL

Alternatively, the so-called Nature Train (Treno Natura; www.trenonatura.terresiena.it) provides a similar atmosphere. This service runs through countryside, covering routes where towns are peripheral. The Nature Train generally does the Val d'Orcia run on Sundays in spring and autumn. At other times of the year, the train service focuses on quirky local festivals, including the olive-oil festival in San Quirico d'Orcia, or the pork festival in Vivo d'Orcia. During the autumn white truffle season, one special train travels round the Crete moonscape to San Giovanni d'Asso (http://museotartufo.museisenesi.org), culminating in truffle tasting over lunch.

attests to the vitality of Kamars and shows a distinct bias in the outstanding female Canopic jars, cinerary urns and rounded *cippi* tombstones. The containers have Egyptian-style lids resembling human or animal heads. The Etruscans borrowed freely from the Greeks and Egyptians; the imitation Greek vases are less rational but more vigorous than the originals.

A speciality of Chiusi is *bucchero*, glossy black earthenware, often in the form of vases with figures in relief. This pottery has a sophisticated metallic finish that cannot be reproduced by modern craftsmen. Although much of the domestic pottery has a naturalness verging on the commonplace, the sarcophagi, the cinerary urns and the crouching sphinxes reveal an underlying obsession with death and the appeasement of shadowy spirits.

A visit to the **Etruscan tombs**, 3km (2 miles) outside town, can be arranged with the museum staff or pre-booked (tel: 0578-20177). The tombs contain sarcophagi, cinerary urns and, in the case of the **Tomb of the Monkey**, rare wall-paintings of athletic games and domestic scenes.

Three civilisations are visible at once in Chiusi's **Duomo**: the Romanesque Cathedral is built from Etruscan and Roman fragments. The **Museo della Cattedrale** (Feb–mid-Mar Sat–Sun 10am–noon and 3–4.30pm, mid-Mar–mid-Oct Mon–Fri 10am–12.10pm, Sat–Sun 10am–12.10pm and 3–4.30pm) is of limited appeal, but your ticket entitles you to a tour of a fascinating labyrinth beneath the Cathedral. The recently excavated tunnels are part of an Etruscan water system cut into the rocks, which provided natural filtration. After being led through tunnels to a large Roman cistern dating from the 1st century BC, you emerge, blinking, at the bottom of the Cathedral bell tower. Climb to the top to gaze at Monte Amiata, the Val d'Orcia, and even Lake Trasimeno.

CHIANCIANO TERME

After underground Chiusi, **Chianciano Terme ⓫** is a breath of fresh air. Italians have flocked to this spa town since Roman times to enjoy the unique powers of Acqua Santa. The innovative

The thermal pool in Bagno Vignoni.

Terme Sensoriali is just one of a new breed of swish thermal day spas that have appeared across Tuscany in recent years, replacing the more old-fashioned clinical baths.

Although better known for its spa than for its culture, a new museum aims to put Chianciano on the artistic map. The **Museo d'Arte di Chianciano** (280 Viale della Liberta, www.museodarte.org; summer only Wed–Sun 10am–12.30pm and 3–7pm) presents a collection by the Realists, Surrealists and Post-Impressionists, as well as staging international exhibitions.

Southern Siena province is positively bursting with Etruscan remains, and digging produces a continual flow of exciting finds. In Chianciano, well-marked walks lead to several recently discovered tombs and temples, and an excellent **Museo Archeologico** (www.museoetrusco.it; Apr–Oct Tue–Sun 10am–1pm and 4–7pm, Nov–Mar Sat–Sun same hours) contains an intact monumental tomb of a princess, lined with bronze and adorned with gold and bronze artefacts. The museum also features the remains of a spa complex dating from the 1st century BC, which was discovered in Chianciano and is thought to be the sacred magic spring that cured Emperor Augustus in 23 BC from a life-threatening stomach ailment.

AROUND LA FOCE

Near the town are some of the loveliest walks and drives in Tuscany. Many walks start from **La Foce** ⑫, a 15th-century farmhouse that overlooks the fertile Val di Chiana and the desolate craters of the Val d'Orcia. The superb gardens here (www.lafoce.com; guided tours only: late Mar–Oct Wed 3pm, 4pm, 5pm and 6pm, Sat–Sun 11.30am, 3pm and 4.30pm) were designed by the famous British landscape gardener Cecil Pinsent. There are views across an Etruscan site to Monte Amiata and Monte Cetona. Its excellent strategic position meant that its owners, the Anglo-Italian Origos, allowed it to be used as the partisans' refuge during World War II. Excavations on the property have uncovered some 200 Etruscan tombs. From here, a rough track leads to Petraporciana, the partisans' hidden headquarters, and to a primeval

The famous cypress-lined road leading to La Foce.

forest full of giant oaks, cyclamens, wild orchids or snowdrops: a perfect short spring or autumn walk.

Beside La Foce is **Castelluccio**, a castle – and summer concert venue – that commands the best-loved view in the province: a sinuous line of cypresses plotting an Etruscan route across the craters. When Prince Charles stayed at La Foce, proud locals were not surprised to see him painting this view.

A short walk leads to **Pocce Lattaie** and prehistoric caves with dripping stalactites shaped like teats or nipples. These pagan caves were used in fertility rites and when propitiatory offerings were made to the gods. Be prepared to hire a guide from Chianciano.

AROUND MONTE CETONA

From Chianciano, an idyllic rural drive leads via La Foce to Sarteano and Cetona, two small medieval and Etruscan towns. These views of desolate *crete*, fortified farmhouses and hazy Monte Amiata are captured by Paolo Busato in his celebrated photographs. It is worth sacrificing a hired car to the dirt roads, but the nervous can take the more direct route to Sarteano.

Castiglioncello sul Trionoro is a tiny village with a *castello* and a church containing a Trecento Madonna. The village is set amid vast expanses of abandoned countryside in which Etruscan remains are regularly uncovered.

Spilling over its double ring of city walls, **Sarteano** ⓭ is a popular spa centre that has retained its traditional identity. The town offers Etruscan remains, a grandiose 13th-century Rocca and crumbling Renaissance palazzi built into the city walls. There is an interesting **Museo Etrusco** (tel: 0578-269 261; Apr–Oct Tue–Sun 10.30am–12.30pm, 4–7pm, Nov–Mar Sat–Sun same hours) but, contrary to rumours, the tomb of the Etruscan king Porsenna has never been discovered. In August each year, Sarteano holds a famous *Giostra* or jousting tournament.

Cetona ⓮ clings to a richly wooded hill. The grand 18th-century houses on the plains are a relic of past prosperity, but Cetona is a refreshingly authentic Tuscan community. The broad traffic-free square is filled with locals going about their daily lives, free (as yet) of the quaint wine, food and craft shops that predominate in touristic towns such as Pienza. Although Cetona is noted for its textiles and copies of Etruscan vases, it now relies on *agriturismo* to keep its population from leaving. A short stay in a local farm with mountain walks, local cheeses and *bruschetti* drenched in olive oil is highly recommended.

A very scenic route, the Via della Montagna, goes from Cetona to the spa town of **San Casciano dei Bagni** ⓯ (take the high road north out of town and follow signs to Mondo "X"). En route, it's worth stopping at the beautifully restored **Convento di San Francesco**. It now houses a rehabilitation centre (Mondo "X"), but if you ring the bell, one of the occupants of the *comunità* will be happy to show you round.

A bather at Bagni San Filippo.

⊙ Fact

Radicofani is linked to the exploits of Ghino di Tacco, the "gentle outlaw" immortalised by Dante and Boccaccio. Exiled Ghino controlled the town from Radicofani Castle, built by Hadrian IV, the only English pope. A fierce basalt sculpture of Ghino stands in this forbidding town of low stone houses with external stairways, blind alleys and severe facades.

The view towards Abbadia San Salvatore.

The **Fonteverde spa resort**, on the edge of San Casciano dei Bagni, is one of Tuscany's most alluring destination spas, with the Medici villa at the heart of the stylish resort. Fortunately, you can also use it as a day spa, and wallow in the hot pools while gazing over a sea of greenery (www.fonteverdespa.com).

ROUTES UP TO MONTE AMIATA

The journey to Monte Amiata, southern Tuscany's highest peak, is at least as rewarding as the arrival. The fast Pienza to Abbadia San Salvatore route allows for a detour to the thermal baths at **Bagni San Filippo**, where you can float along on faded charm in a friendly, affordable time-warp spa, or dine in the good-value restaurant (www.termesanfilippo.it)

The alternative route, via Sarteano and **Radicofani** ⑯, was the one taken by both Dickens and Montaigne to a location second only to Volterra for natural drama. While the mountain villages have walking and food trails to thank for their revival, the villages on the edge of Amiata seem to be in permanent limbo, trapped rather than enhanced by a medieval identity. Dickens found Radicofani "as barren, as stony, and as wild as Cornwall, in England". Perched on a craggy basalt rock, it is the only place in Italy to possess a triple Medicean wall. The town overlooks *"Il Mare di Sassi"*, the "Sea of Stones", suitable only for very hardy sheep. Although an 18th-century earthquake destroyed much of the town, enough atmosphere remains.

The drive from Radicofani up to **Abbadia San Salvatore** ⑰ is via Le Conie, a tortuous road known as "Amiata's sentry". For those not interested in skiing, mountain walks and disused mercury mines, Abbadia is best known for its overrated **Abbazia** (abbey) and its medieval "high town". The Romanesque **San Salvatore** (daily summer 8am–8pm; winter until 7pm; free) is all that remains of a once-magnificent abbey, but it has been clumsily restored. A 12th-century *Crucifix* and the crypt with 36 columns remain relatively unspoilt. Geometric symbols, grapes, palm leaves, animals and Gordian knots decorate the pillars.

From Abbadia, a winding road with sharp bends and sheer drops leads to the top of **Monte Amiata**, 1,738 metres (5,700ft) high. The wooded area around the extinct volcano has attractive walks. The Fosso della Cocca, a leafy tunnel, is the best place to spot unusual wildlife and vegetation.

Castel del Piano, set among pine forests and wild raspberries, is the oldest settlement in the area, but **Piancastagnaio** is a better base. Perched among chestnut groves, the town has a newly restored Rocca and Franciscan monastery.

Arcidosso ⑱ was the birthplace of David Lazzaretti, "The Prophet of the Amiata". In the 19th century, Lazzaretti created a revolutionary social and religious movement with its headquarters on **Monte Labro**, a lonely peak. Now a nature reserve where deer, chamois and wolves roam, the park is best visited in autumn, when the crowds have left and the wild mushrooms appear.

Santa Fiora is particularly delightful, and has fine works of art in the 12th-century Santa Fiora and Santa Lucilla churches, including some della Robbia ceramics.

MONTALCINO

In both temperament and identity, **Montalcino** ⑲ is certainly the most Sienese town in the province. In essence, its history is a microcosm of Sienese history. From a distance, Montalcino even looks like a Sienese Trecento painting: the landscape could be a background to a saint's life; in the foreground would be the fortress and scenes of rejoicing and celebration after a historic victory.

Montalcino has been known as "the last rock of communal freedom" since its time as the Sienese capital-in-exile between 1555 and 1559. After the fall of Siena, exiles gathered around Piero Strozzi and the Sienese flag. As a reward, Montalcinesi standard-bearers have the place of honour in the procession preceding the Palio in Siena.

The magnificent 14th-century **Fortezza** (www.enotecalafortezza.com; daily 9am–8pm) is the key to Montalcino's pride. The approach is through olive groves and the slopes famous for Brunello wine. But the asymmetrical fortress, astride a spur of land,

A Sienese shepherd.

A view of Montalcino.

Brunello di Montalcino is one of Italy's best wines. Opportunities abound to taste and buy Brunello and the younger Rosso di Montalcino.

The Romanesque abbey of Sant'Antimo.

dominates the landscape. From its gardens, there is a sense of boundless space and absolute freedom. In winter, the wind howls over the massive walls and drives visitors to a different type of fortification in the *Enoteca* bar inside. This "National Wine Library" naturally serves Brunello, a magnificent wine whose reputation is slightly tarnished after some producers were charged with illegally blending it with other grapes.

Architecturally, Montalcino offers a neoclassical cathedral, a Gothic loggia, a Romanesque church and myriad intriguing alleys. The Duccio and della Robbia schools are well served by the Civic and Sacred museums. Most significant is the Palazzo Comunale, a mass of *Fiorentinità* finished off by a Sienese tower to prove that the Sienese always surpass the Florentines.

In spring, the area is very green, but yellow rapeseed, poppies, sunflowers and grapes soon take over. Before leaving, try *pici*, home-made spaghetti, in the Grappolo Blu or sweet *sospiri* ("sighs") in a *fin-de-siècle* bar.

SANT'ANTIMO

Nearby is **Sant'Antimo** ⑳ (www.antimo. it; daily Nov–Mar 10am–5pm, Apr–Oct until 7pm), the remains of a Romanesque abbey founded by Charlemagne, set amidst cypress trees in a peaceful valley. Designed in the French and Lombard style, the abbey is built from local travertine, which resembles alabaster or onyx. The interior has a translucent quality that, as the light changes, turns luminous shades of gold, white and brown.

The community of Augustinian monks who tend the church sing the Gregorian chant at Mass every Sunday afternoon. From here there are many superb marked trails through timeless countryside.

Not far away, **Sant'Angelo in Colle**, a fortified hilltop village, once cast a dramatic shadow over Grosseto and other enemies. Until 1265, it was a Sienese outpost, but the tower is all that remains. Today it is a quiet medieval village.

Modern Siena province ends just there. As a frontier castle, Sant'Angelo looked down on to the plain that falls into Grosseto. After Siena province, Grosseto can look deceptively flat.

Montalcino at dusk.

The tufa town of Sorano.

THE MAREMMA AND MONTE ARGENTARIO

Grosseto province has some of the most beautiful stretches of coast and wilderness areas in the region. The Maremma, "the marsh by the sea", is Tuscany's Wild West, where cowboys and long-horned cattle roam. Inland, the marshy plains give way to densely wooded hills, where towns seem to grow from the tufa.

Tuscany's southwestern corner offers a wonderfully varied landscape, ranging from the flat coastal plains to the wooded, snow-capped peak of Monte Amiata, or to the gentle hills bordering Siena province. The coastline has an unrivalled mix of Mediterranean flora and fauna, but the region is dominated by the marshy plain of the Maremma, stretching from the Piombino headland to Tuscany's border with Lazio. Backed by striking hills, this coastal marshland is famous for its horse-breeding, wild-boar hunting, Etruscan sites and austere inland villages, not to mention its rich cuisine.

Abundant remains reveal that the Etruscans thrived in this area, cultivating the land and exploiting the mineral wealth on Elba. However, while the Romans continued to mine Elba for the iron they needed to make swords, they allowed the drainage and irrigation systems the Etruscans had put in place on the mainland to decay. By the Middle Ages, the Maremma had become a malarial swamp and the population had migrated to the hills. It wasn't until the mid-19th century, with the draining of the swamps and land reclamation, that the revival of these evocative lowlands began, spearheaded by the return of the *butteri* (Tuscany's tough cowboys) with their herds of long-horned cattle.

The harbour at Porto Ercole.

GROSSETO

The provincial capital, **Grosseto ❶**, is a commercial and administrative centre, with little to recommend it, unless you are passing through and have an interest in things Roman and Etruscan. The **Museo Archeologico e d'Arte della Maremma** (Piazza Baccarini 3; Apr–May Tue–Fri 9.30am–4pm, Sat–Sun 10am–1pm and 4–7pm, June–Sept Tue–Fri 10am–6pm, Sat–Sun 10am–1pm and 5–8pm, Oct–Mar Tue–Fri 9am–2pm, Sat–Sun 10am–1pm and 4–7pm) is one of the richest museums

Main attractions
Roselle
Parco della Maremma
Monte Argentario
Giglio
Cosa
Scansano
Saturnia
Pitigliano
Sovana

Map on page 234

The pink-and-white candy-striped facade of Grosseto's Cathedral overlooks Piazza Dante, the hub of the town.

in the area. It has a fine collection of pre-Etruscan, Etruscan and Roman artefacts from the archaeological sites of Roselle, Vetulonia, Talamone, Pitigliano and Saturnia to the south.

The excavations at **Roselle ❷** (daily Nov–Feb 8.30am–5.30pm, Mar–Apr and Sept–Oct until 6.30pm, May–Aug until 7pm; follow signs to the ruins, not the town of Roselle), about 10km (6 miles) northeast of Grosseto, reveal one of the most important Etruscan cities in northern Etruria. The paved streets, ruins of Etruscan taverns and workshops, and the nearly intact circuit of Romano-Etruscan walls, as well as the outlines of the Roman forum and amphitheatre, are all very evocative. Most of the finds are on display in Grosseto's archaeological museum.

On the other side of the old Roman Via Aurelia (also less romantically known as the N1), about 20km (12 miles) north of Grosseto, the hilltop village of **Vetulonia ❸** lies above another ancient Etruscan city, Vetluna. The small excavated area (the *Scavi Città*) is more Roman than Etruscan. More

interesting are the tombs (www.museidimaremma.it; Tue–Sun Oct–Feb 10am–4pm, Mar–May until 6pm, June–Sept 10am–2pm and 4–8pm, also Mon July–Aug; archaeological park same hours; free), 3km (2 miles) from the *Scavi Città*.

THE COAST

This stretch of coast ranges from the mundane to the magical, often with little in between. South of the rural delights of the Maremma reserve, the decidedly chic Monte Argentario peninsula is dotted with charming coves and small beaches. Instead, north of Castiglione della Pescaia, the Gulf of Follonica represents tawdry, cheap-and-cheerful tourism aimed at the local market. Ignore the unprepossessing **Marina di Grosseto** in favour of the old fishing village of **Castiglione della Pescaia ❹**.

The boat-lined harbour is believed to be the Etruscan Hasta, or Portus Traianus in Roman times. Overlooking the port is the Rocca Aragonese, with its walls and towers dating back to the 14th century. This low-key resort has pleasant, family-friendly hotels tucked away in the pine groves bordering the beach.

The coastal stretch from Castiglione della Pescaia south to the Parco della Maremma is bordered by a magnificent forest of umbrella pines known as the **Pineta del Tombolo**. You can leave your car by the roadside and take any of the footpaths through the umbrella pines to the lovely beach.

From here the road leads north to the brash Gulf of Follonica. The gulf's southern promontory is occupied by **Punta Ala** ➎, an elite summer resort with a flashy marina, upmarket hotels, golf clubs, horse riding and polo facilities. It's an attractive spot, and offers an amusing window on the lemming-like habits of moneyed Italians at leisure.

If you are in Bay of Follonica area and yearning for the seaside, **Cala Violino** is a quiet bay just before the resort. Alternatively, there are some good beaches between Follonico and Piombino. Otherwise, at this point you're better off heading inland to Massa Marittima, or back south to the beautiful Parco della Maremma.

PARCO REGIONALE DELLA MAREMMA

Also known as the Parco dell'Uccellina, the **Parco Regionale della Maremma** ➏ covers an area of around 60 sq km (150 sq miles), including about 20km (12 miles) of coastline.

Evidence of human settlement here can be seen in the remains of a castle, the Benedictine monastery of **San Rabano**, and lookout towers used for the unfortunate soldiers posted here to watch for Saracen pirates and Spanish galleons.

The main entrance to the park is at **Alberese** ➐, where you have to leave your car. The helpful visitor centre (www.parco-maremma.it; daily 8.30am–2pm), where you buy your entrance ticket, is full of information on the flora and fauna, and activities within the park. With your ticket you'll be given a map of clearly explained waymarked trails you can follow, of various levels of difficulty and duration,

Beach at Castiglione della Pescaia, with Rocca Aragonese above.

Tip

The beaches within the Parco dell'Uccellina are among the most beautiful and unspoilt in Tuscany. To preserve this wilderness, the number of visitors is limited during the summer, and apart from the road to Marina di Alberese, cars are not permitted in the park. Transport from Alberese is arranged on buses. Visiting in the height of summer is ill-advised, as the weather becomes hot and humid, and there are tiny insects, *serafiche*, whose bite is painful.

from gentle two-hour walks to day-long treks. Shuttle buses into the park leave from outside the visitor centre at regular intervals, but be sure to check the time of the last bus back down.

Activities within the nature park include canoeing on the Ombrone River, sailing along the coast, riding across the mountains, birdwatching beside the salt marshes, and visiting the noble ruins of San Rabano and other towers strung out along the mountain tops and overlooking the sea, each with its story of marauding pirates and hidden treasures, going back to the times of the Saracens and the Spanish galleons.

If time is limited or you'd rather not walk, you can take the one access road (you still need a ticket) from Alberese to **Marina di Alberese**, a 6km (4-mile) stretch of beach.

Just outside the southern boundaries of the park is the walled village of **Talamone** (18km/11 miles from Alberese), a low-key resort with decent hotels and restaurants. You can gain access to local trails around here from nearby Caprarecce.

MONTE ARGENTARIO

It's a short drive from Talamone along the Aurelia-Etrusca (Grosseto–Rome highway) to **Monte Argentario ⑧**, a craggy peninsula that was once an island, thought to have been occupied by Roman money lenders in the 4th century – *argentarius* in Latin is money lender. From 1556 until 1815, Argentario existed as a separate state from the Grand Duchy of Tuscany, under Spanish rule. This kingdom encompassed the whole promontory and the existing ports of Orbetello, Talamone and Porto Azzurro, on the island of Elba. The Spanish legacy lingers on in the medieval watchtowers that still hug the coast.

Monte Argentario gradually became attached to the land by two long sandbanks: Tòmbolo della Giannella and **Tòmbolo di Feniglia**. Both have fine beaches, but while Giannella is backed by a main road, Feniglia is traffic-free and backed by protected pine forest. It's a 7km (4-mile) walk or bike ride to the mainland.

Like two outstretched arms holding on to the mainland, the sandbanks embrace

⊙ PARCO DELLA MAREMMA

As the last virgin coast on the Italian peninsula, Tuscany's most beguiling park is extraordinarily precious and thus well cared for. The landscape ranges from salt marshes, sand dunes and open plains to rocky mountains, sheer cliffs, pine forests and Mediterranean maquis – dense scrubland characterised by rosemary, broom, sea lavender and holm oaks. Wild deer, boar and small mammals thrive in the undergrowth, while it is incredibly rich in birdlife. Wading birds flock to the marshes around the mouth of the Ombrone River, and birds of prey circle the hills. The park is also an important resting place for birds migrating between Europe and Africa. Depending on the habitat and the season, you can see flamingoes, falcons, ospreys, herons and black-winged stilts.

Down on the open fields and low-lying olive groves, herds of long-horned cattle and horses graze. They are reared by *butteri*, the tough Tuscan cowboys who settled in the region in the 19th century, after the swamps were drained and the land could be used for cattle grazing.

One of the loveliest marked routes leads to a high cliff overlooking a forest of umbrella pines cascading all the way down to a sea, and beach, that looks almost Caribbean.

The park headquarters in Alberese (Via del Bersagliere 7/9, tel: 0564-407 098, www.parco-maremma.it) has launched a series of interesting itineraries, notably a scenic cycling trail (18.8km/12 miles) from Alberese to Marina di Alberese. There are also specific marked horseriding trails. The park offers birdwatching canoe trips and there is even a night-time trip during which you can listen to animal sounds under the stars. For those not eager or unable to walk, the park organises horse-drawn carriage excursions as well.

The park is open year round. However the information centre in Talamone and the Talamone Aquarium, which concentrates on the Orbetello lagoon sealife, are open Mar–Oct only (tel: 0564-887 173).

Last but not least, there is a tasting zone where visitors can try selected local produce for free, including wine, honey and cheeses. (Naturalmente Toscana, tel: 0337-106 5079, www.naturalmentetoscana.it).

a lagoon, an important wintering spot for migrating birds. The lagoon is cut in half by a central causeway that links Argentario to the town of **Orbetello**, which juts into the lagoon. The town's Baroque architecture reflects its history as a 16th-century Spanish garrison, where the sea laps the city walls. Visitors come from afar for the excellent fish restaurants found here and on Monte Argentario.

The rugged peninsula rises to a height of 635 metres (2,000ft) and is cloaked in Mediterranean maquis, olive groves and vineyards. Apart from **Porto Santo Stefano** ❾, the mountain has been spared from the property developers, but the exclusive villas outside the port towns remain the preserve of the rich. Sadly, most of this delightful coastline is inaccessible, unless, of course, you are the owner of a yacht. The best way to enjoy Argentario is to stay in a hotel with a private beach. Otherwise, of the few beaches with public access, the nicest are Le Cannelle (roughly opposite Isola Rossa) and the beach to the left of the luxury hotel Il Pellicano, near Porto Ercole.

Porto Santo Stefano's busy harbour is crowded with fishing boats and yachts. It is an atmospheric town, lined with upmarket boutiques, bars and fish restaurants. For a breathtaking and often hair-raising drive, the scenic coastal road from here (follow signs to La Panoramica) takes you along the clifftops.

Porto Ercole is Santo Stefano's smaller, more exclusive sister, but what was once a quiet fishing village is often overwhelmed by all the traffic that converges on it from sea and land. Its main attractions for landlubbers are the *centro storico* and the 16th-century Spanish fortress overlooking the harbour.

ISLAND EXCURSIONS

Santo Stefano has ferry connections with Giannutri and Giglio, two of the seven islands in the Arcipelago Toscano. The archipelago was declared a nature reserve in 1996 – not that all the regulations are interpreted as strictly as one might imagine. Crescent-shaped **Giannutri** is a tiny, flat, virtually uninhabited island 22km (14 miles) away, where day-trippers go to visit the ruins

Umbrella pines line many of the long, straight roads through the Maremman plains.

Porto Santo Stefano.

of a Roman villa – columns, mosaics, baths and a private pier.

Giglio ⑩, an hour's sail from Porto Santo Stefano, has more to offer. It is a playground for sailors and divers, and the second-largest island in Tuscany after Elba. It has an almost impenetrable coastline, with only one easily accessible port, Giglio Porto. A rocky road uphill leads to Giglio Castello, which dominates the landscape. Set among vineyards (which produce grapes for the very strong, distinctive local wine, Ansonica), it is a picturesque settlement, with archways, alleyways and stairs carved from the rock. Giglio abounds in sandy beaches on its western side and is covered in typical Mediterranean vegetation: aromatic herbs and plants, and orange and lemon groves.

COSA TO CAPALBIO

Back on the mainland coast, across the Aurelia from the town of **Ansedonia** are the important Roman remains of **Cosa ⑪** (www.cosaexcavations.org; museum daily May–Sept 10.15am–6.30pm,

Oct–Apr 8.15am–4.30pm; site free, guided tours possible in June) built on top of an Etruscan settlement. Excavations have revealed a main street, a forum, a walled acropolis and *capitolium* with magnificent views out to sea. After a long break which saw the site get overgrown, new excavations have begun there.

Below the promontory is the silted-up Roman port and the Tagliata Etrusca, the Etruscan Cut – a canal in fact built by the Romans to drain the **Lago di Burano** reserve.

Inland lies **Capalbio**, one of the first towns on the hills bordering Lazio. Capalbio is a fashionable, foodie haunt among wealthy Italians. Nearby is the magical **Giardino dei Tarocchi ⑫**, or Tarot Garden (http://ilgiardinodeitarocchi.it; daily Apr–mid-Oct 2.30–7.30pm), created by French sculptor Niki de Saint-Phalle, who died in 2002, and inspired by the arcane symbolism of the Tarot. The park displays 22 fantastic, brightly coloured sculptures covered in mirror and mosaic, glinting in the sun among the flowers and fountains.

The harbour at Porto Ercole.

FORTIFIED TOWNS

Across the densely wooded hills north of Capalbio is the drained Albegna plain, which leads to the castle of **Marsiliana** ⓭, once an Etruscan town and now the only property left belonging to the Corsini family, who originally owned the entire area. Most of these swamps were expropriated by the state, drained and then distributed to small landowners.

North of here lies **Magliano in Toscana** ⓮, a fortified medieval village perched above olive groves. Both civil and religious architecture shows a strong Romanesque influence, with Gothic and Renaissance additions. A perfect example of the blend of styles is San Giovanni Battista, a Romanesque church with Gothic side windows and a Renaissance facade.

A few kilometres further inland, **Scansano** ⓯, a breezy hill village with a fortified section *(oppido)*, was once the summer capital of the province, when the administrative powers were moved from malarial Grosseto during the hot season. Now famous for the fine wine Morellino di Scansano, there are several *cantine* for wine tasting.

SPA RESORT

Travelling eastwards across hills and moors inhabited by *butteri* (cowboys) and Maremman cattle, you come to Montemerano, another typically Tuscan walled town, with 15th-century fortifications. From here you can head to the ancient Roman spa centre of **Saturnia** ⓰. On the approach to the town, around a sharp curve, you will glimpse the **Cascate del Gorello**, a steaming waterfall where you can bathe in hot sulphur springs. Alternatively, soak car-weary limbs in the upmarket thermal swimming pools of Terme di Saturnia. Saturnia, drowsy under the weight of its Etruscan and Roman past, is centred around a large oak-ringed piazza with one or two notable trattorias.

TUFA TOWNS

Pitigliano, Sovana and Sorano are three southern Tuscan jewels situated above dramatic cliffs of soft, porous tufa covered in a thick jungle of fern, ivy and

Bathing in the Cascate del Gorello.

⊘ SPA THERAPY

Tuscany has an ancient spa tradition. Etruscans worshipped water and were believers in water rituals and herbal cures, but it was the Romans who perfected water cures, pioneering the virtues of moving between the hot and cold of the *caldarium*, *tepidarium* and *frigidarium*. The steaming thermal waters that gush from the ground are channelled into spa pools. These waters stimulate, re-mineralise, relax and revive the body, with sodium and magnesium nourishing bones, while the therapeutic mud is collected at the source of the spring and used in natural face and body treatments. The top Tuscan spas are pampering as well as curative.

Ciborium of the 8th or 9th century inside Sovana's exquisite Romanesque church of Santa Maria.

Pitigliano at night.

evergreen trees. The roads here, hewn out of the hills, are an experience in themselves. The winding stretch between Sovana and Pitigliano, which rises spectacularly above it, is particularly memorable.

In the middle of the 18th century, **Pitigliano** ⑰ was one of the most important settlements in southern Tuscany. This majestic town is built on a hill of volcanic tufa and straddles a vast aqueduct with wine and olive-oil cellars carved out of the hillside below. The town is centred around a magnificent medieval citadel built by the Orsini. Laid out around two parallel streets, Pitigliano is crossed by countless atmospheric alleys.

Pitigliano used to be called "little Jerusalem", as it was a refuge for Jews fleeing from religious persecution in the Papal states. Even today, the Jewish quarter of the city, which has the oldest Italian synagogue, remains distinct. It is one of the few places in Italy where you can find kosher cakes, from a Jewish bakery no less. The **Museo Ebraico** (Jewish Museum) (via Zuccarelli; Sun–Fri Apr–Sept 10am–1pm, 2.30–6pm, Oct–Mar 10am–noon and 3–5pm) is utterly compelling. Although resident in the former ghetto, Pitigliano's Jewish community were never persecuted. Before leaving town, dip into Slow Food Il Tufo Allegro inn and enjoy a glass of Bianco di Pitigliano from the tufa wine cellars.

Sovana ⑱, situated a few kilometres away, is a perfectly formed one-street village with two outstanding proto-Romanesque churches. The surrounding area is scattered with Etruscan tombs, hidden in the woods, as well as evocative Etruscan streets, carved into the rock.

Situated above a deep ravine with a roaring stream and waterfall is medieval **Sorano**, which is also built on a tufa outcrop.

Visible from all corners of the Maremma on a clear day, is **Monte Amiata**, the highest peak in Tuscany south of Florence. It is a dormant volcano, with hot geysers and underground waters that supply the spa at Saturnia. Monte Amiata is a refreshing escape during the summer months and a ski resort in winter.

Monte Amiata.

AREZZO AND EASTERN TUSCANY

Known for its gold, art and antiques, Arezzo can feel removed from tourism. The province is also blessed with prosperous farms, castles and abbeys tucked into deep woods. For all its wealth, there is a spirituality in the air that feels more akin to mystical Umbria.

Arezzo province is rugged, with steep, thickly wooded valleys that shield its towns and villages from view. The source of the Arno is here, too, in an area of great natural beauty known as the Casentino. This remote, northern area of chestnut woods, vineyards and monasteries leads to the farms of the fertile Val di Chiana. To the west, across the Pratomagno ridge, lies the Arno valley. At the heart of the province, its capital, Arezzo, was one of the most important towns in the Etruscan federation, thanks to its strategic position on a hill at the meeting point of three valleys. Today, it is one of Tuscany's wealthiest cities, as witnessed by the proliferation of jewellers, goldsmiths and antique shops on the city's streets.

AREZZO

Arezzo ❶ abounds in monuments and works of art from all eras, but tourism is mostly muted. The old, hilly part of the city is the most picturesque, with its massive main square, the **Piazza Grande Ⓐ**, barely on an even keel. On the first Sunday of every month, this square welcomes an antiques market, the largest of its kind in Italy. Stalls cover the square, run around the base of the Duomo, and spill into the cobbled **Corso Italia**, the city's main shopping street. After being tempted by the jewellery shops, linger over a leisurely

Giostra del Saracino, Arezzo.

lunch around Piazza Grande, ideally at **La Torre di Gnicche** (Piaggia di San Martino, tel: 0575-352 035), a rustic inn serving salami, cheese platters and stuffed pasta.

Spiritual duties await in one of the loveliest Romanesque churches in Tuscany. Rising from the southern side of the square, sitting on the Corso, is the **Santa Maria della Pieve ❸** (daily 8am–noon and 3–7pm; free), with its "tower of a hundred holes", so named because of the filigree pattern of arches that pierces the belfry.

Main attractions

Piero della Francesca
  Frescoes, San Francesco,
  Arezzo
Sansepolcro
Monterchi
The Casentino Countryside
Monastero di Camaldoli
Castello dei Conti Guidi,
  Poppi
Lucignano
Cityscape, Cortona
Museo Diocesano, Cortona

Maps on pages
245, 246

The Corso.

A SPIRITUAL TRAIL

Just west stands the cavernous church of **San Francesco** ⑥ (summer Mon–Fri 9am–7pm, Sat until 6pm, Sun 1–6pm, winter Mon–Fri 9am–6pm, Sat until 5.30pm, Sun 1–5.30pm) which contains Piero della Francesca's restored *Legend of the True Cross* (1452–66) (advance booking necessary; tel: 0575-352 727). This haunting fresco cycle weaves together a complex story in which the wood of the *Tree of Knowledge* (from which Adam and Eve ate the apple) becomes the wood of the cross on which Christ died, and which was later discovered by the Empress Helena, mother of the Emperor Constantine the Great, who converted to Christianity and made it the state religion of the Roman Empire, AD 313. What matters more is the spirituality that suffuses his art, a transcendent quality that elevates his work beyond the mere mastery of perspective and space. Look for his graceful figures framed by idealised depictions of Arezzo and Sansepolcro.

Medieval monuments cluster together in the northern part of the city, where you will find the **Duomo** ⑩ (daily 6.30am–12.30pm and 3–6.30pm; free), sheltered by the encircling walls of the Grand Duke Cosimo's 16th-century Fortezza, now a park with fine views of the town and the Casentino beyond. The lofty Duomo, dating from the late 13th century, boasts a Gothic bell tower but still feels stranded on its hilltop site. Inside you can see 16th-century stained-glass windows and the 14th-century tomb of Guido Tarlati, which flanks the *St Mary Magdalene* fresco by Piero della Francesca. This work can be contemplated in comparative peace, unlike the frescoes in San Francesco. The **Museo Diocesano** (daily Apr–Oct 10am–6.30pm, Nov–Mar 10am–5pm), behind the Cathedral, contains medieval crucifixes and some Vasari frescoes.

VASARI TRAIL

Further west is the **Casa del Vasari** ⑥ (www.museistataliarezzo.it; Mon, Wed–Sat 8.30am–7.30pm, Sun 8.30am–1.30pm), the attractive house that Giorgio Vasari – Mannerist painter, architect and author of *The Lives of the Artists* (1550)

– built for himself and decorated with frescoes painted by the artists he most admired. The 500th anniversary of his birth was celebrated with much pomp in Arezzo in 2011, including the painstaking restoration of a Vasari altarpiece before visitors' very eyes.

Close by is the **Museo Statale d'Arte Medievale e Moderna ⓕ** (www.museistataliarezzo.it; Tue–Sun 10am–noon and 4–6pm; free), housed in the 15th-century Palazzo Bruni. Its varied collection includes an excellent display of majolica pottery, a selection of frescoes and fine examples of the Arezzo goldsmiths' work, featured alongside paintings by Vasari and modern works by local artists.

ROMAN AREZZO

Last but not least, in the flat southern part of the city, you will find the **Anfiteatro Romano ⓖ** (daily 8.30am–7.30pm, request to be accompanied by museum custodian). The Roman Arretium was originally an Etruscan city, but in 294 BC it became a Roman settlement, a convenient resting post on the Via Cassia between Rome and Florence. The site was later plundered to build the city walls and churches, and the perimeter wall is all that remains.

A section of the amphitheatre walls was incorporated into an Olivetan monastery (near the station), now occupied by the excellent **Museo Archeologico ⓗ** (www.museistataliarezzo.it; daily 8.30am–7.30pm). This museum features the Aretine ware for which Arezzo has long been famous. This Roman pottery once competed with the more famous Samian ware as the crockery of choice on the dinner tables of Roman aristocrats.

PIERO DELLA FRANCESCA TRAIL

East of Arezzo, the Upper Tiber valley is tightly enclosed at its northern end by the Alpe di Catenaia and the Alpe della Luna. Two important towns for Piero della Francesca enthusiasts are here. **Sansepolcro ➋** is famous for two things: as the town where Buitoni pasta is produced; and as the birthplace of the great Renaissance artist. The old town, huddled behind crumbling ramparts,

Piazza Grande is the scene of the Giostra del Saracino, a historic jousting tournament held twice a year, in June and September.

The Loggia Vasari in Arezzo.

is an important artistic centre. The quiet, narrow streets are linked by four ancient gates, the best preserved of which is the Porta Fiorentina.

In the town centre, at the junction of Piazza Torre di Berta and Via Matteotti, is the **Duomo** (daily). Dedicated to St John the Evangelist, it began life in the 11th century as a monastic abbey. A wide range of excellent artworks cover the walls of the interior, including a tabernacle by the della Robbia school. Perugino's *Ascension of Jesus* is also here.

However, the reason most people make the pilgrimage here is to see Piero della Francesca's greatest work, *The Resurrection*. The fresco, created in 1463, was nearly destroyed by

the Allies during World War II as they bombarded Sansepolcro, believing the Germans were still occupying the town. The fresco was thankfully saved from destruction by the villagers, who surrounded it with sandbags. Today, this intense, brooding work is displayed in the **Museo Civico** (www.museocivicosan sepolcro.it; daily mid-June–mid-Sept 10am–1.30pm, 2.30–7pm, mid-Sept– mid-June 10am–1pm, 2.30–6pm), in Via degli Aggiunti, alongside the *Madonna della Misericordia*, another Piero della Francesca masterpiece.

Also stop to admire the 16th-century Palazzo delle Laudi (the Town Hall) and the Gothic Palazzo Gherardi, both in Via Matteotti, and the Palazzo Pretorio opposite Piazza Garibaldi.

From Sansepolcro, the Piero della Francesca trail leads south to **Monterchi ❸**, where a former schoolhouse displays his striking *Madonna del Parto* in the **Museo Madonna del Parto** (www.madonnadelparto.it; Apr–Oct 9am–1pm and 2–7pm, Nov–Mar 9.30am–12.30pm and 2–5pm). The Madonna, heavily pregnant and aching, has unbuttoned the front of her dress for relief, while above, two angels hold up the entrance to the tent in which she stands.

MICHELANGELO'S BIRTHPLACE

Northwest of Sansepolcro, on a steep slope above the Tiber, is the hamlet of **Caprese Michelangelo ❹**, birthplace of Michelangelo. Protected by an almost complete set of walls, this cluster of rustic buildings – which includes the Buonarroti house, the old town hall where Michelangelo's father was the Florentine governor, and the tiny chapel in which Michelangelo was baptised – are interesting more for their connections than for their contents. The views over Alpine countryside explain why Michelangelo attributed his good brains to the mountain air he breathed as a child.

THE CASENTINO

The Casentino is the name given to the little-known region of the Upper Arno valley that runs from the eastern side of the Consuma Pass down to the source of the river just north of Arezzo. It is an area of great natural beauty, enclosed by high mountains, cloaked in fir, chestnut and beech woods, and concealing ancient monasteries and farming villages. The narrow, winding, rural roads are slow going, and with views at every turn, the temptation to stop and admire them is hard to resist.

At its remoter edges, this region is rooted in the 13th century, when St Francis took to a desolate crag on the wooded slopes of **Monte Penna** at **La Verna ❺**, using a niche between two huge boulders as a hermitage. On this spot in 1224, St Francis is supposed to have received the stigmata while he was praying. Today, in the middle of the ancient forest, a Franciscan sanctuary still occupies the rock. Assembled around a tiny piazza is a collection of monastic buildings, including one large church containing yet more examples of della Robbia terracotta sculptures.

Sixteen kilometres (10 miles) northeast of La Verna, high in the spectacular woodland cut by mountain streams and waterfalls, is another more ancient monastery, **Camáldoli ❻** (monastery church daily 9am–12.30pm, 2.30–6.30pm). It was founded in 1012 by San Romualdo (St Rumbold), a former member of the Benedictine Order, who founded a strict community of hermits. The monastery is still inhabited, and the monks run a welcoming café here. The old cloister pharmacy (9am–12.30pm, 3–6pm), with its mortars and crucibles, now sells soaps and liqueurs made by the monks.

Another 300 metres (1,000ft) up the mountain (a beautiful hour-long

The Resurrection, by Piero della Francesca.

The view across Poppi from the Palazzo Pretorio.

Fiat's classic Cinquecento "Bambino" is still a much-loved runaround, perfect for the narrow streets of small towns such as Poppi.

walk), above the monastery, is the **Eremo**, a hermitage comprising a small Baroque church and 10 cells, each surrounded by a high wall and a tiny kitchen garden. Here the hermits still live in solitude and silent contemplation. The church and St Rumbold's cell are open to visitors (daily 9–11am and 3–6pm), but access to the monks' quarters is closed.

After the silence and isolation of Camáldoli, noisy **Bibbiena** ❼ will bring you sharply back to the modern world. Although hidden by urban sprawl and best known for its tobacco industry and salty salami, Bibbiena is still a typical Tuscan hill town at heart. Buildings of note in the historic centre include the church of **San Lorenzo**, which has some richly decorated della Robbia panels, and the church of **Sant' Ippolito Martire**, which has a fine triptych by Bicci di Lorenzo.

Nearby is the Renaissance Palazzo Dovizi, home of Cardinal Dovizi, who, as Cardinal Bibbiena, became the secretary of Pope Leo X. Bibbiena's central piazza offers distant views to Camáldoli

and Poppi – the latter is the gateway to an interesting area for castles and fortified towns.

CASENTINO CASTLES

This region was continually fought over by the Guelf Florentines and the Ghibelline Aretines. A decisive battle in 1289, which firmly established the dominance of the former over the latter, is marked by a column on a site called Campaldino, just between Castel San Niccolò and Poppi.

Poppi ❽ surveys the surrounding countryside from its hilltop perch, dominated by the brooding **Castello dei Conti Guidi** (mid-Mar–June and Sept–Oct daily 10am–6pm, July–Aug until 7pm, Nov–mid-Mar Thu–Sun 10am–5pm), the most important medieval monument in the Casentino. Built in the 13th century for the ruling Guidi counts, the castle's design was inspired by the Palazzo Vecchio in Florence, and it is thought likely that Arnolfo di Cambio was the architect. The courtyard and stairway are impressive, and the Florentine

⊘ BED, BORGHI AND WINE

Tuscany excels at rescuing medieval hamlets *(borghi)* and turning them into country retreats, often with a castle or wine estate attached. Set in the hills near Arezzo, **Il Borro** (tel: 055-977 053; www.ilborro.it) is part of a patchwork of cypresses, sunflowers, olive groves and vineyards that once inspired Leonardo da Vinci. The setting may feature in fashion shoots, but the Ferragamo fashion dynasty are serious hoteliers and wine producers. As Salvatore Ferragamo says, "It's a wine estate, not Disneyland. The medieval village was in ruins after the war but my father and I had a vision of turning it into a rural resort and wine estate for trailblazing Super Tuscans rather than traditional Chianti Classico." Formerly owned by the Savoia, Italy's former royal dynasty, the estate is unstarry, with craft workshops set up for a goldsmith, carpenter, ceramicist, glassmaker and, of course, a cobbler, a reminder of Ferragamo's shoemaking heritage.

Set in the Val d'Orcia, **Castiglion del Bosco** (tel: 0577-1913 822; www.castigliondelbosco.com) is another medieval borgo

converted into a chic country estate, as smooth as its Brunello vintages. It boasts a prestigious 18-hole golf course designed by one-time British Open winner Tom Weiskopf. **Castello del Nero** (tel: 055-806 470; www.castellodelnero.com) represents rural luxury, with frescoed, vaulted suites, views of vineyards and olive groves, as well as a top of the range spa. **Laticastelli** (tel: 0577-724 419; www.laticastelli.com) is a simpler affair, set in a fortified hamlet outside Rapolano with probably the best panoramic pool in Tuscany. In the Chianti, **Castel Monastero** (tel: 0577-570 570; www.castelmonastero. com) boasts frescoed bedrooms, superb wines, a luxury spa and cookery courses in a former monastery. Just north, **Borgo di Vescine** (tel: 0577-741 144; www.vescine.it) is a medieval hamlet converted into a Chianti wine estate and country resort offering wine-tasting and cooking classes. Near Colle di Val d'Elsa, the latest boutique bolthole is **Castello di Casole** (tel: 0577-961 501; www.castellodicasole.com), combining castle suites with farmhouse hideaways, complete with an excellent spa, pool and fitness centre.

frescoes may be viewed on request. The ancient streets of this quiet town are lined with arcades linked by steep steps and decorated with finely carved capitals and stone seats. There is a Romanesque church and a few shops here selling locally made copper pots.

Off in the distance, on a hill above the village of **Pratovecchio ❾**, birthplace of Paolo Uccello, is the 11th-century **Castello di Romena** (Apr–June Thu–Sun 10am–1pm, 2–6pm, July–Aug daily 10am–1pm, 2–7pm, Sept–Oct Thu–Sun 10am–1pm, 2–5pm), another Guidi castle. The noble family gave refuge to Dante here after his expulsion from Florence at the beginning of the 14th century. Of the 14 towers that Dante would have seen at the castle, only three remain.

Standing on a lonely slope, a stone's throw from the castle, **Pieve di Romena** (visits by appointment with the custodian; tel: 0575-582 060; free) is one of the most important Romanesque churches in Tuscany. Beneath its apse, which dates from 1152, excavations have revealed the remains of an Etruscan building as well as two earlier churches. The finely carved capitals atop the gigantic granite columns in the nave make reference to the four Evangelists and to St Peter.

Back down in Pratovecchio, you'll find the headquarters of the **Parco Nazionale delle Foreste Casentinesi** (Casentino national park) (Via G. Brocchi 7; tel: 0575-50301; www.parcoforeste casentinesi.it; free).

To the north and guarding the source of the Arno (Monte Falterona) is the medieval town of **Stia ❿**, with a pretty porticoed piazza. Here stand the ruins of the **Castello di Porciano** (www.castel lodiporciano.com; May–Oct Sun 10am–noon, 4–7pm, or by appointment; tel: 337 671 277; free), another Guidi stronghold that once watched over the Arno valley.

The **Castello di Romena** is visible from up here. Whereas most monuments are easily accessible, the fortified remains at Castel Castagnaia, with the nearby ruined Roman temple, both to the west of Stia, are harder to reach. The road peters

In Tuscany, shop decoration is an art form.

⊘ VAL DI CHIANA CATTLE

The Val di Chiana, the most extensive valley in the Apennine range, is rich farmland mainly used for cattle-rearing. Here graze herds of one of Italy's most prized breeds of beef cattle – the Chianina, which is native to Tuscany. (Its only rival is the Razza Piemontese from Piedmont.) The cream-coloured Chianina cow grows quickly to a large size, so that it is butchered when the steer is a grown calf. The meat is firm and tasty, with a distinctive flavour. For any beef-loving Italian, *bistecca alla Fiorentina* – a huge, tender Val di Chiana T-bone steak, grilled over an open fire and seasoned with nothing more than crushed peppercorns, salt, and a hint of garlic and olive oil, served very rare – is the ultimate steak.

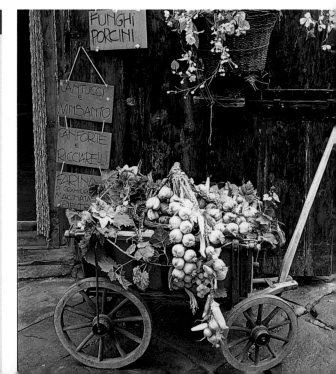

⊙ Tip

East of the Arno, and skirting the western edge of the high Pratomagno ridge, is the panoramic road known as the Strada dei Sette Ponti, or Road of the Seven Bridges. The winding route passes through several medieval towns, including Castelfranco di Sopra, Loro Ciuffena to the south and the abbey at Vallombrosa to the north.

out, and they can only be reached on foot through rough, stony countryside.

Remains of yet another Guidi castle can be seen in the tiny village of Montemignaio. There's not much left to see, but the village church does have Ghirlandaio's *Virgin and Child with the Four Church Elders*.

On the slope of the forested Pratomagno ridge, south of Bibbiena, is the restored castle at **Chitignano**. The medieval remains were rebuilt in the 18th century. There are other ruined castles located at Talla and Subbiano.

THE VALDARNO

The most scenic route to Florence skirts the Pratomagno ridge on the eastern side of the Arno. It's full of twists and turns, but the views are rewarding. In the Middle Ages, the Valdarno was bitterly fought over by the Ghibellines and the Guelfs. At the close of the 13th century pressure was exerted on the Florentines by the warlike Aretine bishops, who controlled powerful strongholds in the Arno valley. In an effort to resist them,

the Florentines built three fortresses, which were really fortified towns, at San Giovanni Valdarno, Terranuova and Castelfranco di Sopra.

Halfway between Florence and Arezzo, **San Giovanni Valdarno** ⑪ was fortified as a bulwark against the Aretines, but little evidence remains of its former military function. The central piazza and arcaded **Palazzo Comunale** were designed by Arnolfo di Cambio. The nearby church of **Santa Maria della Grazia** (daily; free) contains a *Virgin and Child with the Four Saints* by Masaccio, who was born here in 1401. Just outside the town, the Renaissance monastery of Montecarlo houses an *Annunciation* by Fra Angelico.

In prehistoric times, the Arno basin was one big lake, and farmers today frequently dig up fossil remains and bones of long-extinct animals. At **Montevarchi**, south of San Giovanni Valdarno, is a castle housing the **Accademia Valdarnese** (tel: 055-981 1227; June–Aug Thu 10am–7pm, Fri–Sun 10am–1pm and 4–7pm, Sept–May Thu–Sun 10am–1pm and 3–6pm), an important museum of prehistory. It is home to an impressive collection of fossilised remains of the Pliocene period discovered in this stretch of the Arno valley.

Unlike San Giovanni Valdarno, **Castelfranco di Sopra**, across the Arno (also fortified for the Florentines by Arnolfo di Cambio), retains its military character: the Porta Fiorentina gate is as forbidding as it ever was, and many of the 14th-century streets and buildings have survived.

About 10km (6 miles) south of Castelfranco, on the scenic **Strada dei Sette Ponti** (Road of the Seven Bridges), is **Loro Ciuffena** ⑫, a medieval village positioned on a chasm cut by the Ciuffenna river. A couple of kilometres away is the rural Romanesque church of Gropina, dating from the early 13th century, noted for the carvings of animals, figures

The white Chianina cattle are prized for their beef.

and geometrical patterns on the pulpit and columns. From here the picturesque route to Talla, where you'll find another ruined castle, crosses into the Casentino.

VAL DI CHIANA

Surrounded by hills and charming towns, the fertile **Val di Chiana** plains south of Arezzo supply Florentine restaurants with the raw ingredient of *bistecca alla Fiorentina*. **Monte San Savino** ⑬, on the edge of the Val di Chiana, has been a citadel since Etruscan times, although the existing fortifications date from the Middle Ages. In 1325 the inhabitants were unable to fend off a ruthless Aretine mob, who razed the town as punishment for their Guelf sympathies. It was subsequently rebuilt. Its once large Jewish community was wiped out – many were burnt at the stake – for resisting the French army in 1799. "Progress" has hardly touched Monte San Savino; it retains medieval and Renaissance houses, of which the **Palazzo Comunale**, with a facade by Antonio da Sangallo the Elder and a fine museum (Nov–Mar Wed–Fri 9am–1pm, Sat–Sun 9am–1pm and 4–7pm, Apr–Oct Tue 9am–1pm, Wed–Fri 9am–1pm and 4–7pm, Sat–Sun 9am–1pm and 2.30–7.30pm; free), is the most important.

Other important landmarks here include the Loggia del Mercato by Sansovino, and the churches of Santa Chiara and Sant'Agostino.

The wild hills northwest of the town shelter a feudal retreat, the **Castello di Gargonza** ⑭. This 13th-century *borgo*, or walled village, on the western slope of Monte Palazzuolo dominates the Chiana valley and is the centre of a vast wooded estate producing oil and wine. The walled settlement has been converted into a hotel and restaurant complex (www.gargonza.it). The adapted cottages, tiny cobbled streets, a chapel, a baronial tower, attractive gardens and a magnificent view down to the Chiana all make Gargonza a very pleasant retreat.

South of Monte San Savino is **Lucignano** ⑮. Originally an Etruscan stronghold, the concentric arrangement

The church and square in Lucignano, known for its unique concentric street plan.

Piazza Collegiata, Lucignano.

of streets around a fortress make it unique among Tuscan hill towns. With a few exceptions, Lucignano's buildings (13th–18th-century) are perfectly preserved, as is the Gothic church of San Francesco. The 14th-century **Palazzo Comunale** (Apr–Oct Wed–Mon 10.30am–1pm and 2.30–6pm) contains frescoes from the Sienese and Aretine schools, as well as some examples of finely worked gold ornaments for which the province of Arezzo has long been famous, including the beautiful 14th-century *Tree of Lucignano*, richly embellished with jewels.

FORTIFIED VILLAGES

Marciano della Chiana 6km (4 miles) northeast, another tiny village of great character, was also fortified in the Middle Ages. Much of the castle remains intact, as do the walls and a gateway that has a clock tower built into it. Three kilometres (2 miles) to the southeast is the octagonal chapel of Santa Vittoria, designed by Ammannati to mark the spot where the Florentines defeated the Sienese in battle in 1554.

Castiglion Fiorentino.

Foiano della Chiana clings prettily to the side of the hill. Much of it dates from the 15th–16th centuries, though traces of medieval defences can be seen around the edge of the town. At **Cisternella**, about 3km (2 miles) to the northeast of the centre, are the remains of what is believed to have been a Roman bathhouse.

From here, looming large in the distance, is the fortified village of **Castiglion Fiorentino ⑯**, bounded by thick walls and dominated by the **Cassero Fortress** (June–mid-Sept Mon–Wed 10.30am–1pm, Thu–Sun 10.30am–1pm and 3.30–7pm). This well-preserved medieval settlement has an unusually high number of churches. The oldest of these, the **Pieve Vecchia** (the oldest church), has a Signorelli fresco of the *Deposition of Christ* (1451), and the 13th-century church of San Francesco also contains a sculpted version.

Other sacred works and gold, and silverware from the surrounding churches can be seen in the **Pinacoteca Comunale** (tel: 0575-659 457, by appointment). On the old market square Vasari's famous loggias can be found. Their stone arches frame a fine vista of the rooftops and surrounding countryside.

Just outside the village is the fine octagonal temple of **Santa Maria della Consolazione**. Looming beyond the village, and visible from the Cassero Fortress, are the battlements of the **Castello di Montecchio** (tel: 335-7217 315; closed for archaeological works at the time of writing). This crenellated medieval castle once belonged to the legendary English *condottiero* John Hawkwood.

CORTONA

Close to the Umbrian border, 30km (18 miles) south of Arezzo, **Cortona ⑰** is one of the most enchanting hill towns in Tuscany. It was founded by the Etruscans, colonised by the Romans, and, after being sold to the

Florentines in 1409, thrived under the Grand Duchy of Tuscany. The success of the celebrity-studded Tuscan Sun festival, and the book by Frances Mayes, mean that Cortona's quaintly crooked, cobbled streets can be awash with summer visitors.

Cortona is perched majestically on a ridge of Monte Sant'Egidio, dominating the Val di Chiana. The approach road winds its way through terraced olive groves and vineyards, past villas, farms and monasteries. But Cortona's main attraction lies in the steepness of its crooked streets, linked by stone staircases, which work their way painfully to the Medici fortress at the top.

The town is entered from the relatively flat Piazza Garibaldi and Via Nazionale, which lead to Piazza Signorelli, with its 13th-century **Palazzo Comunale** (Town Hall) and the **Museo dell'Accademia Etrusca** (Apr–Oct daily 10am–7pm, Nov–Mar Tue–Sun until 5pm). The highlights are the lovely fresco of Polymnia, generally considered to be a fine Roman painting of the *Muse of Song* until recent research proved it to be an 18th-century forgery; and a genuine Etruscan chandelier dating from 300 BC.

At the bottom of the hill, a new archeological park, the **Parco Archeologico del Sodo**, showcases the Etruscan Sodo Tombs, including a sculpted sacrificial altar.

West of the piazza is the 16th-century Cathedral and its companion, the **Museo Diocesano** (Apr–Oct 10am–7pm, Nov–Mar Tue–Sun until 5pm), which contains some rare masterpieces by Fra Angelico, Lorenzetti and Luca Signorelli.

Before leaving town, seek out **Via Janelli** for its row of brick buildings with overhanging upper storeys – some of Tuscany's oldest surviving medieval houses. Other picturesque streets include the Via Ghibellina and Via Guelfa. It's a steep climb up to the **Basilica di Santa Margherita**,

dedicated to the local saint and follower of St Francis. The citizens of Cortona still make pilgrimages up the winding stone-flagged streets to her tomb to offer her prayers during hard times. The **Medici Fortress** above is overgrown and rarely open, but the views from up here are splendid, and it's a fine spot to stop for a picnic.

One side of Cortona's public gardens opens to a belvedere with sweeping views south, enveloping the **Lago di Trasimeno** ⑱, Italy's fourth-largest lake, which lies in neighbouring Umbria. Its shallow waters are surprisingly clean and popular with swimmers, boaters and windsurfers. There was a day, though, in 217 BC, when the lake waters ran red with the blood of the Roman legions, more than 16,000 of whom were slaughtered by Hannibal's troops.

Today, the scene is considerably more peaceful, especially on the southern shore, with Castiglione del Lago the place to toast farewell to underrated Arezzo province over a lakeside fish feast.

The lofty heights of Cortona.

Classic Tuscan road.

TUSCANY

TRAVEL TIPS

TRANSPORT

GETTING THERE

By Air

From the UK, low-cost airlines such as Ryanair and easyJet operate from many of Italy's smaller provincial airports, making travel between the UK and Italy easy, as well as opening up Italian routes to greater competition. Also, CityJet has a direct flight from London City Airport to Florence (www.cityjet.com).

In addition to the national airline, Alitalia, many major scheduled airlines run direct flights to Italy, as well as charter flights, which tend to offer lower fares and often fly to more convenient provincial airports.

From the US, the main carriers are Alitalia, Delta and United, which fly to Rome, Milan and Venice. European airlines such as British Airways and Air France also fly to Italy, with a stopover.

The country has two airports designed for intercontinental flights: **Roma Leonardo da Vinci** (known as Fiumicino) and **Milano Malpensa**.

Pisa's Galileo Galilei Airport is the usual airport for most international visitors to Florence. Getting from Pisa to Florence is easy and cheap.

Florence's Peretola-Florence Airport (also known as Amerigo Vespucci) is 4km (2 miles) northwest of the city centre. Some international flights land here, but these tend to be more expensive than flights to Pisa. **Bologna Airport** is a further alternative; it is conveniently located for Florence and Tuscany (there's a direct train to Florence and Arezzo).

By Rail

Rail travel is a slow but scenic option, although Italy has improved the speed and quality of its inter-city trains in recent years. (Florence is now only 36 minutes from Bologna and 1 hour 45 minutes from Milan). And the rise of "slow travel" makes rail an appealing option, travelling through Alpine scenery, avoiding the airports, and arriving in the heart of the city. It's both civilised and eco-friendly.

For those under 26, travel is far cheaper if you sign up to the InterRail scheme (providing a month's unlimited rail travel in Europe). When travelling from Great Britain via Paris (the usual route when travelling to Florence), it is necessary to change in Paris (from Gare du Nord to Gare de Lyon).

ES (Eurostar), EC (EuroCity), IC (Inter City) and TEE (Trans Europe Express) trains are top-of-the-range, running between the main Italian and European cities. A supplement is charged and seat reservation is obligatory. You can check your route or book tickets online on the official Italian railway website: www.trenitalia.it.

In the UK, consider booking through **Railbookers** (tel: 020-3780 2222; www.railbookers.com). A week's break includes an independent rail tour staying in Florence, Siena and Lucca.

Alternatively, for train bookings, contact **Voyages-SNCF** tel: 08448-485 848 or consult https://uk.voyages-sncf.com.

Visitors from the US and Canada can also buy tickets and passes in advance through Rail Europe, or holidays through Railbookers. Visit www.raileurope.com or tel: 1-800-622 8600 in the US and Canada.

By Road

When calculating the cost of travelling to Italy by car, allow for the price of motorway tolls as well as accommodation en route and petrol. The quickest cross-Channel car ferries are from Dover to Calais. The Channel Tunnel transports cars on the train between Folkestone and Calais (Eurotunnel, tel: 08443-353 535; www.eurotunnel.com). The usual route from

Santa Maria Novella train station, Florence.

France to Italy is via Paris and the Mont Blanc Tunnel (between Chamonix and Courmayeur), or from Switzerland through the Gran San Bernardo Tunnel (between Bourg St-Pierre and Aosta). Some of the Alpine passes are seasonal, so check the viability of your route with the tourist board or a motoring organisation before setting off.

To take your car into Italy, you will need your current driving licence, your vehicle registration document and insurance certificate. You are also required to carry a warning triangle in case of breakdown. Headlights should be illuminated at all times. Some petrol stations require payment in cash, not credit card. Keep cash handy for *autostrada* tolls, too.

The AA and RAC in the UK give up-to-date advice on Channel crossings, with or without a car, and also driving on the Continent.

In the US, the AAA provides information on travel in Italy.

By Coach

Travelling to Italy from the UK by coach is not much cheaper than flying. National Express Eurolines runs coaches from London Victoria, via Paris and Mont Blanc, to Aosta, Turin, Genoa, Milan, Venice, Bologna, Florence and Rome. To book from London, contact: National Express (www.nationalexpress.co.uk).

GETTING AROUND

On Arrival

Pisa Airport: The international airport, Galileo Gallilei (www.pisa-airport.com; tel: 050-849 111) has its own high-speed automated people mover, launched in 2017. Services operate from 6am to midnight, every five to ten minutes into Pisa Centrale. Airport Bus Express and Sky Bus Lines also link the airport with Florence's Santa Maria Novella train station (www.airportbusexpress.it, www.caronnatour.com; around 1 hour). Car hire is available from the airport, and so are taxis. A toll-free *superstrada* links Pisa airport with Florence. **Peretola (Amerigo Vespucci) International Airport** (www.aeroporto.firenze.it;

tel: 055-306 1830) in northwest Florence is also connected by Volainbus (www.fsbusitalia.it; 20-minute transfer) to central Florence.

By Air

Alitalia offers a huge range of internal flights from Florence and Pisa airports. These are supplemented by Meridiana's domestic services (www.meridiana.it), which are usually a bit cheaper.

By Rail

For information, visit www.trenitalia.it. The state-subsidised railway network is a relatively cheap and convenient form of transport for travelling between major cities in Tuscany. The principal Rome–Milan line is convenient for Bologna (36 minutes), Florence and Arezzo, while the Rome–Genoa line serves Pisa, Livorno and Grosseto. The Florence–Siena route is much faster by coach than by train.

Note that Pisa and Florence both have several train stations: **Pisa Centrale** station serves Pisa city and Pisa San Rossore was under reconstruction at the time of writing. In Florence, **Santa Maria Novella** is the main station for the city, although the second station, **Rifredi**, is served by several Eurostar trains. In Florence, a controversial additional station for high-speed routes designed by Norman Foster is scheduled to open in 2021.

Categories of Trenitalia Trains
Eurocity: these trains link major Italian cities with other European cities – in Germany and Switzerland, for instance. A supplement is payable on top of the rail fare.
Le Frecce: these swish, high-speed Frecciarossa (330kmh/186mph; four classes of carriages; supplements payable), Frecciargento (250kmh/155mph) and Frecciablanca (200kmh/125mph) trains connect major cities across Italy.
Intercity: this fast service links medium-sized and major Italian cities. Intercity Plus is the latest fleet of plush, new fast trains. A supplement is payable; reservations required.
Interregionali: these inter-regional trains link cities within different regions (eg Tuscany and Umbria) and stop fairly frequently.

Regionali: these trains link towns within the same region and stop at every station.
Intercity night: couchettes or sleepers; possibly the best way to travel long-distance in Italy.

In 2012 privately-owned NTV (Nuovo Trasporto Viaggiatori) started operating Italo high-speed trains (three classes of service), competitive to Trenitalia's Frecciarossa, between major Italian cities; www.italotreno.it.

Tickets

Booking
Reservations are mandatory for superior trains (such as Eurostar and Eurocity) and tickets should be purchased in advance. Other tickets with compulsory supplements should be purchased at least three hours in advance. You must date-stamp *(convalidare)* your rail ticket before beginning the journey at one of the small machines at the head of the platforms, or you may be fined. If you wish to upgrade to first class or a couchette, you can pay the conductor the difference.

To avoid long lines for tickets at major stations, book online with Trenitalia or, for a small charge, buy from local travel agencies. There are automatic ticket machines at major stations, although these are often out of order. Payment can be made either by cash or by credit card.

Wagons Lits/Carrozze Letto (sleeper cars) are found on long-distance trains within Italy, as well as on trains to France, Austria, Germany, and Switzerland. Reservations are essential.

Special Offers
There are a wide variety of train tickets and special offers available, which vary constantly and with the season. Some of the more established are:
The Eurail Italy Pass: available for foreign visitors, it allows between 3, 4, 5 or 8 days of unlimited travel on the Italian State Railway network, within a one month's period.
Group fares: groups of between 6 and 24 people can benefit from a 20 percent discount.
Youth fares: students aged between 12 and 26 can buy a yearly Carta Verde – "green card". This season ticket entitles them to a 10 percent discount on national trains

and a 25 percent discount on international trips.

Children's fares: children under four travel free; children aged between 4–12 are eligible for a 50 percent discount on all trains but must pay the full supplement for Intercity and Eurocity trains.

Pensioners' fares: the over-60s can buy a Carta d'Argento (free for over 75s). Valid for a year, this "silver card" entitles them to a 10–25 percent discount on certain train tickets.

Railway Stations

The main railway stations are open 24 hours a day and are integrated with road and sea transport. They provide numerous services, including telecommunications, left luggage, food and drink, tourist information and porters (luggage trolleys are hard to find).

Florence: The train information office at Santa Maria Novella station is next to the waiting room. The train reservation office is just inside the building (daily 6am–9pm). There is a left-luggage counter.

Siena: The railway station has an information office, counter for left luggage (and bicycles), and restaurant. Immediately outside the station is a bus ticket office and a tourist office. However, Siena's railway station is outside the town centre. More useful, and with faster services and a greater range of local destinations, is the coach service, with coaches leaving from Piazza San Domenico to Florence and various other Tuscan towns.

The ferry at Livorno.

By Coach

Coaches are very comfortable and often quicker than trains. Especially convenient is the Rapida bus to Siena, running several times a day. Provincial bus companies include (websites in Italian only, except for Sita and sena):

cpt, Pisa; tel: 050-5205 133 or free phone line: 800-570 530; www.pisa.cttnord.it (for travel in Pisa Province).

cap, Piazza Duomo 18, Prato; tel: 0574-608 218; www.capautolinee.it (for travel in Tuscany and elsewhere).

Sita, Via S. Caterina da Siena 15, Florence; tel: 800-373 760; www.sita-bus.it (for travel in Tuscany and Italy in general).

sena, Sottopassaggio (Underpass) la Lizza, Siena; tel: 0861-199 1900; www.sena.it (travel to and from Tuscany, great for Siena–Rome).

Tuscan Island Ferries

Numerous ferries ply the waters between the mainland and the islands of the Tuscan archipelago (Elba, Giglio, Capraia, Gorgona and Pianosa). Services from Piombino to Elba are regular throughout the day – every half-hour in the summer – but during the peak months, especially August, you should book in advance. At other times you can turn up and buy your ticket direct from the harbour office. The journey time for the car ferry is under an hour. Hydrofoil services for foot passengers only are less frequent but take around 35 minutes.

The biggest operator is **Toremar**, which connects Piombino to Portoferraio, Rio Marina and Cavo. For information and online bookings, go to www.toremar.it and see www.visitelba.com. Alternatively, book Toremar services through www.traghetti-toremar.com; tel: 0565-31100 (Piombino office). **Moby Lines**, the other main operator, runs a regular service between Piombino and Portoferraio as well as to Rio Marina and Cavo. For information and bookings, see: www.moby.it.

If you are booking from the UK, or you want to compare the two main ferry operators to Elba, consult www.ferrysavers.com. Toremar also operates services from Livorno to Capraia, from Piombino and Rio Marina to Pianosa, and from Santo Stefano on the Argentario peninsula to the island of Giglio.

City Transport

Local Buses/Trams

Buses within each province are cheap and plentiful. Tickets can be bought at designated offices, tobacconists, bars and newspaper stands. They are purchased in booklets (of usually 10) or as singles, and have to be stamped by a machine on the bus at the start of a journey. Failure to do so risks a fine. All provincial bus services are routed past the railway station in every town.

In **Florence**, a range of tickets for the city's buses and new tram system is available from the ATAF office (Piazza Stazione; tel: 800-424 500; www.ataf.net). One of the handiest options is the three-day Firenze Card Plus (see page 98), which includes museum access and public transport on buses and trams.

Siena's city/regional bus service is called Tiemme.

Pisa province bus times are displayed on a board in Pisa's APT office on Piazza Garibaldi. Just outside Pisa Centrale Station, on the left, is a window for bus tickets.

Sightseeing Buses

Numerous sightseeing tours are offered in all the main cities.

Florence: **City Sightseeing Italy** (Piazza Stazione; tel: 055-290 451; www.city-sightseeing.it) offers tours of Florence with multilingual commentary. Given the gradual pedestrianisation of parts of the city, the routes are subject to change. Tickets are valid for 24, 48 or 72 hours, allowing you to hop on and off at numerous points around the city. City Sightseeing Italy also offers many guided tours of Florence (as well as tours of Livorno). However, far more interesting are the thematic Florence walking tours booked through the Link guiding service (see page 102).

Taxis
Taxis are plentiful in all towns and tourist resorts. They wait in special ranks at railway stations and main parts of the city but can be contacted by telephone. If you book one by phone, the cost of the journey begins then. (In Florence, tel: 055-4242, 055-4390 or 055-4798). Meters display fares: the fixed starting charge varies and extra charges are payable for night service, Sunday service and public holidays, luggage and journeys outside the town area. In Florence, there are taxi ranks in Via Pellicceria, Piazza di San Marco and Piazza Santa Trinità, and outside Stazione di Santa Maria Novella.

Cycling and Mopeds
Mopeds and bicycles are the most efficient way to get around the narrow streets of Florence, Siena and Lucca. They can be hired in the main cities. Try to find one with good brakes and a stand. You may have to leave an identity card or passport as security.
Florence: Mobike bike-sharing initiative, https://mobike.com, allows cyclists to borrow one of 4,000 bikes at very reasonable prices from many points in the city. You can also can rent a bike from Florence by Bike, Via San Zanobi 54r; tel: 055-488 992; www.florencebybike.it or **Alinari**, via San Zanobi 38r; tel: 055-280 500; www.alinarirental.com.
Siena: Perozzi, Via del Romitorio 5 (near the Lizza park); tel: 0577-280 839; www.perozzi-siena.com. Amici della Bicicletta di Siena, c/o Comitato Associazioni Sportive Sensei, Via G. Di Vittorio 12; tel: 0577-333 333; www.adbsiena.it.
Lucca: Rent Bike Lucca in the square in front of the railway station (www.touristcenterlucca.com); Chrono, Corso Garibaldi 93; tel: 0583-490 591; www.chronobikes.com; Cicli Bizzarri, Piazza S. Maria 32; tel: 0583-496 682.

Driving
To ease traffic, many city centres are closed to most vehicles.

Since cities such as Florence, Montepulciano and Pistoia have introduced partial or complete city-centre driving bans (at least for non-residents), it makes sense to leave the car in the car parks on the edge of the historic centre. Florence, in particular, has extended its pedestrianised areas to include Via de Tornabuoni, the Palazzo Pitti area and parts of the Oltrano.

State highways in Tuscany include the No. 1 "Aurelia", which runs north–south, to the west of Pisa. National motorways *(autostrade)*: the A11, the "Firenze–mare", and the A12, the "Sestri Levante–Livorno". Both of these are toll roads. The two *superstrade* (Florence–Siena and the Florence–Pisa–Livorno) are toll-free.

Car Hire
The major rental companies (Hertz, Avis, Europcar, etc.) have representation in most cities and resorts. The smaller local firms offer cheaper rates but cars can only be booked on the spot. Booking online, or in advance, often as part of a fly-drive package, is usually cheaper than hiring on arrival.

Rates normally allow unlimited mileage and include breakdown service. Basic insurance is included but additional cover is available at fixed rates. Most firms require a deposit and often take and hold a credit-card payment until the car is returned. You will usually be asked to return the car with a full tank; do so, as if the rental company has to fill it, they charge a premium for the petrol.

Licences and Insurance
Licences: Drivers must have a driving licence issued by a nation with a reciprocal agreement with Italy. The pink EU licence does not need an Italian translation. All other licences do need a translation, obtainable (free) from motoring organisations and Italian tourist offices. You are legally required to keep documents related to the car and driver on you.
Insurance: If you are bringing your own vehicle, check that your insurance covers Italy. A Green Card, obtainable from your insurance company, is not obligatory within the EU and does not provide extra

cover, but it is internationally recognised, which may be useful if you have an accident.

Rules of the Road
Italy drives on the right. Road signs are international, with a few local differences:
Road signs: ALT is a stop line on the road for road junctions; STOP is for a pedestrian crossing.
Precedence: At crossroads, motorists must give precedence to vehicles on their right, except on recently built roundabouts, when those already on the roundabout have priority. If a motorist approaching a crossroads finds a precedence sign (a triangle with the point downwards) or a Stop sign, he/she must give precedence to all vehicles coming from both the right and left.
Parking: Outside cities and towns, parking on the right-hand side of the road is allowed, except on motorways, at crossroads, on curves and near hilly ground not having full visibility. Illegally parked vehicles will be towed away, and incur a hefty fine. To understand the parking options in Florence, look at the clear advice and map on www.visitflorence.com. To find a car park in an Italian town online, look on www.parcheggi.it; for Florence go to www.firenzeparcheggi.it. There is a *"parcheggio scambiatore"* in Viale Europa (south Florence) – drivers can park their cars here and get a bus, hire a bike or take part in the car-sharing scheme to get into the centre. Special "tourist" rates (24 hours and nightly tickets) are available at the "Parterre" (Piazza della Libertà), "Oltrarno" (Porta Romana), and "Beccaria" garages.
Breakdowns and accidents: In case of a breakdown, dial 116. On motorways, telephones are 2km (1 mile) apart, with buttons to call for the police and medical assistance. Both have to be contacted if an accident involves an injury.

Motorways
Access signs to the motorways, unlike in other European countries, are in green, not blue. Motorway tolls can be high. There is rarely a hard shoulder on motorways, and often there are only two lanes. Accidents are frequent, so take care.

A

Accommodation

The quality and choice of accommodation in Tuscany is extremely varied. Visitors can choose between a city palazzo, grand country villa, or a historic family-run hotel, a rented apartment or villa, a bucolic farm-stay holiday (agriturismo) or even, in the most popular cities, a private home stay. (This is not known as bed and breakfast since breakfast is not usually provided.)

Hotel rooms generally need to be booked well in advance in Florence and Siena. During local summer festivals, particularly the Sienese Palio and Arezzo's Giostra, it can become very difficult to find a room.

Attractive accommodation in the centre of Volterra and San Gimignano is popular, so early booking is advisable.

There is a huge variation in what you get for your money. A moderately priced hotel in Florence may be somewhat underwhelming, whereas the same money could buy you a luxurious 4-star room in a grand country house off the tourist track.

Generally speaking, "high season" in Tuscany is May to September. However, in towns this does not necessarily include August. In Florence, for instance, many of the more expensive hotels reduce their prices during this month. It can sometimes pay to bargain.

Many hotels with restaurants insist on a half- or full-board arrangement, especially in the high season. This ploy is particularly prevalent on the islands (eg Elba), in seaside resorts (eg Forte dei Marmi), in spa resorts (eg Montecatini Terme and Chianciano Terme), and where accommodation is in short supply.

Private Home Stays

This is a fairly new development in Tuscany, but it is a good way of meeting the locals while paying modest prices. In Florence and Siena, the homes are carefully graded from simple to luxurious.

In Florence, contact www.firenzealloggio.com for B&B accommodation booked online directly with the owners, and no booking charge. For B&B accommodation in Florence, Lucca, Pisa and Siena, book online through the reliable American website: www.bedandbreakfast.com. Also try **ANBBA** (Associazione Nazionale Bed & Breakfast e Affittacamere): www.anbba.it.

In Siena, request the *Affittacamere* (private lodgings) booklet of addresses from the tourist office (APT, Piazza Campo 56, Siena; tel: 0577-280 551). The list includes private accommodation in the whole of Siena Province, including San Gimignano, Montalcino and the Sienese Chianti.

Agriturismo

Farm stays (agriturismo) are an excellent way of experiencing the Tuscan countryside while staying on a farm or a wine estate. Standards vary widely from simple, rustic accommodation at low prices to relatively luxurious surroundings, complete with swimming pool. Before booking, check the website if they have one, or insist on a description or a photo, since many may be modern and fail to match up to the visitor's romantic image of Tuscany. Some farms, however, are genuine 16th-century wine and oil estates. There is usually the opportunity to buy local produce on site and meals are sometimes provided. For obvious reasons, you will normally need a car to make the most of a farm stay.
Reservations: During peak season, it is best to book in advance. Official accommodation tends to be booked for

a minimum of one week, but individual arrangements for weekends and overnight stays are often possible, especially during mid- and low season.

Every local tourist authority produces farm-stay booklets. Or you can browse the following websites: www.agriturismo.com; www.agriturismo.net; and www.agriturist.it. Also try Terranostra, tel: 064-899 3209; www.terranostra.it.

Rural Stays

These overlap with farm stays but can include country houses or even entire restored medieval villages (such as Sovicille, near Siena). In general, there is a working farm attached to the accommodation, or at least the opportunity to sample or buy wine, oil and local produce grown on the estate. As with farm stays, the accommodation offered can vary from simple rooms to self-contained apartments. The owners often use the profits from letting to reinvest in the restoration of the family estate or village. With rural stays, the emphasis is on country living in traditional buildings rather than in luxurious villa accommodation.

Many of the owners may speak basic English, French or German, but at least a smattering of Italian is appreciated. Always request detailed descriptions and directions.

Local tourist offices are a good source for recommendations (see page 267). Extensive listings, supported by images, can also be found on www.agriturismo.com and www.agriturismo.net. The following are some typical examples of rural stays, but are just a handful among countless options:
La Ripolina, Località Pieve di Piana, 53022 Buonconvento, Siena Province; tel: 0335-573 9284; www.laripolina.it. Most of the holiday apartments are in converted farmhouses; one is in a fortified abbey with a

10th-century wall. Fresh farm produce available.

Agriturismo Podere San Lorenzo, Via Allori 80, 56048 Volterra, Pisa; tel: 0588-39080; www.agriturismo-volterra.it. Podere San Lorenzo is a working olive farm that has nine guest apartments in the farmhouse. Organic produce from its garden is used in the preparation of delicious meals served in an old Franciscan chapel. Cooking classes are available and there is a chemical-free swimming pool.

San Savino, Val di Chio, Località Santa Lucia 89/a, 52043 Castiglion Fiorentino, Arezzo province; tel: 0575-651 000; www.agriturismo-san savino.it. This restored 11th-century monastery overlooks, a lake, olive groves and woods and offers several apartments (plus pool and stables).

Villa Igea, Torre Alta, 55060 Ponte del Giglio, Lucca province; tel: 0583-353 122; www.villa-igea.biz. This charming traditional Tuscan villa and cottage is set among woodland and olive groves overlooking a valley. Home-produced extra-virgin olive oils and tastings.

La Parrina, km 146 Via Aurelia, Località Parrina, 58010 Albinia, Grosseto province; tel: 0564-862 626; www.parrina.it. This long-established agricultural estate is set among vineyards, olive groves and orchards. The rooms and dining rooms are decorated with an unfussy elegance that makes you feel right at home. To prove you're on a working farm, you may be woken early by the sound of tractors. Rooms and apartments; swimming pool; chapel; farm shop; restaurant and wine tasting; and bicycles.

Villa and Apartment Rentals

One of the most popular ways of visiting Tuscany is to stay in a rented villa or apartment. They do not come cheap, but you have the benefit of independence, and the freedom to cook for yourself using delicious fresh Tuscan produce. Prices vary enormously, depending on the season and the luxuriousness of the accommodation. The following agencies deal with rentals:

To Tuscany: UK: (+44) 12276-46 040. US/Canada: (toll-free) 1800 454-5922; www.to-tuscany.com. This recommended, well-established company is well known for its customer service. Specialising in the Chianti, it offers cottages, villas with pool and entire estates, and has a UK office.

The Best in Italy, tel: 055-223 064; www.thebestinitaly.com. A

Florence-based lettings agency offering luxurious villas and palazzi with pools, tennis courts, stables, domestic staff and other such luxuries.

Cuendet, tel: (+39) 041-251 6100; www.cuendet.com. A good selection of Tuscan villas and apartments.

Hello Italy, tel: (+44) 01983-508 923; www.helloit.co.uk: recommended for the Lunigiana region.

Simpson Travel, tel: (+44) 020-3740 4570; www.simpsontravel.com. A good selection of luxury villas. UK-based and established.

The following are some typical examples of villas:

Casa Glyn, Cotto, Lunigiana, tel: 0585-92098; www.merrioncharles.com. Lovely setting with striking views of the Apuan Alps and the Carrara hills. A tempting base for walks in the Apennines and foodie forays to Lucca. Unwind in a modest family retreat with great character and comfort. Pizza oven, pool, gardens and south-facing terrace.

Gargaricus Palazzolaccio: Val d'Orcia, tel: (+44) 01803-290 958; www.private-travel.co. Beautifully restored rustic villa stunning views of the Val d'Orcia. A lovely pool on site. Foodie forays to Pienza for pecorino cheese and oil, and Montalcino and Montepulciano for red wines.

Villa Rignana: Via di Rignana 7, Greve in Chianti, Chianti; tel: 055-852 137; www.villarignana.com. Set among vineyards, this former monastery is now a villa retreat with the air of a minor stately home, dotted with heirlooms. Sleeps 18, with a chapel that makes it popular for wedding parties.

Castles and Monasteries

Accommodation is available in a variety of castles and palaces. Standards will vary from very simple to luxurious. Many convents, monasteries and other religious institutions offer simple accommodation for tourists and pilgrims. Monte Oliveto Maggiore is just one example. Each provincial tourist office should be able to supply you with a full list.

Youth Hostels

A list of youth hostels is available from ENIT (Italian National Tourist Offices (see page 267) and places can be booked through them or through local Tuscan tourist offices. Alternatively, contact the Associazione Italiana Alberghi per la Gioventù, Viale Mazzini 88, 00195

Rome; tel: 06-9826 1462; www.aig hostels.it.

Camping

For a free list of campsites, contact the Confederazione Italiana Campeggiatori, Via Vittorio Emanuele 11, 50041 Calenzano, Florence; tel: 055-882 391; www.federcampeggio.it.

Admission Charges

The price of admission for an adult to major museums such as the Uffizi or Pitti Palace, is generally around €10–20, while for smaller museums it's usually around €5–10. Admission is free or discounted to public museums and monuments for European Union citizens aged under 18 or over 65. Private museums have their own charges (around €8–15) and discounts for older and younger visitors. Nearly all the major museums now have websites that allow you to book tickets online. This is highly advisable for big attractions, such as the Uffizi, especially in peak seasons, as demand is high and booking online allows you to miss some of the queues.

The Firenze Card (www.firenzecard. it) provides one entry to each of the 72 museums of Florence Circuit and is valid for 72 hours (€72).

Admission to churches and religious buildings is usually free, but some charge an entry fee (generally €5–12, with reductions for children) to cover maintenance costs. In addition, the number of visitors allowed per day to see some major sights in churches is limited for conservation reasons, so you need to book a visit. This can often be done online, as well as through local tourist offices. Also, you need to carry some change when visiting churches, to feed the coin-in-slot machines that illuminate frescoes and other details.

B

Budgeting for your Trip

The cost of travelling in Italy varies enormously depending on where you go and how you travel. Florence is a notoriously expensive place. Hotel prices vary enormously by season. In general, though, prices overall, even in the countryside, tend to be a bit higher north of Rome than south of it and in the islands.

If you order a drink or a meal at an outside table you will always pay more than inside, and more if you have a coffee at any table than standing at the bar Italian-style. The amount added on for *terrazza* service varies, so the price of sitting on the most celebrated terraces of Florence is astronomical. Hence people take their time. Beer is peculiarly expensive in Italy, especially at outside tables, often at around €4–6 for a smallish glass, and so is drunk relatively little; wine bought by the glass is similarly expensive, often around €5, except in traditional basic wine bars (*enoteche* or in Venice *bacari*), so in many cases you might as well order a bottle or a carafe. To eat, in most cities – even well-touristed ones – you can find unfussy restaurants that provide *tavola calda* lunch menus for around €15–20, while a generous pizza costs around €8–10. An enjoyable three-course meal with wine in mid-range restaurants can be found in Florence or Siena for around €50, in less fashionable places for closer to €30. Gourmet restaurants will cost from around €70–80 per person and upwards, although again in less trodden spots you can often find remarkable food for much less.

Hotel rooms, especially attractive ones, are expensive in Florence and it's hard to find a pleasant double room in a hotel for much under €80 a night. Comfortable mid-range rooms cost around €150, while Florence and rural Tuscany have a great deal of luxury accommodation for an indulgent splurge, with rooms for €400 and upwards. Hence travellers seek out more economical options, such as monastery stays, apartment rentals, B&Bs or bland but good-value business hotels like those of the NH chain. B&B rooms on farms (*agriturismi*) are economical in most areas, often around €60, but there are also luxurious variations.

For long-distance travel, train fares are very reasonabl. A daytime taxi journey within the centre of most cities should cost around €10. In most cities and towns a single transport ticket costs €1.20–1.50, but most have systems that allow you to buy multiple tickets, saving time and money. The Firenze Card Plus (www.firenzecard.it), beside free entry to top museums, offers free transport on buses and trams for three days (€77).

Children

Italy is a very child-friendly country and few restaurants ever object to admitting them, even very grand ones (although they will be expected to behave and sit at table properly). Few restaurants have special children's menus, but then Italian cuisine is full of things kids like – pasta, pizza, ice cream. Accompanied small children (generally under 6, or more traditionally under 1 metre (3ft) tall) travel free on most public transport. Admission is also free to most public museums and monuments for EU citizens aged under 18, and there is usually a reduced price for non-EU under-18s (some museums now also offer free entry to non-EU citizens under 18).

Many hotels have family rooms or offer the option of an additional bed in the parents' room. Hotel bed-sitting services, however, are fairly scarce except in more expensive hotels. An exception are the family-oriented holiday hotels (often called a *centro de vacanze* rather than a hotel) around the Italian coasts, lakes and islands, usually open in summer only, which have play areas, kids' pools and many other facilities.

Climate

The Tuscan climate is pleasantly mild in the spring and autumn, cool and wet in the winter, and very hot near the sea and on low-lying land in the summer, with a pleasant warmth in the hills. There is very little wind except for on the Tyrrhenian coastline around Marina di Pisa and Tirrenia, but surprise storms can be

very heavy at any time of the year, and flooding in a number of places has caused severe damage in the past. The rainfall in Tuscany is generally higher than in most other parts of Italy. The temperature is slightly lower than in other areas, making it more agreeable in summer but somewhat colder in winter.

The weather in Florence can be extreme. The city is situated in a bowl, surrounded by hills, with the Arno cutting through it, and this accounts for the high degree of humidity that is often a feature of midsummer. The worst of the humidity is likely to occur between mid-July and mid-August, with temperatures climbing well into the 30s Celsius (90s Fahrenheit).

Crime and Safety

Although violent crime is rare, in recent years, much crime in the north has tended to be gang- or drug-related. With an influx of immigrants in Italy recorded since 2015, the harassment of so-called "foreigners" (essentially immigrants from Asia or Africa) is unfortunately on the increase in a country traditionally unused to dealing with immigrants.

The main problem for tourists is petty crime, from pick-pocketing and bag-snatching to the theft of objects left unattended in cars; it is wise to have insurance coverage against this and to take basic, sensible precautions against theft. If driving, lock your car and never leave luggage, cameras or other valuables inside. This applies particularly in major cities.

If you are the victim of a crime (or suffer a loss) and wish to claim against your insurance, it is essential to make a report at the nearest police station as soon as possible and get documentation to support your claim. When you need a policeman, dial **113** (or **112** for the *Carabinieri*, the national police force). Or, in Florence, call the Tourist Aid Police, 055-203 911.

Customs Regulations

Examination of luggage, passports, currency and hand baggage may take place on both entering and leaving Italy at airports, ports and borders. Formalities may also be carried out on trains. Registered luggage may be sent to towns with Customs Offices: examination takes place at the destination.

It is no longer possible to buy duty-free or tax-free goods on journeys within the EU; VAT and duty are included in the purchase price. Shops at ports and airports will sell goods duty- and tax-paid to those travelling within the EU; in practice, many shops have chosen not to pass on price increases since the sale of duty-free goods within the EU was abolished.

There are no longer any limits on how much you can buy on journeys within the EU, provided it's for your own personal use. But there are suggested limits, and if you exceed them Customs may seize your goods if you can't prove they are for your own use. The guidance levels are:
800 cigarettes or 400 cigarillos or 200 cigars or 1 kg of smoking tobacco;
10 litres of spirits; 20 litres of fortified wine; 90 litres of wine; 110 litres of beer.

Duty-frees are still available to those travelling outside the EU.

Professional photographers must carry an ata Carnet (issued in the UK through the London Chamber of Commerce, 33 Queen Street, London EC4R 1AP; tel: 020-7248 4444) for temporary importation of equipment.

Disabled Travellers

Despite difficult cobbled streets and poor wheelchair access to many tourist attractions and hotels, many people with disabilities visit Florence and Tuscany every year.

However, unaccompanied visitors will usually experience some difficulty, so it is best to travel with a companion.

Conditions and disability awareness are improving slowly in Tuscany (as well as in Italy in general), although the situation is certainly not ideal, and access is not always easy. More museums now have lifts, ramps and adapted toilets; newer trains and buses are accessible (although wheelchair users may need help when boarding); and recent laws require restaurants, bars and hotels to provide the relevant facilities. These laws, however, do not always cover access to those facilities. Information about the facilities offered at sights and museums is provided at tourist information centres. A lot of information is also available online at www.visittuscany.com in the Accessible Tourism section.

The Accessible Guide to Florence, by Cornelia Danielson, provides very detailed information on museums, restaurants, hotels and more for disabled travellers to Florence. Also, visit www.sagetraveling.com, the site of the European Disabled Travel Experts, tel: (+44)) 2035-406 155 (UK), +1-888-645 7920 (US), where you can order bespoke comprehensive guides to Florence, Siena, Livorno and the Tuscany region.

For drivers with disabilities, there are plenty of reserved parking places in towns, and these are free.

In the UK, you can obtain further information from Disability Rights UK, Plexal, East Bay Lane 14, London E20 3BS; tel: 0330-995 0400; www.disabilityrightsuk.org. In the US, contact SATH, tel: 212-447 7284; www.sath.org.

Eating Out

Tuscan cuisine is highly revered throughout food-focused Italy. In general, the food is rustic and simple, relying heavily upon fresh vegetables, legumes (pulses), meat and game.

Where to Eat

Italy has three traditional types of place to eat: a *trattoria*, a *ristorante* or an *osteria*. At first they may appear to be similar, and this is increasingly true, but to Italians they signify different types of dining experiences. A *trattoria* is more casual, serving basic regional dishes in an informal setting. *Trattorie* are often family-owned and have no frills. A *ristorante* implies somewhat fancier décor, more formal service, and more elaborate and expensive food. To make things more confusing, the *osteria* is historically a tavern-like wine shop where you can buy a glass of wine and perhaps a hunk of cheese, but the word is now used almost interchangeably with *ristorante* or *trattoria*.

Yet another type of eating establishment is the *tavola calda* or *rosticceria*, both of which are cafeteria-style places where several selections of hot dishes are prepared daily and served from a counter. You generally pay in advance and show the receipt to someone working behind the counter, who prepares a plate for you.

Although pizza has become a national dish, it is not one for which Tuscany is particularly famous. Eating in a *pizzeria* costs considerably less than in a *ristorante* or *trattoria*, and they generally serve only pizza and appetisers.

In general, a *ristorante* or *trattoria* serves both lunch and dinner. Lunch is generally from 12.30 to 3pm, and dinner from 7.30 to 11pm. Most establishments close one day a week and occasionally for lunch or dinner immediately preceding or following that day. Most Italian eating establishments close for holidays *(ferie)* once or even twice a year. Many restaurants close for at least two weeks around 15 August and sometimes another week or two in the winter.

What to Eat

You will notice that just about all menus are divided into more or less the same categories: *antipasti* (appetisers), *primi* (first courses), *secondi* (second courses), *contorni* (side dishes) and *dolci* (desserts).

Antipasto means 'before the meal', and these selections are usually served in small portions. Many restaurants offer an *antipasto misto* (mixed appetiser) that is often served buffet-style from a table laden with such dishes as *melone con prosciutto* (ham and melon) or grilled vegetables, and *insalata caprese* (mozzarella, tomatoes and fresh basil). Typical Tuscan *antipasti* are *crostini*, tomatoes or liver pâté on toasted bread; *prosciutto di cinghiale*, ham from wild boar; *finocchiona*, pork sausage laced with fennel.

Il primo is the first course, and in Tuscany that generally means hearty soup or pasta (increasingly you will also find risotto). Typical Tuscan *primi* include: *acquacotta*, onion soup that is a speciality of Arezzo; *minestrone alla fiorentina*, a vegetable soup with beans; *panzanella*, a bread salad often found on summer menus, whose ingredients also include tomatoes and basil; *pappardelle con lepre* or *con cinghiale*, broad noodles topped with a rich sauce made from hare or wild boar; *ribollita*, a rich vegetable soup with bread mixed into it; *cacciuco*, a rich fish soup that is reason in itself to travel to Livorno.

Il secondo is the main dish of meat or fish, usually meat, and often beefsteak, pork, rabbit or game birds. Some typical dishes are *porchetta*, roast suckling pig; *cinghiale*, wild boar; *fritto misto*, a mixed grill including lamb chops and sweetbreads; *anatra*, duck; and *girarrosto*, a spit of roast game birds; *trippa alla fiorentina*, tripe with tomato sauce; *baccala alla livornese*, salt cod, a speciality of Livorno; and *bistecca alla fiorentina*, a T-bone steak grilled rare.

Il contorno is the vegetable course. It's always ordered separately. *Fagioli*, beans – especially white beans – are a favourite. Salads *(insalate)* are straightforward and tend to come in two varieties: green *(insalata verde)* or mixed *(insalata mista)*.

Il dolce is dessert, a course that is not among Italy's greatest culinary achievements, but ice cream *(gelato)* is reliably delicious when it is home-made, and *biscotti* are sweet biscuits, often almond flavoured, that are dipped in *vinsanto*, a sweet wine. Most restaurants offer *tiramisù*, and many towns have their own sweet specialities.

Electricity

Italy uses 220v and two-pin plugs. Adaptors for British three-pin appliances can be purchased from airports or department stores in the city. You will need a transformer to use 100–120 volt appliances.

Embassies

Australian Embassy: Via Antonio Bosio 5, 00161 Rome; tel: 06-852 721; http://italy.embassy.gov.au.
Canada: Via Zara 30, 00198 Rome; tel: 06-85444; www.canadainternational.gc.ca.
Ireland: Villa Spada, Via Giacomo Medici 1, 00153 Roma; tel: 06-585 2381; www.embassyofireland.it.
New Zealand: Via Clitunno 44, 00198 Rome; tel: 06-853 7501, www.nzembassy.com.
South Africa: Via Tanaro 14, 00198 Rome; tel: 06-852 541; www.dirco.gov.za.
UK Embassy: Via XX Settembre

80a, 00187 Rome; tel: 06-4220 0001; www.gov.uk/world/organisations/british-embassy-rome.
US Embassy: Via Vittorio Veneto 121, 00187 Rome; tel: 06-46741; https://it.usembassy.gov.
US Consulate: Lungarno A. Vespucci 38, 50123 Florence; tel: 055-266 951.

Emergencies

Useful Florence Contacts
Ambulances *(Misericordia)* – tel: 118
Italian Red Cross Medical Service – Ungarno Soderini 11; tel: 055-293 801.
Tourist Medical Service (Guardia Medica Turistica), with English-, German- or French-speaking doctors: Piazza del Duomo; tel: 055-212 222, no need to book if 8am–8pm (normal cases) or call any time for emergencies.
Lost Property, Via Circondaria 19; tel: 055-328 3942/43; but first report to the Police (Questura, tel: 055-49771).
Automobile Club d'Italia (ACI) tel: 803-116.
Car breakdown, call ACI Road Service, tel: 116.
Police Headquarters (Questura) – the place to visit in the event of thefts, stolen cars, lost passports, etc., Via Zara 2; tel: 055-49771.
Tourist Police *(Polizia Assistenza Turistica)* are at Via Pietrapiana 50r (Piazza dei Ciompi); tel: 055-203 911, and have interpreters on hand to assist.
Associazione Volontari Ospedalieri, Florence; tel: 055-234 4567. This group of volunteers will translate (free) for foreign patients.

Useful Siena Contacts
Siena Hospital Nuovo Policlinico di Siena, Località le Scotte, Viale Bracci; tel: 0577-585 111.
Police Station *(Questura)*, Via del Castoro 6; tel: 0577-201 111 – 24 hours a day.
Pronto Soccorso *(Misericordia)*, Via del Porrione 49; tel: 0577-21011, or dial 118 in an emergency.
Lost Property Via Casato di Sotto 23; tel: 0577-292 230.
Associazione Volontari Ospedalieri, Siena; tel: 0577-247 869.
See the Siena Town Hall website for all key numbers: www.comune.siena.it.

Etiquette

Tuscans are generally friendly and will appreciate efforts to speak the language. Any attempt to rush or

pressurise them, however, will be regarded as the height of bad taste, and whatever you want will take longer. Almost everything is done on the basis of personal favours or contacts, so any personal recommendations you can muster will always come in useful.

F

Festivals

Arezzo
Last Sunday in June and first Sunday in September: Giostra del Saracino – Jousting match in which mounted knights attack a wooden effigy of a Turk.

Chianciano Terme
September: The Chianciano Biennale is a celebration of contemporary art, staged in uneven years (www.museodarte.org).

Cortona
June: The Tuscan Sun Festival features concerts, stars, wine and food events, and art exhibitions (www.tuscansunfestival.com).
Mid-August: Sagra della Bistecca – "Feast of the Beefsteak".
End of August/beginning of September: antiques fair.

Florence
Easter Day: Scoppio del Carro, the "Explosion of the Carriage" (actually fireworks on a float). Colourful musical processions.
Ascension Day: Festa del Grillo, Festival of the Crickets in the Cascine park - sale of crickets and sweets.
End of April: Flower Show, Parterre, near Piazza Libertà – a riot of colour.
End of April, May and June: Maggio Musicale Fiorentino – performances of opera, ballet and classical music.
June: Calcio in costume (Calcio Fiorentino) – football in medieval costume in Piazza Santa Croce.
June–September: Estate Fiesolana in Fiesole (just outside Florence) – music, dance, opera, cinema and theatre.
24 June: San Giovanni – Florence's patron saint's day, with a holiday in the city and an evening firework display near Piazzale Michelangelo.
July–August: Estate Fiorentina – Florence's summer festival.

7 September: night festival of the Rificolona (lanterns) – procession of carts, lanterns and singers.

First three weeks of December: German Christmas Market – Piazza Santa Croce becomes a festive German market with decorations, mulled wine, sausage and beer, and other German specialities. For Florence events, see www.comune.fi.it.

Lucca

July: Lucca Summer Festival, one of Tuscany's best festivals – with big-name international bands in Piazza Anfiteatro and a range of venues around town.

September – first weekend. Festival of Flowers.

September: Luminaria di Santa Croce – a religious procession.

Lucignano

Last two Sundays in May: Maggiolata Lucignanese festival that includes a procession of carts decorated with allegorical scenes in flowers.

Massa Marittima

Sunday following May 20 and the second Sunday in August: Balestro del Girifalco – crossbow competition.

Montalcino

Last Sunday in October: Sagra del Tordo – Thrush Festival. Pageant, costume ball, banquet and archery at the fortress.

Monticchiello

End of July–early August: Il Teatro Povero – "The Poor Theatre" presents a performance written by locals about locals.

Pienza

First Sunday of September: Fiera del Cacio – a fair devoted to Pienza's famous cheese.

Pisa

May and June: concerts at various annual festivals and fairs, especially during the Gioco del Ponte on the last Sunday of June.

16–17 June: Luminaria di San Ranieri – thousands of candles light up buildings along the Arno. Boat race in the evening of the second day.

Last Sunday in June: Gioco del Ponte.

September–October: The annual Anima Mundi International Festival of Sacred Music takes place in Pisa Cathedral. Tel: 050-835 029; www.opapisa.it/en.

Pistoia

25 July: Giostra dell'Orso – a mock battle between a wooden bear and 12 knights in costume on Piazza del Duomo.

San Gimignano

July–September: Summer Fair – varied programme of events, including ballet, concerts and cinema.

Siena

28–30 April: Feast of St Catherine.

2 July and 16 August: Il Palio traditional horse race. For tickets and hotel bookings, plan six months in advance (www.ilpalio.org).

July–August: International Summer Festival for Opera & Chamber Orchestra – performances of opera, symphonies and chamber music.

End of July: Incontri in Terra di Siena – chamber-music festival featuring top-quality concerts held in stunning settings south of Siena.

13 December: Festa di Santa Lucia – ceramics festival.

Torre del Lago

July and August: Puccini Opera Festival, Torre del Lago, near the composer's villa on Lake Massaciuccoli (www.puccinifestival.it).

Viareggio

February: Carnevale – one of the best carnivals in Italy.

Volterra

First Sunday in September: Torneo di Tiro con la Balestra – crossbow tournament.

Health and Medical Care

UK visitors are entitled to medical treatment in Italy provided they have a European Health Insurance Card (tel: 0300-330 1350; visit www.nhs.uk; or obtain an application form from the post office). There are similar arrangements for citizens of other European Union countries. As few Italians have faith in their own state health service, it may be advisable to take out insurance for private treatment in case of accident.

Visitors from outside the EU are strongly advised to take out adequate holiday and medical insurance to provide full cover during their stay abroad.

In high summer, the weather can be very hot; sunscreen, shady hats and mosquito repellent are recommended.

Medical Services

Pharmacies: The staff in chemists (*farmacie*) are usually very knowledgeable about common illnesses and sell far more medicines without prescription than in some other countries (even so, most drugs still require a prescription). Pharmacies are identified by a cross, often red or green and usually in neon.

Normal pharmacy opening hours are Mon–Fri 9am–1pm and 4pm–7pm. Every *farmacia* posts a list of the local chemists who are on emergency duty in their window. The following are chemists that are open 24 hours in Florence:

Farmacia Comunale 13, in Florence station; tel: 055-216 761.

Farmacia Molteni, Via Calzaiuoli 7r; tel: 055-215 472.

Farmacia all'Insegna del Moro, Piazza San Giovanni 20r; tel: 055-211 343.

In addition, you can call 800-420 707 to find out which chemists are on the night rota.

First Aid Service (*Pronto Soccorso*) with a doctor is found at airports, railway stations and in all hospitals. See page 264 for numbers to call in an emergency.

Internet

Most large hotels offer Wi-Fi, email and fax facilities. There are numerous internet cafés around Florence, and most other cities, including the chain Internet Train, which allows you to connect using its computers or your own laptop. Most main post offices, travel agencies and hotels have fax facilities.

LGBTQ Travel

Gay life in Italy is becoming more mainstream, helped by increasing numbers of club nights and festivals such as Toscana Pride in June. Attitudes are generally more tolerant in the north: Bologna is regarded as Italy's gay capital, but Florence and Siena also have a lively gay scene. The Bologna-based Arcigay network (tel: 051-095 7241; www.arcigay.it) and www.gayfriendlyitaly.com provide all kinds of information.

Maps

Touring Club Italiano does a good fold-out map of the Tuscany region showing major and minor roads. The Siena and Florence tourist offices supply reasonable city maps. *Insight Guide Fleximaps* are also available for Florence and Tuscany.

Media

Each large Italian town has its own newspaper. The centre-right *Il Corriere della Sera*, and the centre-left *La Repubblica* also have a national following. *La Nazione* is the paper favoured by most Tuscans for regional matters.

Television is deregulated in Italy. In addition to the state network, rai (which offers three channels), there are about 1,000 channels, of which the main ones are Canale 5, Rete 4, Italia 1 and Telemontecarlo.

There are several useful publications for visitors to Tuscany, including *The Florentine*, a bi-weekly English-language paper focusing on current events and city life (www.theflorentine.net), *and Firenze Spettacolo*, a monthly listings magazine in Italian (with some listings also in English), focusing on nightlife, clubs, bars and the live arts in Florence (www.firenzespettacolo.it).

Money

In common with the other eurozone countries of the EU, Italy's monetary unit is the euro (€), which is divided into 100 cents. The currency is available in 500, 200, 100, 50, 20, 10 and 5 euro notes, and 2-euro, 1-euro, 50-cent, 20-cent, 10-cent, 5-cent, 2-cent and 1-cent coins.

Italy is a society that prefers cash to credit cards, except for large purchases, or, for instance, hotel bills. In the case of petrol stations, more modest restaurants and smaller shops, it is usual to pay in cash. Check beforehand if there is any doubt. Most shopkeepers and restaurateurs will not change money, so it is best to change a limited amount at the airport when you arrive, especially if it is the weekend, when banks are closed. Try to avoid changing money in hotels, where the commission tends to be higher than in banks.

Cash Machines and Credit Cards

Given the long queues for money-changing in Italy, it is simplest to get cash from cashpoint machines. Most main cards work in Italian machines, with your normal PIN number, though you may sometimes have to look for particular "Bancomats" (cashpoint machines) that take your card.

In cities, many restaurants, hotels, shops and stores will take major credit cards, but in rural areas especially, you may be able to pay only in cash.

Banks

Banks offer the best exchange rates (small exchange booths often charge up to 3 percent commission) and are normally open Mon–Fri 8.30am–1.30pm. Some banks also open in the afternoon, 2.30pm–4.30pm. Outside these hours and at weekends you can use automatic exchange machines to change cash, which helps to avoid bank queues. There is a high concentration of banks in Florence, including foreign banks, to the west of Piazza della Repubblica, around Via de'Tornabuoni.

☉ Public Holidays

1 January *Capodanno* (New Year's Day).
6 January *La Befana* (Epiphany).
Easter *Pasqua*.
Easter Monday *Pasquetta*.
25 April *Anniversario della Liberazione* (Liberation Day).
1 May *Festa del Lavoro* (Labour Day).
24 June *San Giovanni* (St John the Baptist) – in Florence only.
15 August *Ferragosto* (Assumption of the Virgin Mary).
1 November *Ognissanti* (All Saints' Day).
8 December *Immacolata Concezione* (Immaculate Conception).
25 December *Natale* (Christmas Day).
26 December *Santo Stefano* (Boxing Day).

Florence

Banca d'Italia, Via dell'Oriuolo 37/39.
Banca Toscana, Via del Corso 6.
Banca CR Firenze, Via Bufalini 4.
UniCredit, Via Vecchietti 11.

Siena

Banca Nazionale del Lavoro, Viale Vittorio Veneto 43.
Cassa di Risparmio di Firenze, Piazza Tolomei 11.
Monte dei Paschi di Siena, Via Banchi di Sopra 84.
UniCredit, Via di Calzoleria 44.

Exchange Offices

Florence

Omega Viaggi, Piazza della Stazione 14, Int. 37 (under the station).

Siena

Viaggi Seti, Piazza del Campo 56.
Forexchange, Via di Città 80-82.

O

Opening Hours

Shops in the main cities open Monday to Friday 8.30am–1pm and 3.30–7.30pm. The majority open on Saturday, and several are open on Sunday, too, especially in high season. Some shops in coastal resorts and tourist centres now stay open all day throughout the summer and have Saturday and Sunday opening. Stores in most cities will close for at least two weeks around the *Ferragosto* holiday on 15 August. This is especially true of smaller cities not on the coastline.

Food shops are closed on Wednesday afternoons in winter and Saturday afternoons in summer. Clothes shops are closed on Monday mornings.

Offices are usually open 8am–1pm and 2–4pm, although many have more extensive opening hours.

On Italian national holidays, all shops and offices are closed.

P

Postal Services

Main post offices in major towns are open all day; otherwise the hours are 8am–1.30pm (12.30pm

Saturday). Stamps are sold at post offices and tobacconists (tabacchi).

There is also a courier service for sending important documents worldwide in 24/48 hours. This service is only available at major post offices. In Florence, these are at Via Pellicceria 3 (main post office) and Via Alamanni 14/16 (by the station).

Religious Services

In general, the Italians are very tolerant of other faiths and accepting of the tourists that visit their churches. However, behaving appropriately when visiting churches is important: wear respectful attire (your shoulders and knees should be covered), switch off mobile phones and keep noise levels down, especially during services.

Roman Catholic Mass is celebrated every day and several times on Sundays in Italian. Some non-Catholic churches hold services in English. St Mark's Anglican church in Florence celebrates mass on Sunday at 10.30am and almost every day at 5.30pm. Mass is also said at St Peter's church in Siena on last Sunday of every month at 3.45pm. Ask at the local tourist office about places of worship in the area.

Shopping

What to Buy

The quality is exceptionally high, especially in terms of craftsmanship, but prices are generally reasonable. Suggested buys are:

Fashion: dresses, suits, hats, gloves, linen, silk ties and shirts, scarves, knitwear, designer labels and jewellery.

Leather goods: prices are not rock-bottom but the quality is often excellent and the designs appealing. Shoes and handbags are particularly good buys, but there are also boxes and belts, luggage, briefcases and wallets.

Fabrics: silk, linen, wool and cotton.

Handicrafts: lace and tablecloths; pottery, ceramics and porcelain; gold-and silverware; alabaster and marble objects; woodwork; straw and raffia goods; glass and crystal work; art

books and reproductions; marbled paper; rustic household goods; prints; antiques; reproduction furniture.

Alcohol: regional wines – along with the well-known Chianti, Montalcino and Montepulciano, wines from the coastal Maremma such as Sassicaia and Ornellaia are celebrated Super Tuscans; also try Vin Santo, Tuscan dessert wine.

Food: extra-virgin olive oil, herbs, locally made pasta, farmhouse cheeses, bottled vegetables, truffles, dried mushrooms, cured ham, salami etc.

Shopping Hours

Food stores and general shops open 8.30am–1pm and 3.30 or 4–7.30pm. They stay open a little later in the summer. Many of the bigger supermarkets stay open through lunch and close at around 8pm. Department stores and other shops in bigger cities stay open all day (9.30am–7.30/8pm), and there is now limited Sunday trading in some places. Many clothes shops are closed on Monday mornings

Telephones

Public telephones are now virtually nonexistent as Italy has one of the highest ownerships of mobile phones in Europe. Annoyingly, many people, including small companies, only use their mobile phone, thus making calls to them more expensive. European standard gsm mobile/cell phones are widely used. Americans will need a tri-band phone. To keep costs down, if you intend to stay for more than a few weeks, it's worth getting an Italian SIM card while there, or keeping a second mobile for this purpose. For citizens of 31 European Economic Area countries, including the UK and Ireland, roaming charges for temporary roaming were abolished in mid-2017 yet under a fair use policy some restrictions on the free use of mobile phones are still in place.

For directory enquiries, dial 12. For international enquiries, call 176, and to make a reverse charges (collect) call, dial 170.

When dialling Italy from abroad, dial the country code (0039) and the area code **including** the initial zero.

In Italy, when calling numbers either inside or outside your area, dialling must always be preceded by the area code including the zero. Key area codes are: Florence (055); Pisa (050) and Siena (0577).

Tipping

Most Italian restaurants levy a *coperto* of around €2 per person – a cover charge for linen, bread and service – and so tipping isn't as common as in other countries. However, in pricier places, a tip of around 10 percent is an appropriate indication of appreciation of good service. Only in the finest hotels, and for lengthy stays, is it customary to tip bellboys, maids and head waiters. You may wish to note that according to Italian law, you should keep the bill with you until you are at least 100 metres (300ft) from the restaurant.

Tourist Board

The Italian State Tourist Board, known as ENIT (Ente Nazionale per il Turismo), provides tourist information. ENIT's headquarters are in Via Marghera 2/6, 00185 Rome (tel: 06-49711; www.enit.it).

In the UK, ENIT, Princes Street 1, London W1B 2AY; tel: (+44) 020-7408 1254.

In the US, ENIT, 686 Park Avenue, New York, NY 10065; tel: 212-245 5618. There are also offices in Chicago, Los Angeles and Toronto, Canada.

The ENIT website for all offices worldwide is: www.enit.it.

Tourist Offices

The current local tourist office details in each Tuscan province are listed below. If you are unable to contact them, consult www.visittuscany. com, Tuscany's official tourism website, which should list all the new contact details for each province as they emerge in connection with the restructuring of the Tuscan tourism system. This umbrella website also contains useful information about the region, offered in several languages.

In addition to the institutional tourist offices, there are also dynamic tourism consortia that act as tourist offices in many places. The best are also listed throughout the book, as here below.

Arezzo Province

Arezzo: Piazza della Repubblica 28; tel: 0575-26850.
Cortona: Piazza Signorelli 9; tel: 0575-637 223.

Florence Province

Florence: Via del Termine 11; tel: 055-315 874; Via Cavour 1r; tel: 055-290 832; Piazza San Giovanni 1; tel: 055-288 496; and Piazza della Stazione 4; tel: 055-212 245. www.firenzeturismo.it
Fiesole: Via Portigiani 3/5; tel: 055-596 1311. www.comune.fiesole.fi.it

Grosseto Province (including the Maremma)

Grosseto: Corso Carducci 5; tel: 0564-488 573. http://quimaremmatoscana.it
Maremma park (Parco della Maremma):
Alberese: Via Bersagliere 7/9; tel: 0564-407 098; www.parco-maremma.it

Livorno Province (and Etruscan Coast with Elba)

Livorno: Via Pollastrini 5; tel: 0586-820 454. www.comune.livorno.it
Elba: Calata Italia 44, Portoferraio; tel: 0565-938 209. www.visitelba.co.uk

Lucca Province (Lucca, Garfagnana and Versilia Coast)

Lucca: Vecchia Porta San Donato, Piazzale Verdi; tel: 0583-583 150, Palazzo Santini, via Cesare Battisti; tel: 0583-4422. www.turismo.lucca.it and www.luccaturismo.it
Bagni di Lucca: Viale Umberto I 97; tel: 0583-583 745.

Versilia (including the Viareggio and Forte dei Marmi coast)

Viareggio: Viale Carducci 10; tel: 0584-962 233. www.luccaturismo.it

---

⏱ Time Zone

Italy works on GMT + 1 and switches to DST – daylight saving time, GMT + 2 – at the same time as the rest of Europe.

Massa-Carrara Province

Marina di Massa: Lungomare Vespucci 24; tel: 0585-240 063.
Marina di Carrara: Viale XX Settembre, 152a; tel: 0585-844 136. www.aptmassacarrara.it

Pisa Province

Pisa: Piazza del Duomo 7; tel: 050-550 100. www.turismo.pisa.it
Volterra: Piazza dei Priori 20; tel: 0588-87257; www.volterratur.it

Pistoia Province

Pistoia: Viale Adua 128; tel: 0573-991 502.
www.pistoiaturismo.it
Montecatini Terme: Viale Verdi 66/68; tel: 0572-772 244. www.montecatiniturismo.it
San Marcello Pistoiese: Via Marconi 70; tel: 0573-630 145.

Prato Province

Prato: Piazza Buonamici 7; tel: 0574-24112. www.pratoturismo.it

Siena Province

Siena: Piazza del Campo 56; tel: 0577-280 551.
www.terresiena.it

Chianciano Terme (and Val d'Orcia area)

Piazza Italia 67; tel: 0578-671 122.

Tour Operators and Travel Agents

Agencies specialising in tours of every corner of Tuscany abound. Tourist offices and hotels can provide lists of these companies. In Florence, Florence Guides, an organisation of professional tourist guides authorised by the city council, includes many English-speaking native Florentines who delight in introducing visitors to their city. Details of their tours can be found at the website, www.florenceguides.com. Another company is Context Florence (www.contexttravel.com/cities/florence), which offers mini-seminars and city walks with international scholars specialised in areas like art, architecture and social history.

Many tours to the region include some interesting educational opportunities. Some language programmes that welcome students of all ages for courses ranging from two weeks to several months include the British Institute of Florence, Piazza Strozzi 2, 50123 Firenze, tel: 055- 267 781, www.britishinstitute.it.

V

Visas and Passports

Citizens of EU countries require either a passport or a Visitor's Identification Card to enter Italy. A visa is not required. Holders of passports from most other countries do not require visas for stays of less than three months, except for nationals from Belarus, the Russian Federation or Ukraine, who need to obtain visas from the Italian Embassy in their own country.

Police Registration

A person may stay in Italy for three months as a tourist, but police registration is required within three days of entering Italy. If staying at a hotel, the management will sort out the formality.

You are legally obliged to carry a form of identification (passport, driving licence, etc.) with you at all times. This rule is often flouted but it would be unwise to call the police or attempt to report a problem (eg theft) unless you are carrying appropriate identification.

W

Websites

Useful websites are given above and throughout the book. The following is just a selection of the many additional sites on Italy, Florence and Tuscany that are available on the web:
Tuscany Tourist Information: www.visittuscany.com
Tuscany tourist attractions: www.discovertuscany.com
What to see in Tuscany: www.tuscanychic.com
Database on all Italian museums: www.italy-museum.com
Florence museums: www.firenzemusei.it; www.polomuseale.firenze.it
Best routes in Italy: www.autostrade.it; www.rac.co.uk; www.theaa.com
Plan your journey from one Italian destination to another.
Information plus hotels and restaurants: www.firenzeturismo.it
Agriturismi (farm-stays) in Tuscany: www.visittuscany.com; www.agriturismo.com
Events: www.firenzespettacolo.it; www.theflorentine.net

Weights and Measures

Italy uses the metric system.

LANGUAGE TIPS

In Tuscany, everyone speaks the Italian language but regional dialects and accents survive. The Tuscan accent features a strongly aspirated "h", much like in Spanish. In major centres, many people speak English, French or German. It is well worth buying a good phrase book or dictionary, but the following will help you to get started. Since this glossary is aimed at non-linguists, we have opted for the simplest options rather than the most elegant Italian.

PRONUNCIATION AND GRAMMAR TIPS

Italian speakers claim that pronunciation is straightforward: you pronounce it as it is written. This is approximately true but there are a couple of important rules for English speakers to bear in mind: c before e or i is pronounced "ch", eg *ciao, mi dispiace, coincidenza*. Ch before i or e is pronounced as "k", eg *la chiesa*. Likewise, sci or sce are pronounced as in "sheep" or "shed". Gn in Italian is rather like the sound in "onion", while gl is softened to resemble the sound in "bullion".

Nouns are either masculine (il, plural i) or feminine (la, plural le). Plurals of nouns are most often formed by changing an o to an i and an a to an e, eg *il panino, i panini; la chiesa, le chiese*.

Words are stressed on the penultimate syllable unless an accent indicates otherwise, generally speaking.

Like many languages, Italian has formal and informal words for "You". In the singular, *Tu* is informal while *Lei* is more polite. For visitors, it is simplest and most respectful to use the formal form unless invited to do otherwise. There is, of course, rather more to the language than that, but you can get a surprisingly long way towards making friends with a few phrases.

BASIC COMMUNICATION

Yes *Sì*
No *No*
Thank you *Grazie*
You're welcome *Prego*
Alright/OK/That is fine *Va bene*
Please *Per favore* or *per cortesia*
Excuse me (to get attention) *Scusi* (singular), *Scusate* (plural)
Excuse me (to get through a crowd) *Permesso*
Excuse me (to attract attention, eg of a waiter) *Senta!*
Excuse me (sorry) *Mi scusi*
Could you help me? (formal) *Potrebbe aiutarmi?*
Certainly *Ma, certo*
Can I help you? (formal) *Posso aiutarLa?*
I need ... *Ho bisogno di ...*
I'm sorry *Mi dispiace*
I don't know *Non lo so*
I don't understand *Non capisco*
Could you speak more slowly, please? *Può parlare piu lentamente, per favore?*
Could you repeat that please? *Può ripetere, per piacere?*
What? *Quale/come?*
When/why/where? *Quando/perchè/dove?*
Where is the lavatory? *Dov'è il bagno?*

GREETINGS

Hello (Good day) *Buon giorno*
Good afternoon/evening *Buona sera*
Good night *Buona notte*
Goodbye *Arrivederci*
Hello/Hi/Goodbye (familiar) *Ciao*
Mr/Mrs/Miss *Signor/Signora/Signorina*
Pleased to meet you (formal) *Piacere di conoscerLa*

Do you speak English? *Parla inglese?*
I am English/American *Sono inglese/americano*
Canadian/Australian *canadese/australiano*
How are you (formal/informal)? *Come sta/come stai?*
Fine thanks *Bene, grazie*

TELEPHONE CALLS

the area code *il prefisso*
May I use your telephone, please? *Posso usare il telefono?*
Hello (on the telephone) *Pronto*
My name's *Mi chiamo/Sono*
Could I speak to...? *Posso parlare con...?*
Can you speak up please? *Può parlare più forte, per favore?*

IN THE HOTEL

Do you have any vacant rooms? *Avete camere libere?*
I have a reservation *Ho fatto una prenotazione*
I'd like... *Vorrei...*
a room with twin beds *una camera a due letti*
a single/double room (with a double bed) *una camera singola/doppia (con letto matrimoniale)*
a room with a bath/shower *una camera con bagno/doccia*
for one night *per una notte*
for two nights *per due notti*
How much is it? *Quanto costa?*
Is breakfast included? *E compresa la prima colazione?*
half/full board *mezza pensione/pensione completa*
Do you have a room with a balcony/view of the sea? *C'è una camera con balcone/con una vista del mare?*
Is it a quiet room? *E una stanza tranquilla?*
Can I see the room? *Posso vedere la camera?*

Can I have the bill, please? *Posso avere il conto, per favore?*
Can you call me a taxi, please? *Può chiamarmi un tassì/taxi, per favore?*

EATING OUT

Bar snacks and drinks

I'd like... *Vorrei...*
coffee *un caffè* (espresso: small, strong and black)
un caffellatte (like *café au lait* in France)
un caffè lungo (weak, served in a tall glass)
un corretto (laced with alcohol, probably brandy or grappa)
tea *un tè*
herbal tea *una tisana*
hot chocolate *una cioccolata calda*
orange/lemon juice (bottled) *un succo d'arancia/di limone*
fizzy/still mineral water *acqua minerale gassata/naturale*
with/without ice *con/senza ghiaccio*
red/white wine *vino rosso/bianco*
beer *una birra*
milk *latte*
a (half) litre *un (mezzo) litro*
ice cream *un gelato*
sandwich *un tramezzino*
roll *un panino*
Cheers *Salute*

In a restaurant

I'd like to book a table *Vorrei riservare una tavola*
Have you got a table for...? *Avete una tavola per ...?*
I have a reservation *Ho fatto una prenotazione*
lunch/supper *il pranzo/la cena*
I'm a vegetarian *Sono vegetariano/a*
Is there a vegetarian dish? *C'è un piatto vegetariano?*
May we have the menu? *Ci dia la carta?*
wine list *la lista dei vini*
home-made *fatto in casa*
What would you like? *Che cosa prende?*
What would you recommend? *Che cosa ci raccomanda?*
home-made *fatto in casa*
What would you like as a main course/dessert? *Che cosa prende di secondo/di dolce?*
What would you like to drink? *Che cosa desidera da bere?*
a carafe of red/white wine *una caraffa di vino rosso/bianco*

the dish of the day *il piatto del giorno*
cover charge *il coperto/pane e coperto*
The bill, please *Il conto per favore*
Is service included? *Il servizio è incluso?*

Menu decoder

Antipasti (hors d'oeuvres)

antipasto misto mixed hors d'œuvres (including cold cuts, possibly cheeses and roast vegetables)
buffet freddo cold buffet
caponata mixed aubergine, olives and tomatoes
insalata caprese tomato and mozzarella salad
insalata di mare seafood salad
insalata mista/verde mixed/green salad
melanzane alla parmigiana fried or baked aubergine (with parmesan cheese and tomato)
mortadella/salame salami
peperonata grilled peppers (drenched in olive oil)

Primi (first courses)

Typical first courses include soup, or numerous varieties of pasta in a wide range of sauces.
il brodetto fish soup
i crespolini savoury pancakes
gli gnocchi dumplings
la minestra soup
il minestrone thick vegetable soup
pasta e fagioli pasta and bean soup
il prosciutto (cotto/crudo) ham (cooked/cured)
i tartufi truffles
la zuppa soup

Secondi (main courses)

Typical main courses are fish-, seafood- or meat-based, with accompaniments (*contorni*) like beans, spinach or roast vegetables.

La carne (meat)

allo spiedo on the spit
arrosto roast meat
al ferro grilled without oil
al forno baked
al girarrosto spit-roasted
alla griglia grilled
stufato braised, stewed
ben cotto well-done (steak, etc.)
al puntino medium (steak, etc.)
al sangue rare (steak, etc.)
l'agnello lamb
il bresaolo dried salted beef
la bistecca steak
il maiale pork
il manzo beef

☺ Emergencies

Help! *Aiuto!*
Stop! *Fermate!*
I've had an accident *Ho avuto un incidente*
Watch out! *Attenzione!*
Call a doctor *Per favore, chiama un medico*
Call an ambulance *Chiama un'ambulanza*
Call the police *Chiama la Polizia/i Carabinieri*
Call the fire brigade *Chiama i pompieri*
Where is the telephone? *Dov'è il telefono?*
Where is the nearest hospital? *Dov'è l'ospedale più vicino?*
I would like to report a theft *Voglio denunciare un furto*

l'ossobuco shin of veal
il pollo chicken
la salsiccia sausage
saltimbocca (alla romana) veal escalopes with ham
le scaloppine escalopes
lo stufato stew
il sugo sauce

Frutti di mare (seafood)

Beware the word *"surgelati"*, meaning frozen rather than fresh.
affumicato smoked
alle brace charcoal grilled/barbecued
alla griglia grilled
fritto fried
ripieno stuffed
al vapore steamed
le acciughe anchovies
l'aragosta lobster
il branzino sea bass
i calamari squid
i calamaretti baby squid
i crostacei shellfish
le cozze mussels
il fritto misto mixed fried fish
i gamberi prawns
i gamberetti shrimps
il granchio crab
il merluzzo cod
le ostriche oysters
il pesce fish
il pesce spada swordfish
il polipo octopus
il risotto di mare seafood risotto
le sarde sardines
la sogliola sole
le seppie cuttlefish
la triglia red mullet
la trota trout
il tonno tuna

le vongole **clams**

I legumi/la verdura (vegetables)

a scelta **of your choice**
i contorni **accompaniments**
ripieno **stuffed**
gli asparagi **asparagus**
la bietola **similar to spinach**
il carciofo **artichoke**
le carote **carrots**
i carciofini **artichoke hearts**
il cavolo **cabbage**
la cicoria **chicory**
la cipolla **onion**
i funghi **mushrooms**
i funghi porcini **ceps best mushrooms**
i fagioli **beans**
i fagiolini **green beans**
le fave **broad beans**
il finocchio **fennel**
l'insalata mista **mixed salad**
l'insalata verde **green salad**
la melanzana **aubergine**
le patate **potatoes**
le patatine fritte **French fries**
i peperoni **peppers**
i piselli **peas**
i pomodori **tomatoes**
le primizie **spring vegetables**
il radicchio **red lettuce**
la rughetta **rocket**
i ravanelli **radishes**
gli spinaci **spinach**
la verdura **green vegetables**
la zucca **pumpkin/squash**
gli zucchini **courgettes**

I dolci (desserts)

al carrello **(desserts) from the trolley**
un semifreddo **semi-frozen dessert (many types)**
la bavarese **mousse**
un gelato **ice cream**
una granita **water ice**
una macedonia di frutta **fruit salad**
il tartufo (nero) **(chocolate) ice cream dessert**
il tiramisù **cold, creamy rum and coffee dessert**
la torta **cake/tart**
lo zabaglione **dessert made with eggs and Marsala wine**
lo zuccotto **ice-cream liqueur**
la zuppa inglese **trifle**

La frutta (fruit)

le albicocche **apricots**
le arance **oranges**
le banane **bananas**
il cocomero **watermelon**
le ciliege **cherries**
i fichi **figs**
le fragole **strawberries**
i frutti di bosco **fruits of the forest**
i lamponi **raspberries**

la mela **apple**
il melone **melon**
la pesca **peach**
la pera **pear**
il pompelmo **grapefruit**
le uve **grapes**

Basic foods

l'aceto **vinegar**
l'aglio **garlic**
il burro **butter**
il formaggio **cheese**
la frittata **omelette**
la grana **Parmesan cheese**
i grissini **bread sticks**
l'olio **oil**
la marmellata **jam**
il pane **bread**
il pane integrale **wholemeal bread**
il parmigiano **Parmesan cheese**
il pepe **pepper**
il riso **rice**
il sale **salt**
le uova **eggs**
lo zucchero **sugar**

SIGHTSEEING

Si può visitare? **Can one visit?**
Suonare il campanello **ring the bell**
aperto/a **open**
chiuso/a **closed**
chiuso per la festa **closed for the festival**
chiuso per ferie **closed for the holidays**
chiuso per restauro **closed for restoration**
Is it possible to see the church? *E possibile visitare la chiesa?*
Where can I find the custodian/sacristan/key? *Dove posso trovare il custode/il sacristano/la chiave?*

AT THE SHOPS

What time do you open/close? *A che ora apre/chiude?*
Closed for the holidays (typical sign) *Chiuso per ferie*
Pull/push (sign on doors) *Tirare/spingere*
Entrance/exit *Entrata/uscita*
Can I help you? (formal) *Posso aiutarLa?*
What would you like? *Che cosa desidera?*
I'm just looking *Sto soltanto guardando*
How much does it cost? *Quant'è, per favore?*
Do you take credit cards? *Accettate carte di credito?*
I'd like... *Vorrei...*

this one/that one *questo/quello*
I'd like that one, please *Vorrei quello lì, per cortesia*
Have you got ...? *Avete ...?*
We haven't got (any) ... *Non (ne) abbiamo...*
Can I try it on? *Posso provare?*
the size (for clothes) *la taglia*
What size do you take? *Qual'è Sua taglia?*
the size (for shoes) *il numero*
expensive/cheap *caro/economico*
It's too small/big *E troppo piccolo/grande*
I (don't) **like it** *(Non) mi piace*
I'll take it/I'll leave it *Lo prendo/Lo lascio*
This is faulty. Can I have a replacement/refund? *C'è un difetto. Me lo potrebbe cambiare/rimborsare?*
Anything else? *Altro?*
Give me some of those *Mi dia alcuni di quelli lì*
a (half) kilo *un (mezzo) chilo*
100 grams *un etto*
200 grams *due etti*
more/less *più/meno*
with/without *con/senza*
a little *un pocchino*
That's enough *Basta così*

Types of shops

bank *la banca*
bureau de change *il cambio*
chemist's *la farmacia*
food shop *l'alimentari*
leather shop *la pelletteria*
market *il mercato*
news-stand *l'edicola*
post office *l'ufficio postale*
supermarket *il supermercato*
tobacconist *il tabaccaio*
travel agency *l'agenzia di viaggi*

TRAVELLING

Transport

airport *l'aeroporto*
arrivals/departures *arrivi/partenze*
boat *la barca*
bus *l'autobus/il Pullman*
bus station *l'autostazione*
car *la macchina*
ferry *il traghetto*
first/second class *prima/seconda classe*
flight *il volo*
left luggage office *il deposito bagagli*
motorway *l'autostrada*
no smoking *vietato fumare*

platform *il binario*
railway station *la stazione (ferroviaria)*
stop *la fermata*

At the station

Can you help me please? *Mi può aiutare, per favore?*
Where can I buy tickets? *Dove posso fare i biglietti?*
at the ticket office/at the counter *alla biglietteria/allo sportello*
What time does the train leave? *A che ora parte il treno?*
What time does the train arrive? *A che ora arriva il treno?*
Can I book a seat? *Posso prenotare un posto?*
Is this seat free/taken? *E libero/ occupato questo posto?*
I'm afraid this is my seat *E il mio posto, mi dispiace*
You'll have to pay a supplement *Deve pagare un supplemento*
Do I have to change? *Devo cambiare?*
Where does it stop? *Dove si ferma?*

You need to change in Firenze *Bisogna cambiare a Florence*
Which platform does the train leave from? *Da quale binario parte il treno?*
The train leaves from platform one *Il treno parte dal binario uno*
When is the next train/bus/ ferry for Pisa? *Quando parte il prossimo treno/Pullman/traghetto per Pisa?*
How long does the crossing take? *Quanto dura la traversata?*
What time does the bus leave for Siena? *Quando parte l'autobus per Siena?*
Next stop please *La prossima fermata per favore*
Is this the right stop? *E la fermata giusta?*
The train is late *Il treno è in ritardo*
Can you tell me where to get off? *Mi può dire dove devo scendere?*

Directions

right/left *a destra/a sinistra*
first left/second right *la prima a sinistra/la seconda a destra*

Turn to the right/left *Gira a destra/ sinistra*
Go straight on *Va sempre diritto*
Go straight on until the lights *Va sempre diritto fino al semaforo*
opposite/next to *di fronte/accanto a*
up/down *su/giù*
traffic lights *il semaforo*
Where is ...? *Dov'è ...?*
Where are ...? *Dove sono ...?*
How do I get there? *Come si può andare? (or: Come faccio per arrivare a ...?)*

On the road

petrol *la benzina*
petrol station/garage *la stazione servizio*
oil *l'olio*
Fill it up please *Faccia il pieno, per favore*
lead free/unleaded/diesel *senza piombo/benzina verde/diesel*
My car won't start *La mia macchina non s'accende*
My car has broken down *La macchina è guasta*

ART AND HISTORY

The Architecture of the Italian Renaissance, by Peter Murray. Thames & Hudson.
Autobiography, by Benvenuto Cellini. Penguin Classics.
Catherine de' Medici: a Biography by Leonie Frieda. Phoenix
A Concise Encyclopedia of the Italian Renaissance, edited by J.R. Hale. Thames & Hudson.
Etruscan Places, by D.H. Lawrence. Olive Press.
The Florentine Renaissance and *The Flowering of the Renaissance*, by Vincent Cronin. Fontana.
The High Renaissance and *The Late Renaissance and Mannerism*, by Linda Murray. Thames & Hudson.
The Italian Painters of the Renaissance, by Bernard Berenson. Phaidon Press.
Lives of the Artists, vols. 1 & 2, by Giorgio Vasari. Penguin Classics.
Machiavelli, by Anglo Sydney. Paladin.
The Merchant of Prato, by Iris Origo. Penguin.
Painter's Florence, by Barbara Whelpton Johnson.
The Rise and Fall of the House of Medici, by Christopher Hibbert. Penguin.
Siena: A City and its History, by Judith Hook. Hamish Hamilton.
Silvio Berlusconi: Television, Power and Patrimony, by Paul Ginsborg. Verso Books.

TRAVEL COMPANIONS

A Room with a View, by E.M. Forster. Penguin.
The Italians, by Luigi Barzini. Hamish Hamilton.
Italian Hours, by Henry James. Century Hutchinson.
Love and War in the Apennines, by Eric Newby. Picador.

The Love of Italy, by Jonathan Keates. Octopus.

⊘ Send Us Your Thoughts

We do our best to ensure the information in our books is as accurate and up-to-date as possible. The books are updated on a regular basis using local contacts, who painstakingly add, amend and correct as required. However, some details (such as telephone numbers and opening times) are liable to change, and we are ultimately reliant on our readers to put us in the picture.

We welcome your feedback, especially your experience of using the book "on the road". Maybe you came across a great bar or new attraction we missed.

We will acknowledge all contributions, and we'll offer an Insight Guide to the best letters received.

Please write to us at:
Insight Guides
PO Box 7910
London SE1 1WE

Or email us at:
hello@insightguides.com

Pictures from Italy, by Charles Dickens. Granville Publishing.
The Stones of Florence, by Mary McCarthy. Penguin.
The Villas of Tuscany, by Harold Acton. Thames & Hudson.
The Birth of Venus, by Sarah Dunant. Random House.
Summer's Lease, by John Mortimer. Penguin.
Death in Springtime, by Magdalen Nabb. Heinemann.
Under the Tuscan Sun and two sequels, by Frances Mayes. Bantam.

OTHER INSIGHT GUIDES

Insight Guides cover nearly 200 destinations, providing information on culture and all the top sights, as well as superb photography and detailed maps. Other Insight Guides to destinations in the region include Italy, Italian Lakes, Sicily and Sardinia.

Italian destinations in Insight's detailed and colourful **City Guides** series include Rome, Florence and Siena, and Venice.

The itinerary-based **Insight Explore Guides**, written by local hosts, come complete with a pull-out map. Titles include Naples and the Amalfi Coast, the Italian Lakes, Venice, Florence, and Rome.

CREDITS

PHOTO CREDITS

4Corners Images 242
akg-images 30, 33, 40, 114BR, 115ML, 115BR, 118BL, 119L
Alamy 12/13, 14/15, 16/17, 113TR, 117TR, 141B, 144, 173
Alinari/Rex Features 120BL
AWL Images 1, 90, 204
Bridgeman Art Library 120/121T
Britta Jaschinski/Apa Publications 7ML, 9BL, 10B, 10T, 22R, 22L, 82, 83L, 83R, 105T, 107, 116BL, 117MR, 117BR, 122, 123, 124, 213B, 213T, 260
Cathy Muscat 171, 176
Chianti Classico Wine Consortium 202ML
Corbis 42, 45, 49, 94, 112BL
ENEL 188B, 250
FLPA 174
Fotolia 66, 129, 138, 143T, 149B, 168, 175, 177, 179, 180T, 203TR
Frances Gransden/Apa Publications 35, 103T
Gentile da Fabriano 58
Getty Images 29, 46, 47, 48, 51, 52/53, 55, 74, 77, 103B, 121T, 131, 151, 170, 172B, 214/215T, 231, 241
Guglielmo Galvin & George Taylor/

Apa Publications 31, 150, 156T, 157
iStock 4, 6BL, 32, 67, 73, 146, 169, 209B, 226, 232, 256B, 258, 273
Jezza Dennis/Apa Publications 111T, 126
Leonardo 140
Lombardi Siena 37
Mary Evans Picture Library 43
Mockford & Bonetti/Apa Publications 79, 101, 106, 108T, 128T, 128B, 130, 152, 154, 155, 156B, 172T, 178T, 180B, 189T, 199T, 200T, 200B, 216, 218, 221, 222B, 223, 229T, 234, 237T, 240T, 244, 245T, 247B, 248, 249, 251T, 251B, 252, 253
Monte dei Paschi di Siena 208
Pitti Gallery, Florence 81
Public domain 26/27, 28, 41, 44, 59, 60, 63, 64, 80, 247T
Robert Harding 6M, 8B
Santa Maria Novella, Florence 61
Scala Archives 7TR, 7BL, 38, 39, 56, 57, 62, 65, 112/113T, 112BR, 113ML, 113BL, 113BR, 114BL, 115TR, 118/119T, 118BR, 119R, 121B
Shutterstock 6MR, 11B, 19T, 19B, 69, 70, 71, 72, 91T, 114/115T, 117BL,

120MR, 125T, 125B, 137, 139T, 143B, 145, 165, 167, 178B, 181, 185, 191, 197, 201, 202/203T, 209T, 212T, 237B, 239, 240B, 243, 245B
Sipa Press/Rex Features 50
Steve McDonald/Apa Publications 7TL, 7BR, 7MR, 8T, 9BR, 9TR, 11T, 18, 20, 21, 23, 24, 25, 34, 75, 78, 84/85, 86/87, 88/89, 91B, 98, 99T, 100, 102, 105B, 116BR, 132, 133, 134, 135, 136, 139B, 141T, 147, 149T, 158, 159, 161, 162, 163, 164, 182, 183, 184T, 184B, 187, 188T, 189B, 190, 192, 193, 194, 195, 196, 198, 199B, 202MR, 202B, 203BL, 203BR, 205, 207B, 207T, 211, 212B, 214BR, 214BL, 215ML, 215BR, 215BL, 215TR, 217, 220, 222T, 224, 225, 227, 228, 229B, 230T, 230B, 233, 235, 238, 254, 256T, 268/269
SuperStock 36
The Art Archive 116/117T
Tom Smyth 68R, 68L, 95, 104, 108B, 110, 111B, 210
Uffizi Florence/Dagli Orti 54
WestEnd61/Rex Features 7MR, 99B

COVER CREDITS

Front cover: San Gimignano *iStock*
Back cover: Val d'Orcia *Shutterstock*
Front flap: (from top) Pitigliano *Shutterstock*; Tuscan landscape *iStock*; Marciana Marina *Shutterstock*; Palatina Gallery, Palazzo Pitti *Shutterstock*
Back flap: Elba island *Shutterstock*

INSIGHT GUIDE CREDITS

Distribution
UK, Ireland and Europe
Apa Publications (UK) Ltd;
sales@insightguides.com
United States and Canada
Ingram Publisher Services;
ips@ingramcontent.com
Australia and New Zealand
Woodslane; info@woodslane.com.au
Southeast Asia
Apa Publications (SN) Pte;
singaporeoffice@insightguides.com
Worldwide
Apa Publications (UK) Ltd;
sales@insightguides.com
Special Sales, Content Licensing and CoPublishing
Insight Guides can be purchased in bulk quantities at discounted prices. We can create special editions, personalised jackets and corporate imprints tailored to your needs.
sales@insightguides.com
www.insightguides.biz

Printed in China by CTPS

All Rights Reserved
© 2018 Apa Digital (CH) AG and
Apa Publications (UK) Ltd

First Edition 1989
Seventh Edition 2018

Every effort has been made to provide accurate information in this publication, but changes are inevitable. The publisher cannot be responsible for any resulting loss, inconvenience or injury. We would appreciate it if readers would call our attention to any errors or outdated information. We also welcome your suggestions; please contact us at:
hello@insightguides.com

www.insightguides.com

Editor: Carine Tracanelli
Author: Lisa Gerard-Sharp
Head of DTP and Pre-Press: Rebeka Davies
Update Production: Apa Digital
Picture Editor: Tom Smyth
Cartography: original cartography Berndtson & Berndtson, updated by Carte

Legend

City maps

	Freeway/Highway/Motorway
	Divided Highway
	Main Roads
	Minor Roads
	Pedestrian Roads
	Steps
	Footpath
	Railway
	Funicular Railway
	Cable Car
	Tunnel
	City Wall
	Important Building
	Built Up Area
	Other Land
	Transport Hub
	Park
	Pedestrian Area
🚌	Bus Station
❶	Tourist Information
✉	Main Post Office
✚	Cathedral/Church
☾	Mosque
✡	Synagogue
⚑	Statue/Monument
⚑	Beach
✈	Airport

Regional maps

	Freeway/Highway/Motorway (with junction)
	Freeway/Highway/Motorway (under construction)
	Divided Highway
	Main Road
	Secondary Road
	Minor Road
	Track
	Footpath
	International Boundary
	State/Province Boundary
	National Park/Reserve
	Marine Park
	Ferry Route
	Marshland/Swamp
	Glacier / Salt Lake
✈	Airport/Airfield
∴	Ancient Site
⊖	Border Control
	Cable Car
⚔	Castle/Castle Ruins
⍥	Cave
⌂	Chateau/Stately Home
†	Church/Church Ruins
⌁	Crater
⚲	Lighthouse
▲	Mountain Peak
★	Place of Interest
☼	Viewpoint

CONTRIBUTORS

This revised edition of *Insight Guide: Tuscany* was managed by **Carine Tracanelli** and updated by **Magdalena Helsztyńska-Stadnik**.

It builds on the excellent foundations created by the writers of previous editions, notably **Lisa Gerard-Sharp**, an experienced travel writer who is knowledgeable about all things Tuscan. Lisa has contributed to many Insight Guides for Italian destinations, after living in several places in the country.

Past contributors also include **Angela Vannucci**, **Adele Evans**, **Sarah Birke**, **Robert John**, **Christopher Catling**, **Russell Chamberlin** and **Rebecca Ford**.

ABOUT INSIGHT GUIDES

Insight Guides have more than 45 years' experience of publishing high-quality, visual travel guides. We produce 400 full-colour titles, in both print and digital form, covering more than 200 destinations across the globe, in a variety of formats to meet your different needs.

Insight Guides are written by local authors, whose expertise is evident in the extensive historical and cultural background features. Each destination is carefully researched by regional experts to ensure our guides provide the very latest information. All the reviews in **Insight Guides** are independent; we strive to maintain an impartial view. Our reviews are carefully selected to guide you to the best places to eat, go out and shop, so you can be confident that when we say a place is special, we really mean it.

INDEX

MAIN REFERENCES ARE IN BOLD TYPE